Graphical Applications
with Tcl and Tk

Eric F. Johnson

M&T BOOKS

M&T Books
A Division of MIS:Press, Inc.
A Subsidiary of Henry Holt and Company, Inc.
115 West 18th Street

New York, New York 10011

Library of Congress Cataloging-in-Publication Data

Johnson, Eric F.
   Graphical applications with Tcl and Tk / Eric Johnson
     p.   cm.
   ISBN 1-55851-471-6
   1. Computer graphics 2. Tcl (Computer program language) 3. Tk toolkit.
  I. Title.
  T385.J618   1996
  005.13'3—dc20   95-51184
                                           CIP

10 9 8 7 6 5 4 3

Associate Publisher: *Paul Farrell*

Managing Editor: *Cary Sullivan*
Development Editor: *Laura Lewin*
Copy Edit Manager: *Shari Chappell*

Production Editor: *Anne Incao*
Technical Editor: *Kevin Reichard*
Copy Editor: *Karen Tongish*

CONTENTS

Chapter 3 • Interacting with the User   71

Chapter 4 • Menus 109

Chapter 5 • Text Editing with Tcl and Tk 143

SECTION II: Advanced Applications

Chapter 8 • Tcl Tricks and Traps: Handling Errors and Debugging   259

Chapter 9 • The Canvas Widget, Bitmaps, and Images   275

Chapter 10 • Launching Applications from Tcl   311

Chapter 11 • Embedding Tcl in Your Applications   321

Chapter 12 • Extending Tcl   335

x

Chapter 13 • Advanced Applications 347

Appendix A • For More Information 357

Appendix B • Installing Tcl and Tk 361

Appendix C • The CD-ROM 367

Index 369

INTRODUCTION

What is Tcl?

Tcl, the **Tool Command Language** (pronounced *tickle*), has captured the hearts and minds of tens of thousands of software developers worldwide. It's an easy-to-learn scripting language that runs under Windows (3.1 and 95), Windows NT, UNIX, and the Macintosh OS.

An associated add-on toolkit, Tk (short for *toolkit*), allows you to quickly create graphical applications, without delving into arcane subjects like Win32, Quickdraw, Object Linking and Embedding, or Motif and the X Toolkit Intrinsics. With a surprisingly small amount of code, you can quickly develop graphical applications.

This book will help you quickly get up to speed creating cross-platform applications with Tcl/Tk.

There are a number of reasons for the great success of Tcl:

- *Tcl is a scripting language.* While there are some Tcl compilers, the vast majority of Tcl users run their programs as scripts. Scripts are easier to develop than full-fledged C or C++ programs because scripting languages such as Tcl tend to stand at a higher level than low-level languages such as C, so you simply have to do less. Furthermore, because the language is interpreted, you get a really quick turnaround when testing your code. You don't have to compile and you don't have to link; all you have to do is execute the Tcl interpreter and run your script.

2

- *Tcl is easy to learn.* At the end of Chapter 1, you'll be ready to go out into the world writing Tcl applications. It shouldn't take you more than a few hours to pick up the basics of the language, as covered in Chapter 2, or the Tk toolkit, introduced in Chapter 3.

- *Tcl works on many different platforms.* Ported to just about every version of UNIX, from Hewlett-Packard's HP-UX to Silicon Graphics' Irix, from SCO UNIX to Linux, Tcl works well in the UNIX environment, particularly because developing graphical applications on UNIX under Motif tends to be a troublesome task.

  On the Windows side, versions of Tcl exist for Windows 3.1, Windows 95, and Windows NT. The latest versions of Tcl also run on Apple's Macintosh platform.

  You can write complicated scripts in Tcl and execute them on multiple platforms with the same results.

- *You can embed Tcl in your programs.* The Tcl interpreter, as you'll find in Chapter 11, is merely a C function that you can link into your applications. This means that you can use Tcl as the application language in your program. For example, if you're developing a spreadsheet program, you can use Tcl as the built-in macro language.

- *Tcl is easy to extend.* As you'll see in Chapter 12, you can easily add commands to Tcl, extending the language. In fact, if you're embedding Tcl in your applications, chances are you'll need to add a number of commands that pertain to your application. This is one of the major uses of Tcl.

- *Tcl is free.* Yep, you can get all this for free on the Internet or a number of on-line services. This book comes with a CD-ROM that contains the Tcl source code (and binaries for Windows), so you should you be up and ready in just a few minutes.

- *Tcl works well with the Internet.* Tcl includes a number of built-in features that make working with Internet World Wide Web pages easier. The x widget, for example supports tags, which help should want to create hypertext links in your text. Tcl is also good for CGI scripts, the code that Web pages execute for image maps and data retrieval.

With all these great reasons, you should now be convinced to hop on the Tcl bandwagon and program away.

When to Use Tcl

All is not roses with Tcl. There are definitely times when Tcl is appropriate and times when it is not.

As an interpreted language, Tcl suffers performance losses because each statement is read in, parsed, and then executed at runtime. You can find a few Tcl compilers that improve this situation somewhat, but because so much of the language is text-oriented (even numbers are stored as text strings), the language suffers from some inherent speed problems. (I should note, however, that in most graphical applications, the speed of the interpreter is not an issue when compared to the time it takes to create windows, draw menus, and so on.)

Tcl provides only the weakest tools for building complex data structures and treats most data items as mere text. Just look at the bizarre way you must simulate multidimensional arrays (as shown in Chapter 2). You can interpret text as a number, but the focus of Tcl is clearly on text and lists of text items.

Part of the beauty of Tcl is that you can choose how much of the application should be written in Tcl and how much in C or C++ (or whatever programming language you use).

If your application does a lot of heavy computations, you can create new Tcl commands and perform the computations in C or C++, inside the syntactic sugar of your new Tcl commands.

Tcl is also strong in both text and list processing. Tcl manages the memory for strings and lists, one of the most troublesome areas for C programmers to handle properly.

Tcl also makes a very effective command language, since it provides most of the handy utility functions that shell scripts do to go through directories and sort the file names, execute commands, and so on.

In this book, the focus is on developing graphical applications using Tcl and Tk on both the Windows and UNIX platforms. Because graphical programs are so hard to create, you'll quickly see for yourself the advantages of the speedy Tcl development model.

This book is not a reference. It does not provide mind-numbing lists of every possible option. That's what the free on-line reference documentation is for. Instead, my goal is to provide you with enough tutorial information to get going with Tcl/Tk applications. When you've finished this book, you'll be at the stage where you won't need a tutorial any more.

There are some differences between Tcl for UNIX and for Windows. Many of these differences lie in the commands you can type in shell windows (called *DOS-prompt* windows for PC users). Since Tcl makes it very easy to execute shell commands and since these shell commands differ between UNIX and Windows, there are bound to be some differences. In this book, you'll find two symbols to help you sort out the differences.

The Windows icon identifies differences that pertain to Windows.

WINDOWS

The UNIX icon, as you'd expect, identifies differences that pertain to UNIX.

UNIX

In Chapter 1, you'll find a basic introduction to Tcl and Tk along with an implementation of the obligatory "Hello world" program in two very short lines of Tcl code.

Chapter 2 introduces the basic syntax of Tcl, covering things such as variables, arrays, flow control and procedures.

Chapter 3 gets back into this book's graphical bent. It introduces most of the Tk widgets and shows you how to start creating graphical applications, the focus of this book.

Chapter 4 covers creating menus, menu bars and the style guide requirements for Windows and UNIX applications.

Just about every application requires some form of text editing, even if it's only for a single-line text-entry field. Chapter 5 delves into this topic with the entry and text widgets. The text widget forms the base of what could be a quickly created HTML web-page browsing widget.

Chapter 6 goes on to discuss lists, listbox widgets, lists of files and lists of directories.

Chapter 7 rounds out the discussion of Tcl basics by covering dialog windows, such as error and warning dialog boxes.

The advanced applications section starts with Chapter 8's concentration on how to debug Tcl and Tk applications. This chapter shows how to track down problems and what help is available to correct the source of the trouble.

Chapter 9 reaches into Tk's strangest bag of tricks and covers the `canvas` widget. In one sense, the `canvas` widget is merely a place to draw graphics such as lines and arcs. In another sense, though, you can embed windows in the canvas and bind events to them turning the `canvas` widget into a complicated application window. Chapter 9 also covers bit maps and images in Tk, including built-in support for GIF images.

Since Tcl is a scripting language, most of your scripts need to execute existing applications on your Windows or UNIX system. Tcl provides a number of commands for launching other applications, as shown in Chapter 10.

Chapters 11 and 12 cover how to embed the Tcl interpreter as an application language within your programs and how to extend the Tcl language from C functions. If you embed Tcl in a spreadsheet program, for example, you need to extend the base set of commands Tcl provides with commands to access the cells in the spreadsheet.

Chapter 13 rounds out the discussion by tackling odds and ends you'll need to create robust finished applications.

Tcl is an ever-changing language. John Ousterhout, the creator of Tcl, and his team keep adding neat new features every day. You can get new versions on the Internet, or use the version that accompanies this book on CD-ROM. You'll quickly find that Tcl and Tk give you the tools to rapidly develop graphical applications.

SECTION I

Writing Applications in Tcl/Tk

This first section introduces all the basics you need to create graphical applications with Tcl and Tk.

Chapter 1 gets the whole thing rolling. Chapter 2 delves into the basic syntax of Tcl, the Tool Command Language. You'll use the commands introduced in this chapter in every Tcl script to come.

Chapter 3 starts with graphical applications and the widgets provided by the Tk extension to Tcl. It covers the basic widgets required of all Tcl applications. This continues in Chapter 4, on menus, and Chapter 5, on text editing and string commands.

Chapter 6 picks up with lists, `listbox` widgets, files, and directories. Chapter 7 rounds out this discussion by delving into dialog boxes.

## CHAPTER 1

Your First Tcl Programs

This chapter covers:

- Starting to program in Tcl
- Basic Tcl syntax
- A few quirks about how Tcl works
- How to look up reference information on Tcl and Tk commands
- Creating a Tcl script file
- Turning a Tcl script into a UNIX command

What is a Tcl Program?

A *Tcl program* is simply a bunch of commands. Like a DOS batch file or UNIX shell script, all you need to do is place commands one after another. There is no `main` function, so familiar to C programmers, nor is there a `WinMain`. There are just commands.

Some key points to remember are that, since Tcl is an interpreted language, every single command is text. You can build new commands at run time by building up new strings and then executing them. *Everything is text.* You'll see this mantra throughout this book because it is the source of most beginners' problems with Tcl.

That said, the way to get your text file to run is to give it to a Tcl interpreter. The most commonly used interpreters are **tclsh** and **wish**.

Both interpreters can be used for two purposes, to execute Tcl script files and to run interactively. In interactive mode, you can type in Tcl commands one at a time. This is very useful for testing out commands. In batch mode, **tclsh** or **wish** will execute a Tcl script and then automatically quit.

The **tclsh** interpreter is built with the Tcl language only, not the Tk toolkit for graphical applications. This means that if you use **tclsh** to execute your Tcl scripts, you won't get any menus, scrollbars, or other graphical elements. However, **tclsh** is good for commonly run nongraphical tasks, such as backup scripts.

On the other hand, the **wish** interpreter comes built-in with Tk, so you can make graphical widgets to your heart's content. Throughout this book, **wish** will be the interpreter of choice in most circumstances.

Make-a-Wish

The first step, then, is to find your **wish** interpreter. Normally, **wish** is named simply that, **wish**. On Windows systems, you may find **wish** named **wish.exe** or **wish41.exe**, following Windows conventions. You can use the Windows Program Manager's search commands to find **wish.exe** on your system. Furthermore, when installing **wish** on Windows, you can choose in which folder the application's icons will appear.

To get the most from this book, you'll want version 4.1 or later of **wish**, although you can still get a lot of use out of older versions. Version 4.1 was the first that officially supported Windows and the Macintosh, an important point in making cross-platform Tcl scripts. In addition, much of the syntax changed from version 3.6 to 4.1. If you're still using an older version, you may need to modify some of the example scripts.

Checking the Version

To check the version number of **wish** you have, run the command (**wish**).

WINDOWS

In Windows, you can select the **wish** program icon in the Program Manager. In Windows NT, you can do this or launch a DOS shell window and run **wish** from there. In regular Windows 3.1, this won't work, because **wish** is a Win32 application that requires Windows. This is one of the differences between Windows NT and regular Windows.

When you run **wish**, you'll see a blank window, as shown in Figure 1.1, and a command prompt, normally a % (percent) character in a terminal or console window.

Figure 1.1 The **wish** window.

At the **wish** prompt, enter the following command:

```
puts $tk_version
```

wish will simply print the response on the next line. Many Tcl commands work like this, especially the puts command (short for *put string*), which prints a text string.

If the response is 4.1 (or higher), you're in business. If the response is something like 3.6, however, you won't be able to run all the programs in this book.

```
% puts $tk_version
4.1
```

Don't worry; the CD-ROM that comes with this book has version 4.1 of **wish** and Tk, along with Tcl 7.5.

CD-ROM

You've just executed your first Tcl command. The next step is to enter your first Tcl program.

A First Tcl Program

You can accuse me of being unoriginal, but the first program is the tried-and-true hello world. Enter the following line at the **wish** prompt:

```
button .b -text "Hello World" -command { exit }
```

In a moment we'll go through each element of this command, which creates a pushbutton widget. When you enter it, you see nothing. You've created a widget; it just isn't visible yet. This brings us to both our second command and our second mantra: *The packer, controlled from the* pack *command, makes things visible.* You'll see this mantra as often as the first.

You must execute the pack command to make the button widget visible:

```
pack .b
```

The pack command takes the name of the widget or widgets, in this case, the single widget named *.b* (yes, the leading period is part of its name), and places the widgets in a window. The key part of the pack command, which you'll see in depth in Chapter 3, is how it places the widgets in the master—or application—widget. (Widgets in Tk appear in a hierarchy, which is described more in the section on widget names later in this chapter.)

Now you should see a widget in the **wish** window, as shown in Figure 1.2.

Figure 1.2 Hello world in Tcl.

A *widget* is an item on the screen that users can interact with. For example, a menu is a widget, as is a menu choice on a menu. So is a scrollbar and, in this case, a button. Virtually all graphical interfaces follow the idea of widgets. In most circumstances, a widget is a window with some smarts attached to it. In Tcl, a widget is a very high-level construct, which frees you from most of the low-level details of programming with widgets. This is one of the advantages of a high-level scripting language.

The First Commands in Depth

The first example uses two Tk commands, `button` and `pack`. Tcl is most useful when its rather small command set gets extended. Tk is one such extension. Tk extends the basic Tcl language with commands to create and manipulate a number of neat widgets (see Chapter 3 for more on widgets). The `button` command creates a button widget. A `button`, as you'd guess, is a simple push-button widget.

Simple enough. The hard part is in all the options available for buttons and in button—and widget—names.

Widget Names

In Tk, all widgets appear in a hierarchy. The main reason for this is the fact that the underlying windowing systems, X and Win32, both follow this model for creating windows. (Each widget typically has its own window.)

An application must have a top-level window. Widgets such as menu bars and pushbuttons then go inside this top-level window, or are nested inside other windows, which are called *containers* because they contain other widgets. You can nest windows to almost any depth (you'll eventually run out of screen space).

Because of this hierarchy, there must be a top-level widget that encapsulates the whole application. In the case of Tk, this widget is named ".". (that's right, a period). A child of the top-level widget (remember, there is a hierarchy, so you can go down many levels) is named *.name*, where *name* is the name of the widget. With container widgets, such as the `frame` widget (see Chapter 3), the full widget name becomes something like *.container.name* or *.container.container2.name*. The idea of using a period to separate parts of the name is purely arbitrary. You just have to learn this.

Similar to dealing with files and directories, *.name* is the full path name of the widget. In most Tk commands, you'll need the full path name of any widgets you use.

In the preceding example, the widget is named *b* and the full path name of the widget is *.b*. Thus our button command creates a button named *.b*.

Button Options

In our example, we created a button with two command-line options, -text and -command. In fact, these are just a few of the options available with the button command (see Chapter 3 for more on these options). For now, though, we'll stick to the -text and -command options.

The -text option specifies the text to display in the button. If we change this option to be "This is new text," as in the following commands, we'll see a different widget, as shown in Figure 1.3.

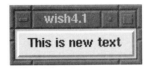

Figure 1.3 A button widget displaying new text.

The following commands create a button widget with different text:

```
button .c -text "This is new text" -command { exit }
pack .c
```

The -command option specifies the Tcl commands, called a **script**, to execute when the user pushes the button. In most user-interface toolkits, the -command option is termed a *callback function*. Since Tcl is a scripting language, this callback can be any set of Tcl code, such as the code we'll examine throughout this book.

In the preceding example, the Tcl code to execute is { exit }, where { and } are used to mark the beginning and end of the code (there's a more technical definition we'll see later) and the command executed is exit, which, as you'd guess, exits a Tcl program. Throughout this book, you'll learn more and more Tcl commands. In addition, you can write your own commands in either Tcl or C.

In Tcl, most commands, such as the button command, are one line long. This comes from Tcl's roots as a command-line interpreter. Therefore, if we have really long text that we want to divide among a number of lines, we need to use a \ (backslash) character at the end of one line as a line-continuation marker. This continues the current line onto the next line. Whenever the backslash occurs as the last character of a line, it is interpreted as a line-continuation marker. The following example shows this:

```
button .d \
  -text "This is longer text" \
  -command { exit }
```

The preceding example shows a single Tcl command that spans a number of lines. To the Tcl interpreter (such as **wish**), the command is simply one line due to the line-continuation markers.

WARNING

Forgetting or misplacing a \ character is a common problem in Tcl scripts.

Looking up Information on Tcl and Tk Commands

You can look up information on every Tcl and Tk command. Tcl comes with documentation in the form of online manual pages on UNIX and a Windows Help file on Windows.

On UNIX, you can use the **man** program to look up more information on the Tk button command:

```
man button
```

You can also use the graphical online manual browsers **xman**, which comes with the X Window System on most UNIX systems and is shown in Figure 1.4, or **tkMan**, a manual browser written in Tcl/Tk.

Figure 1.4 Browsing Tk documentation.

Windows also comes with a graphical help browser, which virtually all Windows applications support. **Wish** is no exception. You can launch this help by clicking on the **Tcl/Tk Manual** icon in the Windows Program Manager. Once the help system starts up, you'll see a list of all the pages in one help topic. When you choose a topic, such as the button command, you'll see a window like that in Figure 1.5.

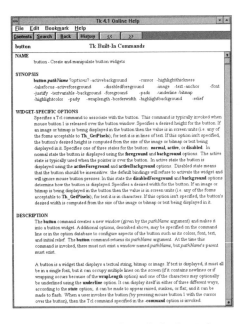

Figure 1.5 Windows help for Tcl.

The Pack Command

The pack command is much harder to explain than the simple button command. The pack command places child widgets, such as *.b*, in a window, usually the main **wish** window, and makes the widgets appear. This command, with its many options, is very useful for controlling the layout of Tcl scripts, as shown in Chapter 3.

Up to now, you've had to type in each Tcl command one at a time. Next, you can place these commands in a file and pass the filename to the **wish** interpreter for execution.

Making a Tcl Script from Our Commands

A Tcl script file is merely an ASCII text file of Tcl commands. You can use any normal text editor, such as Notepad on Windows or **emacs** or **vi** on UNIX, to create a Tcl script file. We can make a simple script from our Tcl commands:

```
button .b -text "Hello World" -command { exit }
pack .b
```

You can place these commands inside a text file and then name the file **hello.tk** (or any name you want, but I'll use **hello.tk**). You can then run this script with the following command:

```
wish hello.tk
```

Older versions of **wish**, such as with Tk 3.6, require an -f flag before the file name, making the command wish -f hello.tk.

N O T E

You should see the same result as when the commands were directly placed on the **wish** command line.

UNIX

On UNIX, virtually all scripting languages (including Tcl), use the # character to mark the start of a comment. (Some scripting languages require the # to be in the first column.) In most UNIX shell scripts, you'll usually see a strange comment on the very first line:

```
#!/bin/sh
```

This comment tells the command shell you're running in, usually **csh** or **ksh**, and which program to run to execute the script (in this case, **/bin/sh**). This is a handy way to request that a shell script be run under the interpreter for which it was designed. For example, I use the C shell (**csh**) for my daily work, but virtually all UNIX shell scripts are written in the Bourne shell (**sh**) language. This initial comment tells my **csh** to run **sh** for the script (rather than running another copy of **csh**).

This is just a convention, but it is followed on most UNIX command shells, including **sh, csh** and **ksh**. This convention is so widely followed that you can take advantage of this to ask the shell (usually **csh** or **ksh**) to run **wish**, the Tcl interpreter, instead, because these Tcl scripts require **wish** or **tclsh** (normally you'll want to use **wish**, because it supports Tk as well as plain old Tcl). In addition, because this first line is a comment, any shell that does not follow the convention will merely ignore the comment, so you're safe either way.

You'll want to place the path to your copy of **wish** in this type of specially formatted comment on the first line of your scripts, provided your script runs on UNIX. The hope is that the UNIX shell will see this and automatically launch the proper interpreter, **wish** in our case. If you put all this together and mark your Tcl scripts as executable files, then you can skip the **wish** part of the command line and merely type in the name of your script as a command, because the **wish** part is in the script, as part of this specially formatted comment. For example:

```
hello.tk
```

Here's what you need to do. First, insert a comment like the following one into the first line of the script:

```
#!/usr/local/tcl/bin/wish4.1

button .b -text "Hello World" -command { exit }
pack .b
```

The **/usr/local/tcl/bin/wish4.1** part is the path to my **wish** interpreter, named **wish4.1** (to differentiate it from **wish** for Tk 3.6). You need to insert the proper path for your system.

Obviously, if you place your **wish** interpreter in a strange location (like I did), your script will not be very portable to other systems. A more common path is:

```
#!/usr/local/bin/wish
```

The **/usr/local/bin/wish** is fairly common, as is **/usr/bin/wish** (for example, on Linux).

Once you've set up the proper starting comment to launch **wish**, the next step is to make your **hello.tk** file an executable file with the **chmod** command:

```
chmod +x hello.tk
```

You should now be able to execute your script from the UNIX command line:

```
hello.tk
```

If you have any problems, chances are your command shell doesn't support this convention. If so, you'll likely get a number of errors, as Tcl commands are not compatible with most UNIX shell commands (some are, which can lead to interesting results if you execute a Tcl script as a Bourne shell script).

There's one main problem with this special first-line comment: some systems, especially Hewlett-Packard's HP-UX, allow only 32 characters in the path. Thus long paths such as **/usr5/local/tcl/Tcl7.5/bin/wish4.1** won't work. In that case, you can use the following trick:

```
#!/bin/sh
# This comment continues on in Tcl,
# but not in sh\
exec /usr5/local/tcl/Tcl7.5/bin/wish4.1 "$0" ${1+"$@"}

# If the above exec doesn't work,
# replace ${1+"$@"} with "$@".

# Place your Tcl code here.
# The file will get re-loaded under wish
# and the above comments will get skipped.
```

```
#
puts "argv0 = $argv0"
puts "argv  = $argv"
exit
```

Save this file as **exectest.tcl** and then mark it executable with **chmod**:

```
chmod +x exectest.tcl
```

Then run it with a different number of command-line parameters to see the Tcl output from the puts commands.

The preceding code asks the shell to run **/bin/sh** to execute the script. From **sh**'s perspective, the first thing that happens is to call **exec** and execute **wish** with the same file and command-line arguments. That is, **wish** will get the same file that **sh** is executing.

The way this trick works is that **wish** will interpret the exec statement as a comment because of the line-continuation backslash on the line above. In Tcl, the line-continuation character, the \, at the end of the comment line causes Tcl to interpret the next line as a comment, too, so Tcl ignores the line that starts with exec. On the other hand, **sh** doesn't understand line-continuation characters on comments, so it tries to execute the exec instruction, which stops **sh** anyway and launches **wish**.

WINDOWS

On Windows NT, you can run scripts from the DOS Command Prompt window; on Windows 3.1, you cannot. On all Windows systems, you can create an icon to launch **wish** with the name of a script as part of the command line. While this isn't as interactive for debugging and testing your scripts, it is easier on the user.

What Happens If You Try This from tclsh?

In addition to problems with UNIX shells, if you try to run the **hello.tk** script under **tclsh** instead of **wish**, you'll get an error message such as the following:

```
invalid command name "button"
```

This is because, of course, **tclsh** doesn't have the `pack` or `button` commands defined. These commands are part of Tk, an add-on to Tcl. (You could add these commands individually to Tcl, but that is exactly what Tk has done.)

Well, you have started the short learning curve of Tcl and Tk scripting. In the next chapter, you'll learn a lot about the basics of the Tcl syntax, including some tricky areas that can mess you up.

Summary

This chapter introduced how to create graphical applications with Tcl and Tk by showing the obligatory "hello world" program. You should also know how to look up information on Tcl and Tk commands. In this book, you'll find the most important options for Tcl commands. This is not a reference, however, so the online manuals will be a big help as you learn Tcl.

In the next chapter, you'll learn what the { and } braces really mean, as well as the basics of Tcl syntax, which is necessary for all Tcl programming.

Tcl/Tk Commands Introduced in this Chapter

```
button
pack
puts
```

CHAPTER 2

Tcl Basics

This chapter covers:

- Starting to program in Tcl
- Tcl syntax
- Tcl variables
- Controlling the flow of the script
- Built-in procedures in Tcl
- Writing your own procedures
- Math in Tcl and math procedures

Tcl Syntax

This chapter and the next are perhaps the most important in this book. In this chapter, you'll cover the basics of Tcl syntax and learn how to get what you want done with Tcl. It may be hard to plod through a chapter on syntax, but you'll use every topic introduced here again and again.

Syntax is usually terribly boring. Tcl makes it much easier because its interpreter is very simple-minded. The Tcl interpreter deals only with commands and arguments. Each distinct line (remember the line continuation marker, \, from Chapter 1) starts with a command. Anything else on the line is an argument that gets passed to that command. *Everything* is text.

While some parts may look like involved syntax (especially for the clever—or deranged—if and while commands shown later in this chapter), a Tcl script is really made up of a set of commands and their arguments.

N O T E You can also place two or more commands on a line if you separate them with a semicolon, ;, as shown in the following example:

```
set var1 marley ; set var2 tosh
```

Commands and their arguments are separated by spaces. That's how the Tcl interpreter divides one part from another. Simple, huh? Unfortunately, it gets more complex. From these simple roots, you start to see some complexity—and quirks—of the language.

Since commands and their arguments are separated by spaces, how can you get spaces into text you want to display? Here comes the first exception to the rules. If you want to place spaces in an argument, you can enclose the full argument in double quotation marks, "".

This handy piece of syntax appeared in an example in Chapter 1:

```
button .c -text "This is new text" -command { exit }
```

The text *This is new text* is treated as a single argument and passed to the button command.

The Tcl interpreter breaks the command up into the following elements:

```
button
.c
-text
This is new text
-command
{ exit }
```

As you can see, the { and } curly braces are a lot like the double quotation marks, in that spaces are preserved inside the braces. These curly braces are the key to Tcl scripting because they defer execution until later.

The curly braces are like double quotation marks except for the following:

- You can nest sets of curly braces, for example, { { } } (not that this particular argument will do much).

- The curly braces delineate code to be executed later.
- The interpreter does not make **substitutions** within the curly braces until executed (later). You'll see more on substitutions later in this chapter in the section on variables and substitutions.

One of the most useful features of the Tcl language is the use of variables.

Tcl Variables

As with virtually all programming and scripting languages, Tcl lets you store a value (or a list of values) into something called a variable. A variable is a lot like the c = a + b you learned back in algebra. Tcl lets you pick a name and then use that name to represent a value. In computer terms, you set the value into the variable.

To set in a value into a variable, you use the set command:

```
set var 6
```

You may want to test this command and the others in the chapter using **wish** (or **tclsh**) in interactive mode. Type in **wish** (or **tclsh**) at you shell command-line prompt. (On Windows, double-click on the **wish** icon or call up **wish** from the **Start** menu.) You should then soon see the **wish** prompt, a percent sign, %, character (or something like tcl>). At the **wish** prompt, you can type in any Tcl command you want.

When you type in the command set var 6, you'll notice that **wish** prints the value set into the variable:

```
% set var 6
6
```

Most Tcl commands print their return values unless the return value is used for some other command.

NOTE

Variables in Tcl are stored as strings, even though the preceding example could fool you into thinking it is a number; it's really stored as a string. A nice part about Tcl is that the string can grow as large as necessary, so you don't have to worry about string lengths or allocating memory (as you do in C and C++ programs).

You can set any type of value into a variable. For example:

```
set var marley
```

You can see what's stored in a variable using the puts (short for put string) command:

```
% puts $var
6
```

(Don't type the % character, **wish** does that.)

Notice the dollar sign, $, in the preceding example. This is our first experience with variable substitution, one of the trickier parts of Tcl.

Variables and Substitutions

The dollar sign signifies variable substitution. That is, if you have $var, this tells the Tcl interpreter to substitute the value stored in the variable in place of the string "$var". Remember, everything in Tcl is text, so the interpreter would have no way of knowing whether you wanted the value held in *var* (6, from our example above), or the string "var" itself. Hence the $ for variable substitution.

Place the $ before the variable name (e.g., $var) to have the interpreter substitute in the current value held in *var*. The trick to remember is that the value substituted is the value held in *var* when it is parsed. You can sometimes get into problems with this, which is why the curly braces defer execution (and parsing) until later.

If $var means to substitute the contents of the variable named *var*, how can you display a string in Tcl with the letters "$var"? Well, you use the backslash (familiar to C programmers) with the dollar sign.

Try the following commands:

```
set var2 $var
set var3 \$var
```

Before you read ahead, you should already know what values will be stored in each of these variables. If you don't, try out the commands:

```
% set var2 $var
6
% set var3 \$var
$var
```

These examples just use the set command. The same concepts apply to all Tcl commands, such as the expr (expression) command:

```
set var4 42
expr 2 * $var4
```

You should see the result 84.

The expr command takes in most kinds of math or logical operations and returns the result.

In addition to *variable substitution*, there's also *command substitution*.

Command Substitution

Many times you need to save the result of a command and use that value as an argument for another command. The way to do this is through the magic of command substitution.

If you see the square brackets, [and], in a command, it means that the contents between the square brackets are to be parsed and executed first, and then the results substituted into the overall command, as shown in the following example:

```
set var5 [expr 2 * $var4]
```

In this code, the [expr 2 * $var4] part gets executed first, and the result, 84, is then substituted to make a new command:

```
set var5 84
```

You can use any valid Tcl command within the [and] command-substitution markers; you aren't limited to the handy expr command. You can also nest the embedded commands. For example:

```
puts [set var6 [expr $var5 + 1] ]
```

If you type this command, you should see the result, 85, printed. Also, the variable *var6* gets set to the same value.

The Tcl interpreter works in what is called *two-phase execution*. In the first phase, the interpreter parses substitutions such as the dollar sign and backslash. In the second phase, the commands get executed. If you nest things, such as with the [and] command-substitution markers, this two-phase process is started again for the data within the [and] characters. This is really very simple, but it can trip you up if you aren't careful.

Table 2.1 shows the various types of substitution in Tcl.

Table 2.1 Variable and Command Substitution

Tc	Meaning
$variable	substitute variable value
${variable}text	Prepend *variable* value onto *text* with no spaces
[expr 1+1]	substitute results of command
"string $variable"	substitute *variable* into quoted text
{string $variable}	don't substitute *variable* into quoted text; defer to later

The ${*variable*} syntax looks rather odd. It allows you to substitute the value stored in a variable into a text string with no spaces, as you can see in the following example:

```
set time_of_day 4
puts ${time_of_day}pm
```

The result of the last command is:

```
4pm
```

There's a much better way to do this using the `format` command, discussed later in this chapter in the section on built-in procedures in Tcl. It's important to know how the *${variable}* syntax is an exception to the normal { and } rules.

NOTE

Worrying about the curly braces, { and }, along with how and when substitutions apply, is the most difficult part of learning Tcl. If you get frustrated now and then, just keep trying different combinations and try to see how the interpreter will treat you code.

NOTE

You can test out how Tcl substitutes with the handy `subst` command, which uses the following syntax:

```
subst -nobackslashes -nocommands -novariables string
```

All the "no" items are optional: `-nobackslashes` means skip backslashes (for multiline commands), `-nocommands` means skip command substitution and `-novariables` means skip variable substitution. Look at the following commands and output:

```
% set var5 84
84
% subst {set var6 $var5 }
set var6 84
% subst -novariables {set var6 $var5 }
set var6 $var5
```

The first `subst` command above performs a full substitution and extracts the value of *var5*, 84, replacing that part of the command. The second `subst` command explicitly turns off variable substitution.

Changing Data in Variables

In addition to the `set` command, Tcl provides other means to modify the values stored in variables, as shown in Table 2.2.

Table 2.2 Changing Data in Variables

Command	Meaning
append variable values...	Append one or more values to variable.
incr variable amount	Increment variable by 1 or by amount.
set variable value	Set value into variable.
unset variable1 variable2...	Unset variables.

With the incr (short for increment) command, the optional *amount* must be an integer value. Otherwise, incr adds 1 to the value stored in the *variable*. This value should be an integer.

You can store individual values into a variable, and you can also store multiple values in an array.

Array Variables

Tcl provides what is called *associative arrays*. You can treat an array as one identifier that represents a set of variables (keys) and values.

N O T E

This is a lot different from most programming languages, except perl, which also offers associative arrays. In most programming languages, an array holds a set of values. In Tcl, an array holds a set of variables and values.

The syntax for accessing an element in an array is:

```
arrayname(variable)
```

where *arrayname* is the name of the array and *variable* is the name of one of the variables (keys) in the array. An example will help:

```
set employee(name) "Eric Johnson"
set employee(city) "St. Paul"
set employee(state) "Minnesota"
set employee(attitude) "Thinks empowerment is a joke"
```

The array *employee* now holds four variables, *name*, *city*, *state* and *attitude*, soon to be on ID cards everywhere.

The standard **$** syntax for accessing the value of a variable still holds, only now the variable name is a bit more complex, as the next example shows:

```
% puts $employee(name)
Eric Johnson
% puts $employee(attitude)
Thinks empowerment is a joke
```

To help you work with arrays, Tcl offers a number of helper commands. The `parray` command prints all the elements of an array:

```
% parray employee
employee(attitude) = Thinks empowerment is a joke
employee(city)     = St. Paul
employee(name)     = Eric Johnson
employee(state)    = Minnesota
```

N O T E

The order of the items in the array is not necessarily the order in which you entered them. Usually the items are alphabetized, but this is not to be depended on. If you need the items in a certain order, you'll need to arrange the output yourself.

The `array` command offers a multitude of options, all of which pertain to—you guessed it—arrays. Table 2.3 lists the basic options for the `array` command, while Table 2.4 lists the search-related options.

Table 2.3 The Basic Options for the Array Command

Command	Usage
array exists name	Returns 1 if *name* is really the name of an array variable.
array get *name*	Returns a list of variable/value pairs of all the items in the array.
array names *name pattern*	Returns all the array item names in the array that match the (optional) pattern.
array set *name list*	Sets values in array from list; list should be in the same format as returned by the array get command.
array size *name*	Returns the number of elements in the array.

To try out these commands, enter the following into **wish** or **tclsh**:

```
% array exists employee
1
% array get employee
attitude {Thinks empowerment is a joke} state Minnesota city {St. Paul}
name {Eric Johnson}
% array names employee
attitude state city name
% array size employee
4
```

The array set command is a little more complex. It expects a list in the same format as returned by the array get command. You can use this, then, to copy one array to another:

```
% array set new_emp [array get employee]
% parray new_emp
new_emp(attitude) = Thinks empowerment is a joke
new_emp(city)     = St. Paul
```

```
new_emp(name)      = Eric Johnson
new_emp(state)     = Minnesota
```

Searching through Arrays

There are also a host of options to the array command for searching through an array, as shown in Table 2.4.

Table 2.4 Searching Arrays with the Array Command

Command	Use
array anymore *name searchid*	Returns 1 (true) if anymore items are in the array for a given *searchId*, 0 (false) otherwise.
array donsearch *name searchid*	Stops an array search.
array nextelement *name searchid*	Returns the name of the next element in the array for the given search ID.
array startsearch *name*	Returns a *searchid* for an item-by-item search in the array.

To better see how the array searching options work, the following example shows how you can fill a list and then search through it, item by item, using the array command options from Table 2.4.

```
# Set values into test array.
set employee(name) "Eric Johnson"
set employee(city) "St. Paul"
set employee(state) "Minnesota"
set employee(attitude) \
    "Thinks empowerment is a joke"

    # Search through all elements of the array.
set searchid [array startsearch employee]
```

```
    # Loop for all items in array from search.
while { [array anymore employee $searchid] } {

    set element \
        [array nextelement employee $searchid]

        # Note use of quotes to
        # make one argument to puts.
    puts "$element = $employee($element)"
}

    # Terminate the search.
array donesearch employee $searchid
exit
```

We cheat a bit by using the `while` command, which is explained later in this chapter in the section on controlling the flow of the script.

Emulating Multidimensional Arrays

Tcl only allows for single-dimensional arrays. That is, you can place only a single element name within the parenthesis. Certain situations cry out for a multidimensional array, such as describing the squares on a tic-tac-toe game, which uses a 3-by-3 square board. A two-dimensional array would allow you to indicate each square on the board by its row and column, the same method used in spreadsheet programs and the Battleship game.

You can fake multidimensional arrays by taking advantage of the fact that the array element names are just text (remember the mantra). So, an element name of 2,3 is perfectly valid:

```
set tic_tac_toe(2,2) X
set tic_tac_toe(3,1) O
```

This makes the `tic_tac_toe` array appear as though it really has two dimensions, but if you print the names in the array with the `array names` command, you'll see the real story:

```
% array names tic_tac_toe
3,1 2,2
```

Special Arrays for Environment Variables

The env variable holds the set of environment variables that the operating system supports.

For example, DOS, NT, and UNIX typically share a **PATH** environment variable. You can access the contents of this environment variable, the same as for any other array. Simply use the name of the environment variable as the item name for the array, as in this example from Linux:

```
% puts $env(PATH)
/usr/local/bin:/bin:/usr/bin:/usr/X11/bin:
/usr/andrew/bin:/usr/openwin/bin:/usr/games:
.:/usr/lib/interviews/bin:/home/erc/bin:
/usr/andrew/bin:/usr/local/tcl/bin:/usr/X11/bin:
/usr/andrew/bin:/usr/openwin/bin:/usr/games:.:
/usr/X11/bin:/usr/andrew/bin:/usr/openwin/bin:
/usr/games:.:/usr/lib/interviews/bin:
/home/erc/bin:/usr/andrew/bin:/usr/local/tcl/bin:
/usr/X11/bin:/usr/andrew/bin:/usr/openwin/bin:/usr/games:.
```

Under Windows NT, you'll see a much different list, depending on what is set up in the **System** choice from the Control Panel (abbreviated here):

```
% parray env

env(COMPUTERNAME)          = YONSEN
env(COMSPEC)               = C:\WINDOWS\system32\cmd.exe
env(DISPLAY)               = localhost:0
env(GLOB)                  = D:\etc\glob.exe
env(HOME)                  = .
env(OS)                    = Windows_NT
env(PATH)                  =
C:\WINDOWS\system32;C:\WINDOWS;D:\BIN;C:\DOS;D:\ETC
env(PROCESSOR_ARCHITECTURE) = x86
env(PROCESSOR_LEVEL)       = 4
env(TEMP)                  = C:\temp
env(USERNAME)              = erc
env(WINDIR)                = C:\WINDOWS
```

You can use the `parray` command to print out your entire environment from within **wish**:

```
parray env
```

This usually results in a lot of output. You can also use the `array startsearch` and `array nextelement` commands to go through the env array.

Most environment variables differ greatly between Windows and UNIX. You'll need to be aware of this for cross-platform scripts.

PORTABILITY

Special Array to Describe Your Computing Platform

The special array *tcl_platform* contains information about your current platform. This array can be useful for determining what kind of system your script executes on. For example:

```
% parray tcl_platform
tcl_platform(machine)   = intel
tcl_platform(os)        = Windows NT
tcl_platform(osVersion) = 3.50
tcl_platform(platform)  = windows
```

On a UNIX system, this looks more like the following:

```
% parray tcl_platform
tcl_platform(machine)   = 9000/715
tcl_platform(os)        = HP-UX
tcl_platform(osVersion) = A.09.03
tcl_platform(platform)  = unix
```

Controlling the Flow of the Script

A Tcl script normally executes from the start to end, top to bottom. Each com- mand is parsed and then executed in turn, although you can defer execution using syntax elements such as the curly braces, { and }.

This situation normally works fine until you want slightly more complex scripts. To aid this, Tcl offers a number of commands that allow for branching and decision-making including if-then statements, for, and while. If you've ever used a programming language before, all these statements will be old hat. All you need to learn is the syntax under Tcl, so you'll probably want to just skim the next sections, but there's one more thing to which you should pay attention.

Even though these statements look like real syntax, be aware that if, while, for, and so on are merely Tcl commands with (usually long) arguments. The most common mistake I make is to think that the Tcl interpreter is smarter than it really is. Tcl is a very simple language. Most of the syntax, such as the if statement, is just for the sake of appearances. The if command is really just a normal Tcl command, although it is very easy to be fooled into thinking the Tcl language supports the idea of an if statement.

The basic format of an if command looks like the following:

```
if {expression} then {body}
```

For example:

```
if {$i < 5} then {
    puts "$i is less than 5"
}
```

NOTE

If you're used to C programming, you may mistake the curly braces, { and } for C's parenthesis, (and) that surround the if expression. Unlike C, Tcl uses curly braces around the expression *and* the body.

The then part is optional. If the expression result is true, that is, if it generates a nonzero value (usually 1), then the body code gets executed. If the expression result is false (0), then the body code does not get executed.

The if command is really getting three arguments (or two, if you omit the optional then part), including an expression and a body. The curly braces allow you to place a lot of Tcl commands within one argument to the if command. Clever, huh?

Expressions

The expression part of the if command can come from the result of any Tcl command or by using one of Tcl's built-in expression operators for comparing values, listed in Table 2.5.

Table 2.5 Expression Operators for Comparing Values

Operator	Meaning
!v1	Returns 1 if v1 is 0, 0 otherwise.
v1<v2	Returns 1 if v1 is less than v2, 0 otherwise.
v1>v2	Returns 1 if v1 is greater than v2, 0 otherwise.
v1<=v2	Returns 1 if v1 is less than or equal to v2, 0 otherwise.
v1>=v2	Returns 1 if v1 is greater than or equal to v2, 0 otherwise.
v1==v2	Returns 1 if v1 is equal to v2, 0 otherwise.
v1!=v2	Returns 1 if v1 is not equal to v2, 0 otherwise.
v1&&v2	Returns 1 if both v1 and v2 are nonzero, 0 otherwise.
v1||v2	Returns 1 if either of v1 or v2 are nonzero, 0 otherwise.

In Tcl, true is 1 (or any nonzero value) and false is 0. The expressions in Table 2.5 allow you to check for a specific condition.

In addition to the basic if command, you can also provide an else part that gets executed if the expression result is false. The syntax is:

```
if {expression} then {if-body} else {else-body}
```

To get even more complex, there's an elseif, which allows you to place multiple expressions in one statement:

```
if {expression1} then {if-body} elseif {expression2} {elseif-body} else
{else-body}
```

If the first expression (*expression1*) is false, then the if command tests the second expression (*expression2*). If that expression is true, the *elseif-body* gets executed. If all tests result in a false value, then the *else-body* gets executed. You can include more than one elseif part. For example:

```
if {expression1} then {if-body}
    elseif {expression2} {elseif-body2}
    elseif {expression3} {elseif-body3}
    elseif {expression4} {elseif-body4}
    elseif {expression5} {elseif-body5}
    elseif {expression6} {elseif-body6}
    elseif {expression7} {elseif-body7}
    elseif {expression8} {elseif-body8}
    else {else-body}
```

You can go for a lot more levels than this. Sooner or later, though, your code will get too complex to be readable.

Better to Switch than Fight

If you have a lot of tests, you can use the switch command. The basic syntax is:

```
switch options string {pattern1 {body1} pattern2 {body2} ... default {bodyd}}
```

NOTE

You can skip the curly braces that surround all of the patterns, but then you must use the line continuation marker, \, if your switch command extends beyond one line.

C programmers should be very familiar with the switch statement. Switch takes a single string and compare it against a number of choices. If it finds a match, it executes the body of Tcl code following the matched choice. For example:

```
set animal cat
switch $animal {
    dog { puts "Dogs make good pets." }
    cat { puts "Cats are better." }
    platypus { puts "Watch out for the Platypus Society" }
    default { puts "Why did you pick a $animal?" }
}
```

If you type in this code into **tclsh** or **wish**, you'll see the following output:

```
Cats are better.
```

The preceding code compares the value held in the variable *animal* against a number of choices: *dog, cat, platypus,* and *default.* Since the value of the variable *animal* was *cat*, the code after the *cat* choice gets executed.

The default section provides an escape clause. If none of the patterns match the initial value, the code body after default gets executed. Since users frequently ignore your careful instructions and enter bad values, you should include the default section in all switch commands.

If you have a number of choices that can use the same code, you can use a shorthand. If you place a minus sign, -, for the body, this means to use the body of the next choice. For example:

```
set animal cat
switch $animal {
    dog -
    cat -
    platypus { puts "A $animal makes a good pet." }
    default { puts "Why did you pick a $animal?" }
}
```

You'll see the following output from the preceding commands:

```
A cat makes a good pet.
```

The *cat* and *dog* choices both execute the same code as the *platypus* choice.

Up to now, all the values have exactly matched the initial string. The Tcl `switch` command is more flexible than that, though. You can also allow for partial matches using special options. The `switch` command allows for three types of matching, as described in Table 2.6.

Table 2.6 Switch Options

Option	Meaning
-glob	Use string-matching syntax (see Chapter 5)
-regexp	Use regex matching syntax
-exact	The choice must exactly match the string

If you're familiar with UNIX shell commands, the `-regexp` and `-glob` options should make sense. The `-glob` option (the default), accepts the special characters shown in Table 2.7.

Table 2.7 Special Globbing Characters

Character	Meaning
*	Matches zero or more characters, of any value
?	Matches one single character, of any value
\c	Matches only the single character *c*
[char]	Matches the single character, any single character between the square braces, or a character in a range in the form of c1-c2

These globbing characters also work with the `string match` command. See Chapter 5.

NOTE

These special characters make more sense with a few examples. The square-bracket syntax is the toughest. Table 2.8 shows some clearer examples.

NOTE

Table 2.8 Globbing Matches

Sequence	Matches
[Cc]	One character: Uppercase *C* or lowercase *c*.
[a-z]	One character: Anything from lowercase *a* to lowercase *z*.

Remember that the square brackets are specifying a single character match, even though you may place more than one character between the brackets.

More Example Globs

In the preceding example switch command, the user must type in cat, dog, or platypus. Anything else is not understood. But what if the user types in Cat, DOG, or pLaTyPuS? The preceding example will fail to detect the input and will use the default case. We can fix the switch example, as shown in the following:

```
switch -glob $animal {
    [dD][oO][gG]* { puts "Dogs make good pets." }
    [cC][aA][tT]* { puts "Cats are better." }
    [pP][lL][aA][tT][yY][pP][uU][sS]*
        { puts "Watch out for the Platypus Society" }
    default { puts "Why did you pick a $animal?" }
}
```

NOTE

Since the -glob option is the default, you can omit the text -glob.

With this example, the *cat* part will match *Cat*, *caT*, *CAT*, or *cats*, along with any combination thereof. The extra star at the end allows for any (or no) characters following, which allows *cats*, with an extra *s*, to match. It also allows *catheter* and *catalog* to match, which is not really a good thing.

We can make another refinement that takes care of plurals:

```
switch -glob $animal {
    [dD][oO][gG]s -
```

```
[dD][oO][gG] { puts "Dogs make good pets." }

[cC][aA][tT]s -
[cC][aA][tT] { puts "Cats are better." }

[pP][lL][aA][tT][yY][pP][uU][sS]es -
[pP][lL][aA][tT][yY][pP][uU][sS]
    { puts "Watch out for the Platypus Society" }

default { puts "Why did you pick a $animal?" }
}
```

As you can see, handling odd user input requires a lot of code (in any programming language).

Regex Matches

In addition to the -glob matches, you can also use the -regexp matches (which are also used with the regexp command on its own). This style of pattern matching, called *regular expressions*, is much looser. A pattern of [a-z] matches any string with a lowercase letter in it.

Table 2.9 shows the special characters for regex-style matching.

Table 2.9 Special Regex-Matching Characters

Character	Meaning
.	Matches any single character
\c	Matches only the character *c*
^	Matches a null string at the start of the value
$	Matches a null string at the end of the value
[*chars*]	Matches any single character from chars. You can use a range, such as a-z, or ^ to match any single character *not* in the remainder of the chars
(*pattern*)	Matches against the *pattern*; allows for grouping

As before, what you can put between the square brackets is the toughest to master. [a-z] matches any string with a lowercase letter, [a-zA-Z] matches any string with a lowercase or uppercase letter, and [a-zA-Z0-9] matches any alphanumeric character.

The ^ character within the square braces acts as a negator as [^a-z] matches any string that does *not* contain a lowercase letter.

So far, the -regexp pattern-matching tools appear to parallel the tools available with the -glob option. So why add the extra confusion? (I'd like to know as well.) One reason is that with -regexp pattern-matching, you can combine patterns to create a much more powerful, if confusing, pattern-matching system. That is, you can match one or more whole patterns, rather than just one or more characters.

Table 2.10 lists the means to match whole patterns.

Table 2.10 Combining Elements in a Regex Pattern

Character	Meaning
*	Matches a sequence of zero or more matches of the preceding element
+	Matches a sequence of one or more matches of the preceding element
?	Matches either a null string or the preceding element
pattern1|*pattern2*	Matches either pattern1 or pattern2; usually used with parenthesis

With this, you can build up complicated patterns of a number of elements. For example, a variable name in Tcl must start with a alphabetic character. It can then be followed by any alphanumeric characters. That is, *var1*, *v1*, and *variable* are all valid variable names, but *1var* is not (the leading numeral is prohibited). Putting this all together in a regexp expression, we get the following:

```
^([a-zA-Z])+[a-zA-Z0-9_]*$
```

Yow. This is complex. Going through this element-by-element, we get:

- ^ matches any null data at the start of the string.
- ([a-zA-Z]) matches any alphabetic character.
- + means that we must have one (or more) alphabetic characters. This takes care of the rule that a variable name must start with an alphabetic character.
- [a-zA-Z0-9_] matches any alphanumeric character or an underscore, _, character.
- * matches zero or more sequences of the preceding rule (any alphanumeric character or an underscore).
- $ matches any null data at the end of the string.

To test this, I'll show the regexp command, which is shorter than the switch command.

The regexp Command

The regexp command takes in a pattern, such as the one given in the preceding section, and a value. It returns 1 (true) if the value matches the pattern, or 0 (false) if the value does not match the pattern. The syntax is:

```
regexp {pattern} value
```

The pattern may be any valid regexp pattern described earlier.

So, to test the pattern —^([a-zA-Z])+[a-zA-Z0-9_]*$—place it in curly braces and compare with values. You must place the regexp pattern within curly braces to prevent the Tcl interpreter from performing variable substitutions with the $ character and so on.

Try the following examples (and compare the results returned):

```
% regexp {^([a-zA-Z])+[a-zA-Z0-9_]*$} var1
1
% regexp {^([a-zA-Z])+[a-zA-Z0-9_]*$} variable
1
```

45

```
% regexp {^([a-zA-Z])+[a-zA-Z0-9_]*$} 1var
0
% regexp {^([a-zA-Z])+[a-zA-Z0-9_]*$} start_value
1
% regexp {^([a-zA-Z])+[a-zA-Z0-9_]*$} a12345bcdef34565

1
```

You can see that *1var* is an invalid name, while *var1*, *variable*, *start_value*, and *a12345bcdef34565* are OK.

Using -regexp in the switch Command

You can use the `regexp` patterns with the `switch` command as well (which is how we got into this mess in the first place), as shown in the following example:

```
set value a12345bcdef34565

switch -regexp $value {

    ^([a-zA-Z])+[a-zA-Z0-9_]*$ { puts "OK variable name." }
    default { puts "$value is not a valid variable name." }
}
```

With a value of *a12345bcdef34565*, you should see the following output:

```
OK variable name.
```

But, if you set *value* to *1var*, you'll see:

```
1var is not a valid variable name.
```

In addition to the `regexp` and `switch` commands, these patterns are used with the `regsub` command.

The regsub Command

The `regsub` command allows you to use regular expressions of the type used by the `regexp` command in replacing values in strings.

The syntax is:

```
regsub pattern string_to_match new_value target
```

The regsub command tries to find the pattern in the *string_to_match*. If so, then regsub creates a new string by replacing the matched value with the *new_value*. This string is then set into the *target* variable. In addition, if this isn't enough, regsub returns 1 if it found a match and 0 if it did not.

Also, you can use the -all option to replace all matches with the *new_value*. The -nocase option tells regsub to ignore the case in the *string_to_match*.

For example, you can use the pattern to find the incorrect element of a string and replace it with a good value. In Minnesota, the native speakers (myself included) often confuse *borrow* and *lend*, leading to such phrases as, "Borrow me a book, please."

You can use regsub to fix this:

```
% regsub borrow "borrow me a book please." lend target

1
% puts $target
lend me a book please.
```

The variable *target* gets set to the new string, "Lend me a book, please."

While this example just used a normal string for the pattern, you can use the regexp-style patterns as well. See the on-line manual page for regsub for even more details on this complicated command. Due to the complexity, I normally shy away from regular expressions if at all possible.

Looping Commands

In addition, to the if and switch commands, Tcl sports a number of looping commands, including the familiar for and while commands.

The for command loops for a set amount of iterations. The basic syntax is:

```
for {start} {test} {next} {body}
```

The *start* code initializes any data needed for loop control. The *test* determines whether to execute the *body* code. If it's true, the *body* gets executed. After each iteration, the *next* code gets executed and the *test* invoked again, until the *test* returns false (0).

To loop 10 times, you can use the following code:

```
for {set i 0} { $i < 10 } { incr i } {

    puts "Index is $i."

}
```

See Table 2.2 for more in the `incr` command, which increments the value by 1. This is a very handy command when working with `for` loops.

You'll see the following output:

```
Index is 0.
Index is 1.
Index is 2.
Index is 3.
Index is 4.
Index is 5.
Index is 6.
Index is 7.
Index is 8.
Index is 9.
```

The `foreach` command is set up to work with lists (see Chapter 6). The basic syntax appears as:

```
foreach varname $list {body}
```

The `foreach` command executes the *body* code once for each element in the given *list*. Each time, `foreach` sets the variable (*varname* in this case) to hold the value of the current item from the list. For example:

```
set l { 1 2 3 4 5 6 seven }

foreach item $l {
```

```
    puts "Current item is $item."
}
```

This example generates the following output:

```
Current item is 1.
Current item is 2.
Current item is 3.
Current item is 4.
Current item is 5.
Current item is 6.
Current item is seven.
```

The while command loops while an expression returns true. Its syntax is very simple:

```
while {expression} {body}
```

For example:

```
set i 10

while { $i > 0 } {
    puts "Current index is $i."

    incr i -1
}
```

Executing this example will generate the following output:

```
Current index is 10.
Current index is 9.
Current index is 8.
Current index is 7.
Current index is 6.
Current index is 5.
Current index is 4.
Current index is 3.
Current index is 2.
Current index is 1.
```

The real difference between the while and for commands is that for the while command, you must modify the value tested against (*i* in the preceding example) in the body of the loop.

50

Jumping Out of Things

If things get too hairy, Tcl provides a number of commands to jump out of a loop, or even out of the Tcl interpreter entirely.

The break command jumps out of the current looping command, instead of jumping back to the top of the loop:

```
set i 10

while { $i > 0 } {

    if { $i == 5 } {
        break
    }

    puts "Current index is $i."

    incr i -1
}

puts "I is now $i."
```

These commands will stop the loop when the variable *i* equals 5.

NOTE

The break command jumps out of the innermost loop. In the following example, the break command will jump out of the inner loop (the while command using the variable *k*) not the outer loop (the while command using the variable *i*).

```
set i 10

while { $i > 0 } {

    set k 10
```

```
while { $k > 0 } {

    if { $k == 5 } {
        break
    }

    puts "Current inner loop index is $k."

    incr k -1
}

    puts "Current index is $i."

    incr i -1
}
```

The continue command jumps from the current position to the top of the loop, continuing on with the next iteration of the loop, as shown in the following example:

```
set i 10

while { $i > 0 } {

    incr i -1

    if { $i == 5 } {
        continue
    }

    puts "Current index is $i."
}
```

These commands will generate the following output:

```
Current index is 9.
Current index is 8.
Current index is 7.
Current index is 6.
Current index is 4.
```

```
Current index is 3.
Current index is 2.
Current index is 1.
Current index is 0.
```

Note that 5 is missing in the above output. That's what `continue` did for us.

NOTE Be careful with `continue`. If you had replaced the `break` in the original example with `continue`, the loop would never terminate. That's because the `incr` command appeared after the `break`. In this example, `continue` appears after the `incr` command (which decrements the value).

To jump out of everything and end the execution of **wish** or **tclsh**, use the `exit` command, which has the following syntax:

```
exit optional_return_code
```

For `exit` (mentioned in Chapter 1), if you skip the optional return code, the default value returned is 0. This follows the UNIX convention that a program terminating successfully returns 0 and one terminating because of errors returns some other value. (Tcl was created in the UNIX environment first, and so follows more UNIX conventions than those for Windows).

As a handy reference guide, Table 2.11 lists the Tcl commands for controlling the flow of execution.

Table 2.11 Controlling the Flow of Execution in Tcl Scripts

Command

```
break
continue
exit optional_return_code
for {start} {test} {next} {body}
foreach varname $list {body}
if {expression} then {body}
if {expression} then {if-body} else {else-body}
if {expression1} then {if-body} elseif {expression2} {elseif-body}
else {else-body}
```

```
switch options string {pattern1 {body1} pattern2 {body2} ...
default {bodyd}}

while {expression} {body}
```

Built-In Procedures in Tcl

Tcl provides a good number of built-in procedures, some of which you've seen, some mentioned only in passing. In the next few paragraphs, you'll see some of the most useful built-in Tcl commands.

The puts command, short for *put string*, prints its argument, a string:

```
puts string
```

In Chapter 6 in the section on files, you'll see that puts can be used to write a string to a file as well as print to the screen.

N O T E

The puts command is very useful for debugging your Tcl scripts. If something seems to be wrong, put in a few puts commands to print values of variables at particular places in the script. You'll find this a great aid in figuring out what the heck is going on.

N O T E

As with all strings, you can take advantage of command and variable substitution, as shown here:

```
set val 1
puts "The value is $val."
puts [set val 1]
```

The first puts will print:

```
The value is 1.
```

The second puts will merely print 1.

By itself, the `puts` command is extremely limited, but you'll most often use it in conjunction with the `format` command.

The `format` command works a lot like the `sprintf` function in C. `format` returns a string that is build from a number of arguments. You can insert values into the string and use expressions to generate the values. The syntax is:

```
format format_string arg1 arg2...
```

The *args* are optional, depending on what you put in the *format_string*.

The following command takes two extra arguments and inserts them in the *format_string*, replacing the *%s* values:

```
% format "My name is %s %s" Eric Johnson
My name is Eric Johnson
```

Sometimes, the format string tends to be obscure:

```
% format "%s's %s is named %s" Eric cat Halloween
Eric's cat is named Halloween
```

You can also insert other values, such as integers, floating-point numbers, and individual characters. Since everything in Tcl is really a string anyway, all you're doing is specifying how you want the value interpreted.

With the complementary ability of using the `$` variable substitution, the `format` command is not as essential as it is in C or C++.

Table 2.12 lists the format values for various types of data.

Table 2.12 Using the Format Command

Format	Meaning
%c	Insert a single character
%d	Insert an integer value
%e	Insert a floating-point value, in scientific notation format
%f	Insert a floating-point value
%g	Insert a floating-point value, in scientific notation format

%i	Insert a signed integer value
%o	Insert an integer in octal (base 8) format
%s	Insert a string value
%u	Insert an unsigned integer value
%x	Insert an integer and display in hexadecimal (base 16) format (%X forces the hexadecimal digits to appear uppercase)

You can also control the number of characters used to format strings or numbers. For example, %5d specifies a five-digit integer value. This allows you to better control how a string gets formatted.

See the on-line manual page for format for more information on how to use the format command.

You can combine format with puts for good effect using command substitution:

```
set i 4
set name file_list
puts [format \
   "Loading the %dth element of the list %s." \
   $i $name]
```

You'll see the following:

```
Loading the 4th element of the list file_list.
```

While the format command acts like the ANSI C printf function, the scan command acts like the ANSI C sscanf function. The purpose of scan is to scan out, or extract, values stored in a string. For example, the following string holds three numbers:

```
"105 42 36"
```

With scan, you can pull out these numbers into three variables:

```
scan "105 42 36" "%d %d %d" var1 var2 var3
```

When you execute this, you'll see:

```
% scan "105 42 36" "%d %d %d" var1 var2 var3
3
% puts "$var1 $var2 $var3"
105 42 36
```

The syntax for scan is:

```
scan string format_string variable1 variable2...
```

The % options used in the *format_string* use the same syntax as the format command does and come from ANSI C.

WARNING

You must ensure you have enough variables for all the values you're trying to extract. Generally, each % item represents a value and requires a separate variable.

The scan command returns the number of values it extracted or -1 on failure. If you save this value, you can check the input string for errors.

In addition to all the built-in procedures in Tcl, you can easily write your own. This is where Tcl really becomes useful.

Writing Your Own Procedures

There are two ways to extend Tcl. You can write procedures strictly within the Tcl language, or you can create new Tcl procedures by writing functions in the C programming language that follow special conventions, which are most useful for application-specific behavior (such as recalculating a spreadsheet). You'll see the latter in Chapter 12. For now, there's a lot you can do by staying strictly within the Tcl language, using the proc command.

The proc command registers a procedure by name and allows you to execute it like any other command in Tcl. The syntax is:

```
proc name {arguments} {body}
```

For example, you can help your human resource department with the following procedure:

```
proc stroke { name } {

    set str [format "%s is a wonderful person!" $name ]
    puts $str
}
```

Once you call proc, then that procedure is ready to be used at any time in the future, as in:

```
% stroke Amanda
Amanda is a wonderful person!
```

In this case, *Amanda* is the argument passed to the procedure stroke. When invoked, the variable *name* will get set to the argument's value (*Amanda*). Every time you invoke the stroke procedure, the *name* variable will get set with a new value, the value passed to stroke as an argument.

Inside a procedure, you can place any number of Tcl commands. You can also use variables and set values.

Using the button command shown in Chapter 1, you can create a procedure to make new buttons:

```
proc make_button { name text } {
    button $name -text $text -command { exit }
    pack $name
}
```

This procedure creates a new button widget and packs it (more on both of these subjects in the next chapter). Note the use of more than one variable (*name* and *text*).

To invoke this procedure, you can use the following example:

```
% make_button .b1 "First Button"
```

After this first button is created, you'll see a window as shown in Figure 2.1.

Figure 2.1 The first button.

You can run the make_button procedure again with:

```
% make_button .b2 "Second Button"
```

Now, you'll see a larger window, as shown in Figure 2.2.

Figure 2.2 The first two buttons.

You'll need to run these commands from the **wish** interpreter because the button command requires Tk, not just Tcl.

NOTE

You can do a lot of work with procedures. In fact, smart use of procedures can make your Tcl scripts much easier to read. You can also reuse Tcl code in new situations.

In conjunction with the proc command, you may need to create a procedure that does more than create widgets or print results. You can use the return statement to return a value from the procedure.

For example, I am relatively bad at estimating how long software projects will take. So, I may need a procedure to multiply my estimate (which is usually far too optimistic) by some constant amount:

```
proc estimate { first_guess } {

   return [expr $first_guess * 2.5 ]
}
```

So now, when I estimate the time it takes to complete a project, I can get a more valid value as I rampage over 30 years of software estimation theory:

```
% estimate 10
25.0
```

In this example, **wish** or **tclsh** will merely print the value. You can instead set a variable to hold the result:

```
set result [estimate 10]
% puts $result
25.0
```

This should look familiar, especially when you look back at the expr and format commands, both of which return a value.

With return, you can optionally pass back error information as well. The full syntax is:

```
return -code code -errorinfo info -errorcode code string
```

All the arguments are optional. The *string* is the value that gets returned. The other arguments are for dealing with error conditions. See Chapter 8 for more on this.

Once you start working with procedures, which you'll need to do for any sophisticated Tcl script, you'll soon discover that variables in the main part of the script are not available within your procedures. You can pass variables into procedures as arguments, but you cannot modify or access variables that exist outside of the procedure.

With the global command, though, you can. global marks a variable as having global scope:

```
proc offset { xoffset yoffset } {
```

```
    global x y

    incr x $xoffset
    incr y $yoffset

      # Return an empty string.
    return
}

set x 10
set y 20

offset 5 2
puts "X is $x and y is $y"
```

You'll see the following output:

```
X is 15 and y is 22
```

Without the global statement, the procedure offset can't access the values of *x* and *y*, which will result in an error such as the following:

```
can't read "x": no such variable
```

When you see such an error, and know that you have indeed defined a variable named *x*, you should suspect that you didn't mark the variable as global in a procedure.

Call by Reference

If you've ever used the Pascal or Modula programming languages, you'll be used to the concept of calling by value or calling by reference (the C language hides the issue: everything is passed by value and you pass a pointer to simulate passing by reference).

Tcl provides the odd command upvar to allow you to simulate calling by reference. upvar allows you to access a variable up one level. (You can also pass the level number, but this is virtually impossible to use generally; it results in a very specific solution to a very specific problem.)

The syntax is:

```
upvar level $variable target
```

The *level* argument defaults to 1, and in virtually all cases, you should skip this argument.

upvar exists mainly to allow you to pass arrays to a procedure. Since an array has no value as is (you must access an element in the array to get a value), you cannot readily pass an array to a procedure.

Because of its widespread use with Tcl arrays, the following example shows how to pass an array and access values in it from a procedure:

```
proc print_name { emp } {

    # Associate var1 with the actual array.
    upvar $emp var1

    puts "Employee $var1(name) lives in $var1(city)."

    return
}

# Store some employee data.
set employee(name) "Eric Johnson"
set employee(city) "St. Paul"
set employee(state) "Minnesota"
set employee(attitude) "Thinks empowerment is a joke"

# Print the name and city values.
print_name employee
```

Note how we call this procedure, print_name, with the array variable *employee* and not the normal value (which would be $employee).

You'll see the following data printed:

```
Employee Eric Johnson lives in St. Paul.
```

In addition to upvar, there's also uplevel, sort of a hybrid cross of eval (covered in Chapter 5) and upvar. You'll usually only need this if you want to create new control statements, such as your own `while` or `for` commands. See the on-line manuals for more on `uplevel`.

Renaming Procedures

The `rename` command allows you to rename a procedure:

```
rename original_name new_name
```

This command allows you to keep old commands while redefining them.

In Tcl, you can simply execute `proc` again with the same name as a command to redefine that command. The problem is that the old command is now lost. With `rename`, you can save the old command, in case you need it later, and then redefine a command.

Procedures with a Variable Number of Arguments

Up to now, you've seen procedures that handle a fixed number of arguments. Even so, the `format` command seems to break this rule in that it can take any number of arguments. As you'd suspect, you can make procedures like this, too.

The special command `args` allows you to use a variable number of arguments in a procedure. The `print_args` procedure, below, takes any number of arguments and prints them:

```
proc print_args { args } {

    foreach value $args {
       puts $value
    }
}

print_args 1 2 3 4
print_args 1 two three 4 5 6 7
```

The `args` value is a list (see Chapter 6 for more on lists) that contains all the remaining (in this case, all) arguments to the procedure.

In some procedures, you may want to have one or two named arguments, and then allow for any number of following arguments. The format command does this. It requires a format string. You can follow this with a number of arguments as well.

To do this, you place the special word args after any arguments you want to name. For example:

```
proc one_arg_plus { first args } {

    puts "the first argument is $first. The rest follow:"
    print_args $args
}
```

The output is:

```
% one_arg_plus 1 2 3 4 5 6 7
the first argument is 1. The rest follow:
2 3 4 5 6 7
```

Note that in this example, you see some of the simplicity of the Tcl interpreter. The one_arg_plus procedure gets the following values. The variable *first* is set to 1. The special variable args is set to the list of 2 3 4 5 6 7, but when print_args gets called from within the procedure one_arg_plus, all these values, 2 3 4 5 6 7, get passed as a single argument to the procedure print_args. The use of the special variable args hasn't changed. It's just that when you pass a list to a procedure like this, you get the value of the list passed as one argument.

If you don't want this behavior, you can use the foreach command shown earlier or one of the list commands in Chapter 6 to extract each item from the list.

While you can write your own procedures in Tcl, it's best to first check if a procedure already exists, so that you don't have to spend the time to write and debug a new one. Tcl comes with a lot of built-in procedures. We've seen some in this chapter. For text string procedures, see Chapter 5. For file and list procedures, see Chapter 6. There's also a whole set of math procedures, which are covered in the next section.

Math in Tcl

Tcl provides a number of built-in math procedures. The workhorse, though, is the expr command. The syntax is:

```
expr expression
```

expr evaluates the expression and returns its value. Such an expression can be a mathematical one, resulting in some value, or a logical one, which results in a true (1 or any nonzero value) or false (0), using the logical expressions from Table 2.5. For example:

```
% expr 2+2
4
% expr (2+4)+5
11
% expr 1<2
1
% expr 2==3
0
```

You can, of course, use variables within expressions:

```
set value 10
expr ($value+2)*2
```

You can use parenthesis to control how the expression gets evaluated. Table 2.13 shows the mathematical expressions that complement the logical expressions in Table 2.5.

Some expressions work with both integer values (whole numbers) and floating-point (decimal) values. Table 2.13 shows the expressions which work with both types of numbers. Table 2.14 shows expressions that work only with integer values.

This is somewhat misleading, in that in Tcl, everything is a text string. Even so, these rules still apply, based on the type of the data you store in the string. For example, if you store a value of 44.5 (with a decimal point), Tcl treats it as a floating-point number (for these purposes, it is still a string). If you store a value of 44, Tcl treats it as an integer.

Table 2.13 Math Expressions in Tcl that Work with Floating Point and Integer Values

Expression	Meaning
-v1	Negative of v1
v1*v2	Multiply v1 and v2
v1/v2	Divide v1 by v2
v1+v2	Add v1 and v2
v1-v2	Subtract v2 from v1

The expressions in Tables 2.13 and 2.14 are listed in the order of precedence, although some, such as * and /, have the same precedence. The idea of precedence is mainly to deal with statements such as:

```
expr $a*$b+$c-$d/$e
```

Because the order in which the operators will be applied is always confusing, it is much better to use parenthesis to clearly show the order you intend the operators to be applied, as in the following example:

```
expr ($a*$b)+(($c-$d)/$e)
```

Comparing these two notations, you'll see different results:

```
% set a 1
1
% set b 2
2
% set c 3
3
% set d 4
4
% set e 5
5
% expr ($a*$b)+(($c-$d)/$e)
1
```

```
% expr $a*$b+$c-$d/$e
5
```

Table 2.14 Math Expressions in Tcl that Work only with Integer Values

Expression	Meaning
~v1	Bitwise complement of v1
v1%v2	Remainder after dividing v1 by v2
v1<<v2	Left-shift v1 by v2 number of bits
v1>>v2	Right-shift v1 by v2 number of bits
v1&v12	Bitwise AND of v1 and v2
v1^v2	Bitwise exclusive or (XOR) of v1 and v2
v1|v2	Bitwise OR of v1 and v2
v1?v2:v3	Returns v2 if v1 is nonzero, otherwise returns v3

If you're familiar with C programming, the expressions in Tables 2.13 and 2.14 should be old hat.

Numeric Notation

Integer values may be defined in decimal, hexadecimal, or octal notation, using standard C conventions (a leading *0x* for hexadecimal and a leading *0* for octal).

Floating-point numbers also follow C language conventions, allowing values such as 4.6, 4.6e+16, 4e6, and so on.

Math Procedures

Tcl includes a range of math functions, most from, you guessed it, standard C. (Did you ever get the feeling that Tcl was written in the C language?)

Unlike most Tcl procedures, you can call the Tcl math functions using standard function notation, such as:

```
set b hypot($a,$c)
```

Table 2.15 lists the major math functions in Tcl.

Table 2.15 Tcl Math Functions

Function	Meaning
acos(a)	Arccosine
asin(a)	Arcsine
atan(a)	Arctangent
atan2(a, b)	Arctangent of a/b
cos(a)	Cosine, using radians
cosh(a)	Hyperbolic cosine
double(integer)	Floating-point value equal to integer
exp(a)	Constant e raised to power a
fmod(a,b)	Floating-point remainder of a/b
hypot(a,b)	Square root of (a squared plus b squared)
log(a)	Natural logarithm of a
log10(a)	Base 10 logarithm of a
pow(a,b)	a raised to power b
sin(a)	Sine, using radians
sinh(a)	Hyperbolic sine
sqrt(a)	Square root of a
tan(a)	Tangent, using radians
tanh(a)	Hyperbolic tangent

Tcl also provides a number of functions to convert from floating-point values to integers, get the absolute value, and so on, as listed in Table 2.16.

Table 2.16 Tcl Math Conversion Functions

Function	Meaning
abs(a)	Absolute value of a
ceil(a)	Smallest integer not less than a
floor(a)	Largest integer not greater than a
int(a)	Integer value of a
round(a)	Integer value of rounded a

In addition to these math functions, you can control the precision used when converting floating-point values to strings. The global variable *tcl_precision* controls this. Normally set to 6, you can increase or decrease it if necessary.

Internally, floating-point values are stored as the C type double, using a 64-bit (or greater) double-precision IEEE floating-point value. Setting tcl_precision to a value larger than 17 doesn't make sense if IEEE floating-point is used.

Integer values are stored as the C type int, normally 32 bits.

Summary

Whew. There's probably more syntax in this chapter than you'd like, but every bit is essential for creating useful Tcl scripts.

Tcl scripts are a set of textual commands. Each command has a number of arguments that are passed to the command for execution. Even statements such as if and while, used to control the flow of a Tcl script, are really just commands with arguments. This is why the curly braces, { and } are so important; they defer execution and substitution within the braces until later. What you want, especially for variables, are the values at the *time of execution*, not the values at the time of parsing.

Square braces, [and], are used to substitute the return value of a command. The dollar sign, $, is used to substitute the value of a variable.

You can control the flow of a Tcl script with the if, while, for, and foreach commands. break and continue jump out of loops, while exit terminates the Tcl script.

You can write your own procedures in Tcl using the proc command to register the procedure. And, you can use Tcl's extensive list of built-in math commands, such as expr, to perform mathematical operations. These math functions become very important in an interpreted language, so that you can take advantage of compiled code (the built-in math functions) when executing numeric-intensive scripts.

In Chapter 3, you'll see a lot more fun graphical applications and meet many of the widgets provided by Tk.

Tcl/Tk Commands Introduced in this Chapter

abs	int
acos	log
append	log10
array	parray
asin	pow
atan	proc
atan2	regexp
break	regsub
ceil	rename
continue	return
cos	round
cosh	scan
double	set
exit	sin
exp	sinh
expr	sqrt
floor	subst
fmod	switch
for	tan
foreach	tanh
format	unset
hypot	upvar
if0	while
incr	

## CHAPTER 3

Interacting with the User

This chapter covers:

- The button widget, making a repeat appearance from Chapter 1
- Common widget options
- The label widget for displaying text
- The message widget, a multiline label
- The frame widget for containing other widgets
- The radiobutton and checkbutton widgets for on/off values
- The scale widget for sliding values
- How the widget packer works
- Destroying widgets

The Tour de Widgets

In this chapter, you'll get a taste of most of the Tk widgets. Some of the more advanced widgets appear in separate chapters, along with the Tcl commands that make the most sense in conjunction with the widgets. For example, the listbox widget makes extensive use of Tcl list commands, so both topics appear in Chapter 6. Even so, this chapter covers most of the Tk widgets necessary for building graphical applications.

Table 3.1 lists the available widgets in Tk.

Table 3.1 Tk Widgets

Widget	Use
button	Pushbutton, calls Tcl code when clicked on
canvas	Drawing area widget
checkbutton	On-off button
entry	Text-entry widget
frame	Frames widgets inside a three-dimensional bevel
label	Displays a text message
listbox	Scrolled list
menu	Menu
menubutton	Pulls down menu from menubar
message	Multiline label
radiobutton	On-off button; only one can be on at a time
scale	Analog value from min to max
scrollbar	Scrollbar
text	Text-entry widget
toplevel	Dialog or application window

This chapter covers button, checkbutton, frame, label, message, radiobutton, and scale widgets.

Chapter 4 covers menu and menubutton widgets. Chapter 5 covers entry, scrollbar, and text widgets, while Chapter 6 delves into the listbox. Chapter 7 tackles toplevel widgets, and Chapter 9 paints on the canvas and covers how to place images and bitmaps into widgets.

Pushing Buttons

One of the simplest, and most illustrative, widgets is the not-so-lowly button widget. The simple two-line **hello.tk** script from chapter 1 created a button widget. While this widget is simple, you can do a lot with a button, for it is the button widget that makes most things happen in a graphical user interface.

Creating Widgets

All Tk widgets are created in nearly the same manner. The basic syntax is:

```
widget name arguments
```

In this case, *widget* is the name of the widget type to create, such as button or scrollbar. *Name* is the widget name, and *arguments* are any options. The most common options appear in Table 3.2.

So, to create a button, you need only the following command:

```
button .name
```

where *.name* is the name of the button. Of course, this leads to a very uninteresting button, which displays no text and does nothing when pushed.

In Chapter 1, the -text and -command options specified what text the button should display and the command it should execute when pushed. Even more options are listed in Table 3.2.

Common Widget Options

Most widgets support a common set of options, as listed in Table 3.2. This is a huge set, and not every widget supports every option.

Table 3.2 Common Widget Options

Option	Meaning
activebackground *color*	Active background color
activeborderwidth *width*	Border width, in pixels, when active
activeforeground *color*	Active foreground color
anchor *anchor_pos*	Positions information within the widget to n, ne, nw, s, se, sw, e, w, and center
background *color*	Sets normal widget background color

Continued

Table 3.2 continued

Option	Meaning
bg *color*	Sets normal widget background color, same as `-background`
bitmap *bitmap*	Display bitmap in widget, one of `error`, `gray50`, `gray25`, `hourglass`, `info`, `questhead`, `question`, `warning`, or `@`*filename*
borderwidth *width*	Sets border width, in pixels
bd *width*	Sets border width, in pixels, same as `-border-width`
command *tcl_script*	Executes *tcl_script* when invoked
cursor *cursor*	Cursor to display when mouse is in widget
disabledforeground *color*	Disabled foreground color
exportselection *state*	True/false value whether selection in widget should be X (UNIX) selection
font *fontname*	Use *fontname* for widget's text
foreground *color*	Sets normal widget foreground color
fg *color*	Sets normal widget foreground color, same as `-foreground`
geometry *widthxheight*	Sets size of widget, normally in pixels, but you may use other units; the x part is required
height *value*	Sets height, normally in pixels, but you can use different units
highlightcolor *color*	Color of highlight rectangle that signifies keyboard focus
highlighthickness *size*	Sets size of highlight area, in pixels, that signifies keyboard focus
image *image*	Image to display in widget
insertbackground *color*	Background color of insertion cursor
insertofftime *milliseconds*	Sets time gap between cursor blinks
insertontime *milliseconds*	Sets duration of cursor blink "on"
insertwidth *size*	Sets width, in pixels, of insertion cursor

jump *on_or_off*	If true, scrollbars delay updating until mouse button is released
justify *justification*	Sets multiline justification to left, center, or right
orient *orientation*	Sets orientation to horizontal or vertical
padx *pad*	Pads extra pixels in *x* direction
pady *pad*	Pads extra pixels in *y* direction
relief *relief*	Sets three-dimensional bevel to flat (no bevel), groove, raised, ridge, or sunken
repeatdeley *milliseconds*	Time threshold before auto-repeat starts
repeatinterval *milliseconds*	Time between auto-repeats once begun
selectbackground *color*	Selected background color
selectborderwidth *width*	Sets size, in pixels, of border when selected
setgrid *on_or_off*	If true, sets resizing grid on, otherwise off
state *state*	Sets state to normal, disabled or active (only for buttons and the like)
text *string*	Sets text to display
textvariable *varname*	Sets variable to use to get text string to display
troughcolor *color*	Sets color for rectangular troughs in widget
underline *which_char*	Underlines character (by position in string)
width *width*	Sets width, normally in pixels, but you can use different units
-wraplength *length*	Maximum length of text string for word wrapping
-xscrollcommand *prefix*	Prefix for command used to communication with horizontal scrollbars
-yscrollcommand *prefix*	Prefix for command used to communication with vertical scrollbars

Widget Examples

Continuing with the lowly button widget, you can get a good sense of what the available options do.

75

N O T E

All the commands in this chapter require the **wish** interpreter, which has Tk built in. The **tclsh** interpreter does not understand Tk commands and will generate errors for all of the commands used in this chapter.

Also, after each set of examples, you may want to exit and restart **wish**, so that none of the previous settings influence the new example.

To create a button with a text string of "*Push me*" and a command that puts the string "*ouch*" when pressed, try the following commands:

```
button .b1 -text "Push me" \
   -command { puts ouch }
pack .b1
```

N O T E

Remember that widgets are created invisible. You must pack them to make then visible.

Colored Buttons

To create a button with some garish colors, try:

```
button .b2 -text "Blue Button" \
   -foreground green -background blue
pack .b2
```

You should see a pretty garish button widget. In addition, you'll note that the first button, *.b1*, with its *Push me* text, is still visible, as shown in Figure 3.1.

Figure 3.1 Two buttons in wish.

Each widget requires a unique name.

NOTE

By using the pack command to pack both buttons, you've just seen how you can combine more than one widget in a window. See the section on how the widget packer works later in this chapter for more on controlling the way widgets get packed. For now, just try out the options and experiment away.

The preceding example set the foreground color and background color. Unless you have a monochrome display, the colors should be readily obvious. If you move the mouse into the widget, the colors change to the active colors, which the example didn't change. To modify these colors, try:

```
button .b3 \
    -text "Active color test" \
    -foreground green \
    -background blue  \
    -activebackground red \
    -activeforeground orange
pack .b3
```

Now, if you move the mouse into this widget, you should see an active foreground color of orange and an active background color of orange.

Color Names

The color names such as *red, orange, green,* and *blue,* come from the X Window System's color names, which are used commonly on UNIX.

UNIX

On most UNIX systems, if you type the **showrgb** command (in Tcl or in your command shell), you'll see zillions and zillions of color names matched with RGB (red, green, blue) color definitions, such as the following:

```
255 250 250    snow
248 248 255    ghost white
```

```
248 248 255    GhostWhite
245 245 245    white smoke
245 245 245    WhiteSmoke
220 220 220    gainsboro
255 239 213    PapayaWhip
255 240 245    LavenderBlush
255 228 225    MistyRose
211 211 211    LightGrey
119 136 153    LightSlateGray
119 136 153    LightSlateGrey
  0 191 255    DeepSkyBlue
 65 105 225    RoyalBlue
 30 144 255    DodgerBlue
```

You can use any of these color names in Tcl. The color names are quite forgiving, and you can mix upper- and lowercase letters, use *gray* or *grey*, and put in or remove spaces. For example, *DeepSkyBlue* or *"dEEp SKY blue"* should both work, but remember to put multiword names inside of quotation marks.

On Windows, Tcl emulates the UNIX colors, usually quite well, so you can use the same color names.

WINDOWS

RGB Colors

You can also define colors in terms of their RGB values, using hexadecimal numbers and an equal number of digits for the red, green, and blue components. Start such a color with a #, as in the following examples: #FF0000 (red), #0000FF (blue), #FFF (white), #FFFFFF (white) #FFFFFFFFF (white). You must always use the same number of digits for the red, green, and blue components.

```
  # Red
.b3 configure -foreground #FF0000
  # Blue
.b3 configure -background #0000FF
```

NOTE

The # character is supposed to start a comment, but for colors, Tk uses the X Window System convention from UNIX, which leads to a more complicated syntax in which the # sometimes starts a comment and sometimes indicates an RGB color value.

Fonts

In addition to colors, you can also specify fonts with the -font option.

UNIX

Unfortunately, font names depend on the operating system, so on UNIX, try this command line:

```
button .b4 \
  -text "Font test" \
  -font fixed
pack .b4
```

Most UNIX font names (which are really X Window System font names) tend to be very long. The UNIX command **xlsfonts** will list zillions of available fonts. Here are a few:

```
-adobe-courier-bold-r-normal--17-120-100-100-m-100-iso8859-1
-adobe-helvetica-bold-o-normal--0-0-75-75-p-0-iso8859-1
-b&h-lucida-medium-i-normal-sans-34-240-100-100-p-192-iso8859-1
-bitstream-charter-medium-r-normal--33-240-100-100-p-183-iso8859-1
-daewoo-mincho-medium-r-normal--0-0-100-100-c-0-ksc5601.1987-0
-jis-fixed-medium-r-normal--24-170-100-100-c-240-jisx0208.1983-0
-sun-open look glyph---10-100-75-75-p-101-sunolglyph-1
lucidasanstypewriter-24
```

The font format used by UNIX is called the X (short for X Window System) Logical Font Description, or XLFD. Few users know about XLFD, but it is responsible for the long font names used on UNIX and Tk on all platforms.

Coming Up with Font Names

XLFD font names include a number of fields, separated by hyphens. The hyphens are important because you'll normally need to place font names in quotation marks so that Tcl doesn't interpret the leading hyphen incorrectly (as an option perchance). Table 3.3 lists the fields in an XLFD font name used by Tk.

Table 3.3 Decoding XLFD Font Names

Field	Example	Description
Foundry	adobe, b&h	The company that created the font
Font family	times, courier	Basic font, usually same as font name on Windows
Weight	bold, medium	How thick the letters are
Slant	i, r	Italic, roman, oblique, etc.
Set-width name	normal, condensed	Width of characters
Additional style	sans	Extra info to describe font
Pixel size	26, 20	Height, in pixels, of characters
Point size	190, 140	Height of characters in points * 10
Dots-per-inch	100-100, 75-75	Dots per inch in x and y directions
Spacing	m, p	Spacing, e.g., fixed-width or proportional
Average width	94, 159	Average width in pixels * 10
Charset registry	iso885-1	Character set encoded in the font

NOTE

Some fields in XLFD font names may have spaces, such as a font family of *Times New Roman*.

The slant field uses one or two letters to describe the slant of the font. Most fonts use *r* for roman (normal) or *i* for italic. Other choices include *o* (oblique), *ri* (reverse italic), *ro* (reverse oblique), and *ot* (other).

The oddly named set-width field describes the width of the characters. Examples include *condensed, semicondensed, narrow, normal,* and *double wide.* Most are *normal.*

The additional style field allows the font designer to place any extra information needed to describe the font's style, usually something like *sans* for a sans-serif font. Most font names leave this space blank (where you'll see two hyphens in a row).

A pixel size of 0 usually indicates a scalable font.

The point size field holds a value 10 times the real size in terms of *points* (1/72 of an inch). Thus, a point size of 190 means a 19-point font.

The spacing field tells you if the font has a fixed width (*m, c*) or proportional (*p*). Generally, proportional fonts look better.

Like the point size, the average width is also inflated. This value is ten times the average width in terms of pixels. The inflation allows for floating point numbers to be encoded as integers (e.g., 9.4 becomes 94).

The character set tells what encoding is used for the characters in the font. The vast majority of X fonts (typically used on UNIX) are encoded using ISO 8859-1 (often called *Latin-1*), which is a superset of US ASCII. Other character sets include ISO 8859-2 for other European languages such as Czech and Hungarian, JIS 0208-1983 for Japanese Kanji, and a number of Windows code pages. Because of this, I usually use a wildcard for this field. Some vendors, such as Hewlett-Packard, support their own supersets of ASCII. In HP's case, this superset is called *HP-Roman-8*, and Hewlett-Packard provides a number of Roman-8–encoded fonts with their systems. You typically won't find these fonts on systems from other vendors.

Wildcards in Font Names

You can use an asterisk, *, in place of most fields. Tk (Windows) or the X server (UNIX) will convert the asterisk to a valid value, providing a match can be found. This allows you to know only part of a font name and still use it.

In Tk, Windows also uses the same font name format as UNIX. Even so, the fonts available on Windows systems differ from UNIX. Furthermore, it is almost impossible to determine the full XLFD font names on Windows without a program like **xlsfonts**, which exists only under the X Window System. What I usually do is load a word-processor program, such as Microsoft Word, and look at a listing of the fonts available. I then use that font name to develop an XLFD name for Tk. For example, with a font name of Arial on Windows (which is typically very close to the Windows default system font), you can generate the following font name:

```
"-*-arial-medium-r-normal--*-*-*-*-*-*"
```

The *medium-r-normal* part is used to get a normal (not bold) font. Note that after the double dash come six asterisks.

Try the following examples, generated from the Courier, Symbol, and Arial fonts, available on most versions of Windows:

```
button .b1 -text "Arial" \
    -font "-*-arial-bold-r-normal--*-*-*-*-*-*"
button .b2 -text "Courier" \
    -font "-*-courier-medium-r-normal--*-*-*-*-*-*"
button .b3 -text "Symbol" \
    -font "-*-Symbol-medium-i-normal--*-240-*-*-*-*"
pack .b1 .b2 .b3
```

The first example uses a bold font in the default size. The second uses a normal font (courier is also usually a monospaced font). The third example uses the Symbol font, usually filled with mathematical (mostly Greek) symbols, in a 24-point italic font.

On Windows—and only on Windows—you can also use a special syntax for font names, based on the Windows idea of what a font is. For this, you can use a three-part font name in the following format:

```
fontname fontsize stylelist
```

For the *fontname* part, you can use any valid Windows font name, including Courier, {Times New Roman} (note the braces for quoting, which allow spaces in the name), or Arial. The *fontsize* is in points, such as 24 points.

The *stylelist* can include any combination of the available styles: bold, extra-bold, extralight, heavy, italic, light, medium, normal, oblique, semibold, strikeout, thin, and underline. (Some fonts don't support all of these styles.)

Try the following Windows-style font name (if you're running on Windows):

```
button .b4 \
    -text "Windows Font Name" \
    -font "{Times New Roman} 24 {bold underline italic}"
pack .b4
```

If you need to create cross-platform applications, you should either stick to the default fonts, or use the X-style XLFD names. Even though the long font names are tedious to type in, they do work on both Windows and UNIX.

Text Options

Most widgets support two main options for text, -text and -textvariable. The -text option sets the widget to display the given text.

The -textvariable option sets the widget to display the value held in a variable, for example:

```
set widget_text "Push more"
button .b5 \
  -textvariable widget_text
pack .b5
```

You'll see a button that looks like the one shown in Figure 3.2.

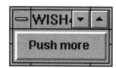

Figure 3.2 A textvariable example.

Now, you can merely change the value of the variable *widget_text* and expect to see changes in the widget itself, because the text displayed in the widget *.b5* is bound to the variable *widget_text*. Try this:

```
set widget_text "new text"
```

The widget should now display new text, as shown in Figure 3.3.

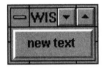

Figure 3.3 A widget with new text.

You can also underline a character in the text. Try:

```
button .b6 \
  -text Underline \
  -underline 0
pack .b6
```

The position value passed with the -underline option starts counting at 0 for the first position, so the *U* in the text *Underline* should have an underline in the preceding example.

The -underline option is normally used with menus, as shown in Chapter 4 on creating menus.

N O T E

Changing Widgets Once Created

Once created, you can change most values stored with a widget. The -textvariable option lets you do this by changing a single text variable. You can also change any option passed at widget creation, using the config-ure option with each widget.

This gets a bit complicated, but Tk automatically registers a new command for each widget you create. Tcl allows you to extend the language with new commands, and Tk does this for you. This new command is the widget name, such as *.b5*, which has now entered the Tcl interpreter as a new command. While Tk does this for you, it doesn't do a lot for the new command it registered.

The `configure` option changes values in the widget. The `cget` option retrieves a value from the widget. Try `configure` first, with the `.b6` widget created earlier. The syntax is:

```
widgetname configure arguments
```

The *arguments* allowed are the same as when you created the widget, such as `-text`, `-foreground` and so on. For example:

```
.b6 configure \
  -foreground white \
  -background black
```

After executing this command, you should see the widget change color.

Try this:

```
.b6 configure \
 -text "Stop It"
```

You should see new text in the widget, and the underline maintained at the first position (position 0).

NOTE If you doubt that a widget is reflecting a new value, try something really garish. For example, set the colors to *pink*, *maroon*, and *limegreen*. This should give you an immediate visual cue as to whether the `configure` option is working.

You can use the `cget` option to retrieve one value:

```
% .b6 cget -text
Stop It
```

```
% .b6 cget -foreground
white
```

Displaying Text Messages with Labels

A label widget is even simpler than a button, for a label displays text (or a bitmap, see Chapter 9 for more on this). As shown in Figure 3.4, a label widget is a simple beast.

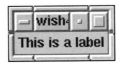

Figure 3.4 A label widget

Use the label command to create label widget:

```
label .l1 -text "This is a label"
pack .l1
```

While it may appear lowly, you'll need a lot of label widgets to place text that explains the interface. For example, an error dialog box displays a label widget (among other widgets) that contains an important error message.

While labels may just seem like glitz in the interface, don't doubt their importance. What good is a user interface that users can't figure out?

Multiline Labels

A message widget holds a multiline label, such as this one:

```
message .m1 \
   -text "This is a test of the\
   Emergency Tcl system. Had this\
```

```
been a real emergency, your widgets\
would blink."
pack .m1
```

The message widget supports the -width option, which allows you to control how much space appears before the message widget wraps to the next line.

The default for units is pixels, but you can also try units such as c (for centimeters), i (for inches) and m (for millimeters). Try the following configure options for the message widget .*m1*:

```
.m1 configure -width 2c
.m1 configure -width 5i
.m1 configure -width 20m
.m1 configure -width 25
.m1 configure -width 100
```

The sizes aren't exact, as many systems cannot accurately calculate exact dimensions when the screen size isn't known. (If you replace a 15-inch monitor with a 17-inch monitor, you typically don't have to perform any configuration, but every dimension will now be off.)

At 2 cm, the widget appears as shown in Figure 3.5.

Figure 3.5 A narrow message widget.

At 5 inches, the widget appears as shown in Figure 3.6.

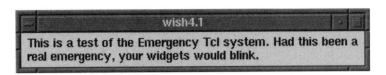

Figure 3.6 A widget message widget.

Framing Widgets

The `frame` widget places a frame, a three-dimensional bevel, around other widgets. This is important for grouping items. Also, due to limitations in the Tk packer (see the packer section later in this chapter), you'll need to group widgets inside frames to properly position them in relation to other frames and other widgets.

The idea of a hierarchy of widgets is hard to get used to, but once you've got the hang of it, you'll be making very complicated hierarchies. Think of the **wish** window as a top-level container widget. Inside this **wish** window, you can place `button`, `label`, `message`, and other widgets. All of these widgets are contained within the **wish** window.

Inside the **wish** window you can also embed other container widgets, such as the `frame` widget. Inside this `frame` widget, you can place widgets such as `button`, `label`, `message`, and even `frame` widgets. If you compare this to files, directories and subdirectories, it should make sense. Treat the `frame` widget as a subdirectory and widgets such as the `button` or `label` as the equivalent of files in this analogy.

Try the following example to see widgets inside of and outside of a `frame` widget:

```
frame .f1 -relief groove \
  -borderwidth 3 \
  -background orange

# Create buttons inside frame.
```

```
button .f1.b1 -text "Inside frame f1"
button .f1.b2 -text "Also inside frame f1"

  # You can pack more than
  # one widget at a time.
pack .f1.b1 .f1.b2

  # Create button outside frame
button .b1 -text "Outside frame"
button .b2 -text "Also outside frame"
pack .f1 .b1 .b2
```

In this example, the frame widget *.f1* encloses two buttons, *.f1.b1* and *.f1.b2*. Note the use of the long names for these button widgets. The naming clearly indicates that *.f1.b1* and *.f1*.b2 are embedded within *.f1*. The frame sports an orange background color to better show its outline.

Figure 3.7 shows the frame widget.

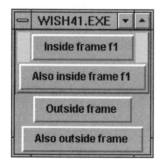

Figure 3.7 A frame widget.

The two buttons outside the frame have names *.b1* and *.b2*. All widget names must be unique, and *.b1* is not the same to Tcl as *.f1.b1*.

Always pack the innermost widgets first, then pack the enclosing frame widget.

N O T E

The frame in the preceding example uses a groove style of relief. You can also use raised (the default for buttons), sunken, flat, or ridge for the relief.

You can use the -relief option with most widgets. It's most commonly used with the frame widget, though.

N O T E

To test this out, try creating the following buttons:

```
button .flat -text "flat" -relief flat  \
    -borderwidth 5
button .groove -text "groove" -relief groove \
    -borderwidth 5
button .raised -text "raised" -relief raised \
    -borderwidth 5
button .ridge -text "ridge" -relief ridge \
    -borderwidth 5
button .sunken -text "sunken" -relief sunken \
    -borderwidth 5
pack .flat .groove .raised .ridge .sunken
```

These examples are shown in Figure 3.8.

Figure 3.8 The relief options.

In the preceding example, the border width was set to a larger value to better show the relief options. For buttons, you can normally use the default border width.

For `frame` widgets, though, if you want any `-relief` option other than flat, you'll want to set a `-borderwidth` to 2 or 3 pixels.

Now that we have the `frame` widget under our belts, you'll see much better-looking examples of the Tk widgets.

Radio and Check buttons

`Radiobuttons` and `checkbuttons` allow you to provide the user with a set of on/off choices. The user can turn each widget on or off. With `radiobuttons`, the user is further limited to having only one radio button, within a given `frame` or **wish** window, on. This is another reason why you'll use `frame` widgets for grouping.

Create a `radiobutton` with the `radiobutton` command, and a `checkbutton` with, you guessed it, the `checkbutton` command. Try the `checkbutton` first, as it's easier to understand.

Create the following `checkbutton`:

```
checkbutton .c1 -text "Check" \
        -variable check1 \
        -command { puts ".c1 holds $check1." }
pack .c1
```

Now, click the button on and off. When it's on, you'll see that the variable *check1* holds a value of 1. When it's off, you'll see a value of 0. This is the default. You can also specify a value for when a `checkbutton` or `radiobutton` is on (`-onvalue`) and when it is off (`-offvalue`), as shown below:

```
checkbutton .c2 -text "Check with value" \
        -variable check2 \
        -onvalue "Print All" \
        -offvalue "Don't Print" \
        -command { puts ".c2 holds $check2." }
pack .c2
```

The -variable option specifies what variable is to hold the checkbutton's value.

A checkbutton typically has its own variable, while a radiobutton usually shares a variable with all other radiobuttons in the same frame.

N O T E

The -onvalue gives a value for the variable when the checkbutton is on, and the -offvalue gives a value for when the checkbutton is off.

Of course, you can skip these options and simply control the activity with the -command option and the Tcl code you give for the -command option. Watch out, though, because the Tcl code gets called when the widget turns on as well as when it turns off.

This is the purpose of the on and off values, to allow you to control the value set when widget gets turned on or off. The default -variable is the widget name. You'll usually want to specify your own variable.

The -indicatoron option allows you to turn the display of the indicator on or off. Try both:

```
.c2 configure -indicatoron 0
```

and:

```
.c2 configure -indicatoron 1
```

With the indicator off, the checkbutton looks more like a button that may get stuck on.

Radiobuttons

Radiobuttons are like checkbuttons, but only one in a frame may be on at any time. This makes radiobuttons harder to work with—at least for testing, since you always need at least two.

The following slightly more complicated code creates a small print options display that determines whether to print all pages or just the current page. Such a set of options is very common in a print dialog boxes in most applications.

To build this, we'll start with a variable to hold the state of how many pages to print: *All* or the *Current Page*. We'll call this variable *print_pages*. One radiobutton will set the variable *print_pages* to *All*, the other will set it to *Current Page*. The radiobuttons won't cause anything to happen, they'll just change the mode of how much to print. In most cases, all radiobuttons in a single frame will share the same variable name because they are all setting different values for the same option.

To actually print a document (or in our case, just display a text message), the user will click on a button widget (labeled *Print*, natch). All together, this makes for one of the most real, but also complex, examples so far. You'll want to look at this one closely:

```
proc print { } {
    global print_pages

    puts "Print $print_pages."
}

label .ll -text "Print Options"
frame .fl -relief ridge \
  -borderwidth 3
radiobutton .fl.rl -text "All" \
        -variable print_pages \
        -value all \
        -anchor w
radiobutton .fl.r2 -text "Current Page" \
        -variable print_pages \
        -value "Current Page"\
        -anchor w

button .print -text "Print" -command { print }

pack .fl.rl .fl.r2 -fill x -expand 1
pack .ll .fl .print
    # Turn on radiobutton on, as a default.
.fl.rl invoke
```

Figure 3.9 shows this example on the screen.

Figure 3.9 A print options window using radiobuttons.

This Tcl example introduces some new concepts, including:

- You almost always place radiobuttons within frames.

- The current frame widget doesn't allow for a text label on the frame itself (a very common option on Windows or Motif), so, we use a label widget above the frame.

- The -anchor w option anchors the radiobuttons to the western side (left) of the widget, within the available space used by the widget.

- Neither radiobutton uses the -command option, but the *Print* button does. The radiobuttons are merely setting a value into a variable.

- The *Print* button calls a Tcl proc for its -command option. Remember, you can call any set of Tcl code from the -command option.

- The proc *print* is forced to use the global statement so that it can access the variable *print_pages*. Inside a proc, you can only access variables that are local to the procedure. If you need to access a variable outside of the proc, you must declare it as being global.

- While checkbutton widgets have -onvalue and -offvalue options, radiobuttons only have a -value option. This tends to be confusing and is an easy mistake to make.

- The -fill x -expand 1 options to the pack command tell the packer to fill widgets in the x (horizontal) direction and that it is OK to expand the widgets. See the section on the packer later in this chapter for more on this.

- The invoke option on the last line of the example turns one of the radiobuttons on. It is always a good idea to start with one button being on, rather than in an indeterminate state.

Flashing Radiobuttons

You can control radio and check buttons from your Tcl scripts using a number of options such as flash, invoke, select, and deselect. All of these options work off the "command" created for the name of the widget. That is, Tk registers a new command for each widget created. So when it creates a widget named *.r1*, Tk also registers a command named .r1. (We've already used this command with the configure and cget options earlier.)

Radiobuttons and checkbuttons add some new options to this widget command.

To make the widget flash, use:

```
.f1.r1 flash
```

(Remember to replace *.f1.r1* with the name of your widget.)

To turn the widget on, use:

```
.f1.r1 select
```

To turn the widget off, use:

```
.f1.r1 deselect
```

To turn the widget on, and invoke the Tcl -command script, use:

```
.f1.r1 invoke
```

To toggle a checkbutton (not a radiobutton) widget (from on to off or off to on), use:

```
.f1.r1 toggle
```

The toggle option generates an error on radiobuttons.

WARNING

The Scale Widget

Use the `scale` widget for sliding values (what a comment on our times). A `scale` widget is a lot like a `scrollbar`, in that it goes from a start position to an end position.

The basic scale goes from 0 to 100 and is aligned vertically:

```
scale .basic
pack .basic
```

This is a pretty simple command, but there are a lot more options you can set.

You can adjust the starting value with the `-from` option and then ending value with the `-to` option:

```
scale .red -from 0 -to 255
pack .red
```

You can add a label to explain the scale (a recommended option):

```
scale .blue -from 0 -to 255 \
  -label "Blue"
pack .blue
```

For scales, the text is stored with the `-label` option, not the more common `-text` option.

Controlling the Scale

A `scale` widget is oriented as either horizontal or vertical. You can control this with the `-orient` option.

You can set up tic marks (really tic numeric labels) at an interval with the `-tickinterval` option. If the `-tickinterval` is too low, you'll see the numbers mashed together, so I usually start out with a `-tickinterval` of 50.

The -showvalue option lets you turn the numeric display of the current value of the scale on (1) or off (0). The scale thumb already gives an approximate value, so you may want to turn this off (I usually leave it on).

Try the following commands to turn the value off:

```
.blue configure -showvalue 0
```

and to turn the display back on:

```
.blue configure -showvalue 1
```

A number of user actions cause a scale to jump. The -bigincrement option controls how far to jump in such a case:

```
.blue configure  -bigincrement 10
```

Controlling Floating-Point Conversions

Since all Tcl values are really stored as strings, the scale widget gives you some control over the conversion process. This really only applies to scales involving very precise accurate numbers.

The -digits option controls the number of significant digits to retain when converting the value.

You normally use the -digits option with the -resolution option, which controls the resolution of the scale, a term that requires some explanation. If you want to set the scale to increment by 0.01 each time, then set the -resolution option to 0.01. If you do so, you'll note that the scale value (if -showvalue is set to 1) will all of a sudden appear as a floating-point number.

The default for the -resolution is 1, so it increments by whole numbers. To change this, use something like the following:

```
.blue configure -resolution .01
```

Executing Tcl Code When the Scale Changes

You can set up a variable to hold the value of a scale, and, of course, this variable will track changes in the scale. Use the familiar -variable option.

You can also use the equally familiar -command option to set up Tcl code to call when the scale changes.

When the user slides the scale thumb, this code can get called many times in a short interval. To maintain performance, you should stick to a short set of Tcl code for the -command option.

NOTE

One tricky part of the scale's -command option is that the value of the scale will be appended to the code. Thus if you write a proc for this case, you should include a variable parameter:

```
proc scale_value { value } {
        puts "New scale value: $value."
}

scale .scale1 -label "Scale Test" \
  -command scale_value
pack .scale1
```

Making Scales Bigger

Often, you want the scale to extend wider than it normally would. To expand a scale, you can use the -length option and specify how wide to make a horizontal scale or how tall to make a vertical scale:

```
scale .green -from 0 -to 255 \
  -label "Green" \
  -length 200 \
  -orient horizontal \
  -tickinterval 50
pack .green
```

Special Scale Widget Commands

The scale widget provides two main special commands, get and set. To use these commands, you need the name of the scale, as in the following example:

```
% .blue get
0.07
```

This returns the value of the scale widget named *.blue*, again using the command that Tk registers that is the name of the widget (just as the config-ure option does).

To set a value into the scale, use the set option:

```
% .blue set .77
```

RGB Scales

You can use the following example to show more about how scale widgets work. The following Tcl code creates three scale widgets and one button. The scales control the familiar red, green, and blue components of a color value, in this case, the background color of the button widget. The border of the button widget appears very wide, so you can see not only the background color selected, but how Tcl creates the top and button three-dimensional shadow colors, as you move the scales.

The example code follows:

```
proc modify_color { ignored } {
        global red green blue

        set color \
            [ format "#%2.2x%2.2x%2.2x" \
                $red $green $blue]

        puts $color

        .test configure -background $color
}
```

```
button .test -anchor w \
  -text "Test Color" \
  -borderwidth 10

scale .red -from 0 -to 255 \
  -label "Red " \
  -variable red \
  -length 300 \
  -orient horizontal \
  -command modify_color \
  -tickinterval 50
.red set 0

scale .green -from 0 -to 255 \
  -label "Green" \
  -variable green \
  -length 300 \
  -orient horizontal \
  -command modify_color \
  -tickinterval 50
.green set 0

scale .blue -from 0 -to 255 \
  -label "Blue" \
  -variable blue \
  -length 300 \
  -orient horizontal \
  -command modify_color \
  -tickinterval 50
.blue set 0

pack .test .red .green .blue
```

Note the lines with the set options. These commands provide an initial value
for the scale.

How the Widget Packer Works

Now we'll get into real widget applications. While single-widget tests illustrate individual widgets, the hardest part is putting widgets together.

In Tk, the **packer** is the main way you have to control how multiple widgets get placed together. In most uses, the packer provides one horizontal or vertical strip of widgets. All widgets inside that packer then appear one after another going either from top to bottom or left to right. Of course, there are a lot of other options, but this is the basic idea.

When you have a complex layout, it's usually best to use a number of nested frame widgets, each holding a horizontal or vertical strip of widgets, and then combine these nested frame widgets.

To pack widgets horizontally, use the -side left option, as shown in the following code example:

```
button .widget1 -text "Widget1"
button .widget2 -text "Widget2"
button .widget3 -text "Widget3"


pack .widget1 .widget2 .widget3 -side left
```

With this option, as show in Figure 3.10, the **wish** window contracts to fit exactly the space needed to hold the widgets. You can add (and pack) more widgets and the window will enlarge.

Figure 3.10 Packing from the left side.

You can reverse this order and pack from the right, although this is not used as often as packing from the left:

```
pack .widget1 .widget2 .widget3 -side right
```

When you do this, the widgets will reverse positions but remain horizontal.

When you want a vertical strip, you can pack from the top or bottom:

```
pack .widget1 .widget2 .widget3 -side top
```

This configuration is shown in Figure 3.11.

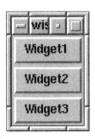

Figure 3.11 Packing from the top.

Inserting Widgets into the Layout

You can insert new widgets into a layout by using the -after and -before options. Try the following code and compare the result, shown in Figure 3.12, with Figure 3.11:

```
button .widget4 -text "Widget4"
```

```
pack configure .widget4 -after .widget1
```

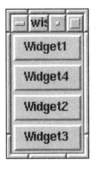

Figure 3.12 Inserting a widget after another.

 The new `pack` syntax uses the `configure` option for all of the preceding examples. You can use it or not. Since Tk is moving in the direction of the `configure` option, you may want to start using it, as shown in the following examples.

You can also pack a widget before another:

```
button .widget5 -text "Widget 5"
pack configure .widget5 -before .widget1
```

This result is shown in Figure 3.13.

Figure 3.13 Packing before another widget.

The same options work horizontally, too.

Filler Up

You can ask that the packer fill widgets out to the available space. This is useful when trying to line up small widgets with large.

The -fill option takes x, y, both, or none (the default) for the value. If you specify to fill x, then you're asking that the widgets be expanded horizontally, if necessary.

Try the following commands:

```
button .w1 -text "Widget—-1"
button .w2 -text "Widget2"
button .w3 -text "Widget3"
pack .w1 .w2 .w3 -fill x -side top
```

You can see this example in Figure 3.14.

Figure 3.14 Filling out widgets.

You can also use -fill y (useful when packing horizontally), -fill both, or the default of -fill none.

Padding

In addition to filling, you can also pad. Padding is placing extra space between widgets. In Tk, there are two kinds of padding, *external* (outside of the widget) and *internal* (within the widget).

External padding goes between widgets. Internal padding makes widgets larger. For external padding, use the -padx and -pady options. For internal padding, use the -ipadx and -ipady options, as shown in the following example, which builds on the previous example:

```
pack configure .w1 .w2 .w3 -pady 10 -ipady 5
```

The -expand option to the packer allows widgets to enlarge, such as when the window gets resized. You can also use the -anchor option, as shown earlier in the section on radiobuttons, to place the widget if there is more space available than the widget will use.

Finding Out about the Packer

The pack info command gives you information about the widgets:

```
% pack info .widget5
-in . -anchor center -expand 0
-fill none -ipadx 0 -ipady 0
-padx 0 -pady 0 -side top
%
```

Finally, to wrap up our discussion of the packer, you can use the pack forget command to undo a packing job:

```
pack forget .widget5
```

This will make the widget named *.widget5* disappear.

Placing Widgets

In addition to the pack command, there's also a command called place. The placer is fairly simple-minded compared to the packer. With the place command, you specify the exact position of the widget. Or, you can use *rubber-band positioning* where you place a widget in relation to another widget. When that other widget moves or changes size, the rubber-band positioning modifies the first widget's placement as well.

To locate a widget exactly, use the `place configure -x` and `-y` options:

```
button .b1 -text "Placed at 50,40"
place configure .b1 -x 50 -y 40
```

The `-anchor` option allows you to control which side of the widget is locked in place. Try the following (after you enter the preceding example):

```
place configure .b1 -anchor ne
place configure .b1 -anchor se
place configure .b1 -anchor w
place configure .b1 -anchor center
place configure .b1 -anchor n
place configure .b1 -anchor s
place configure .b1 -anchor sw
```

You should see the widget move about.

To control the size of the widget, you can use the `-width` and `-height` options. These can be in pixels or other screen units, such as `m` for millimeters, `i` for inches, etc., as shown here:

```
place configure .b1 -width 10c -height 1c
place configure .b1 -width 2i -height 30
place configure .b1 -width 100 -height 5
```

The last example should make the widget really short.

You can also place widgets relatively with the `-relx`, `-rely`, `-relwidth`, and `-relheight` options. The `-relx` and `-rely` use the positions going from 0.0 to 1.0 in the parent window. You pick a relative position from 0 to 1 and the place command will keep the widget in its relative location, even if the parent widget moves or gets resized.

For the `-relwidth` and `-relheight`, the values are similar. For example, 0.5 means half the size of the parent.

Destroying widgets

After expending all this effort creating widgets, you can destroy widgets
with the destroy command:

```
destroy widgetname
```

If you destroy a widget with embedded children, such as a frame widget, all
the child widgets get destroyed, too.

Finally, there's the Tk bell command, which rings the bell, or more likely,
beeps the beeper:

```
bell
```

Summary

Tk comes with a plethora of widgets, include button, label, frame, radiobutton,
and scale. Most widgets accept a set of common options for controlling the
look and feel of the widget.

The frame widget allows you to embed a set of child widgets within a
three-dimensional bevel frame. Using frames allows you to better group
widgets, and also to better place widgets with the pack command.

The pack command controls how widgets are placed. It supports a lot of
options, but the most common ones are -side left for horizontal packing,
-side top, for vertical packing, and -fill x for filling widgets out when placed
in columns.

You can destroy widgets with the destroy command.

In Chapter 4, you'll see how to create menus, menubars and cascading
pullright menus.

Tcl/Tk Commands Introduced in this Chapter

```
bell
button
checkbutton
destroy
frame
label
message
pack
place
radiobutton
scale
```

CHAPTER 4

Menus

This chapter covers:

- Creating menus
- Cascading submenus
- Tear-off menus
- Menu bars
- Keyboard shortcuts, and accelerators
- Standard menus, keyboard shortcuts and accelerators
- The main window
- Option menus
- Pop-up menus

Creating Menus

Just about every windowed application sports a menu bar with pull-down menus. In this chapter, you'll get a close look at how to create Tk menus, cascading submenus, pop-up menus, and almost everything to do with menus.

To create a menu in Tk, you first create a menu widget and then populate the menu with choices. To get the menu to appear, create a menubutton widget, usually on a menu bar. The menubutton widget is a special type of button widget that is intended to pull-down menus. This chapter shows how to create all of these and much more.

Menubuttons Pull-Down Menus

To get going with menus, the first thing you need to do is create a menubutton widget:

```
menubutton .file -text "File" -menu .file.menu
pack .file
```

The most important part of the menubutton is the -menu option, which lists the name of the menu to pull down when the menubutton is activated. This menu must be a child of the menubutton, as you can see from the name *.file.menu* used in the example. This name is purely arbitrary. I find it useful to include the word *menu* in the name, but you don't have to.

Once you have a menubutton, the next step is to create a menu, using the menu command:

```
menu .file.menu
```

Once you create the menu, the next step is to populate it with menu choices.

Populating Menus with Menu Choices

You create menu choices from the menu widget itself, not from any widget command such as button or checkbutton. Instead, use the name of the menu with the add option. You can add a

- command, a normal menu choice
- separator, a horizontal line to help group and separate menu choices
- radiobutton, a lot like the widget of that name
- checkbutton, much like the widget of that name
- cascade, for cascading submenus. A cascade is a lot like a menubutton placed on a menu

The widgets you add to a menu will appear when the user clicks on the menubutton. For example, to create a standard **File** menu, you'd use the following commands:

```
menubutton .file \
        -text "File" -menu .file.menu
pack .file -side left

menu .file.menu

.file.menu add command \
        -label "New" \
        -command { puts "New" }
.file.menu add command \
        -label "Open..." \
        -command { puts "Open..." }
.file.menu add separator
.file.menu add command \
        -label "Save" \
        -command { puts "Save" }
.file.menu add command \
        -label "Save As..." \
        -command { puts "Save As..." }
.file.menu add separator
.file.menu add command \
        -label "Print" \
        -command { puts "Print" }
.file.menu add separator
.file.menu add command \
        -label "Exit" \
        -command { exit }
```

You don't pack menus. The menubutton will handle this task.

N O T E

You can see this menu in Figure 4.1.

Figure 4.1 A File menu.

For each menu choice, the -command option (which is somewhat hard to distinguish from the command type of menu choice) identifies the Tcl script that gets executed when the user chooses this menu choice.

You can also use radiobuttons and checkbuttons in menus:

```
proc change_opts { } {
    global  file_opts

    puts $file_opts
}

proc set_hide_state { } {
    global show_hidden

    puts "$show_hidden hidden"
}

menubutton .view \
        -text "View" -menu .view.menu
pack .view -side left

menu .view.menu

.view.menu add radiobutton \
        -label "Full File Options" \
```

```
        -command { change_opts } \
        -variable file_opts \
        -value full

.view.menu add radiobutton \
        -label "Partial File Options" \
        -command { change_opts } \
        -variable file_opts \
        -value partial

.view.menu add radiobutton \
        -label "File Name Only" \
        -command { change_opts } \
        -variable file_opts \
        -value filename

.view.menu add separator

.view.menu add checkbutton \
        -label "Show Hidden Files" \
        -command set_hide_state \
        -variable show_hidden \
        -onvalue show \
        -offvalue hide

 # Set default values.
set file_opts partial
set show_hidden hide
```

This menu appears as a typical **View** menu for an application, as shown in Figure 4.2.

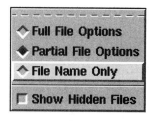

Figure 4.2 A View menu with radio and check buttons.

The radiobutton choices share a variable, while the checkbutton has its own variable. Note also that you can set up initial values by setting a value into these variables. This way, there always is a valid initial state.

Cascading Submenus

Up to now, each menu choice has provided a simple action when invoked. The cascade menu choice complicates this a bit, by allowing a menu choice to pull right a cascading menu.

Even so, the form to create a cascade is very similar to that used by the menubutton and menu commands. First, you create the cascade choice on a menu:

```
menubutton .cascd \
        -text "Cascade" -menu .cascd.menu
pack .cascd -side left

menu .cascd.menu

.cascd.menu add cascade \
        -label "Cascade Test" \
        -menu .cascd.menu.cas
```

Then, you create the cascaded menu itself. A cascaded menu is simply a menu widget.

```
# Note: cascaded menu is
# child of parent menu.

menu .cascd.menu.cas

.cascd.menu.cas add command \
        -label "Cascade Choice1"

.cascd.menu.cas add command \
        -label "Cascade Choice2"
```

That's all you have to do. You can then extend this example, and create cascades that cascade themselves:

```
.cascd.menu.cas add cascade \
        -label "Second Cascade" \
        -menu .cascd.menu.cas.cas2

menu .cascd.menu.cas.cas2

.cascd.menu.cas.cas2 add command \
        -label "Second Cascade #1"

.cascd.menu.cas.cas2 add command \
        -label "Second Cascade #2"
```

Remember that each cascade menu must be a child of the parent menu it pulls right from.

When we're all done, the multicascading menu appears in Figure 4.3.

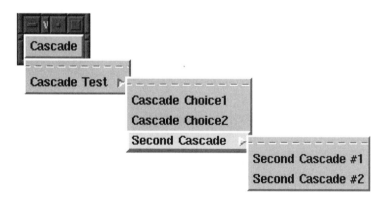

Figure 4.3 Cascaded, or pull-right, menus.

Tear-Off Menus

You can turn any menu into a tear-off menu by using the -tearoff option when you create the menu:

```
menu .file.menu -tearoff yes
```

A tear-off menu displays a small perforated line as the first menu choice, as shown in Figure 4.4.

Figure 4.4 A tear-off menu.

If you click on this line, the menu is "torn off" and appears as a small dialog box, as shown in Figure 4.5.

Figure 4.5 A torn-off menu.

The -tearoff option is all that is needed to convert a menu into a tear-off menu. Long familiar on UNIX from Motif applications, in Tk tear-off menus automatically work on Windows, too.

Since this is such a neat option, you'll probably want to use it, at least for all menus on the menu bar.

Up to now, all the examples merely placed the menubuttons horizontally using the pack -side left option discussed in Chapter 3. But what's really needed is a menu bar.

Making Menu Bars

In older versions of Tk, you'd call the tk_menuBar command to put together a menu bar. Now, you can just use a frame widget. The following code creates a working menu bar:

```
frame .menubar -relief raised \
  -borderwidth 2

menubutton .menubar.file \
  -text "File" -menu .menubar.file.menu
pack .menubar.file \
  -side left

menu .menubar.file.menu

.menubar.file.menu add command \
  -label "Exit" \
  -command { exit }

menubutton .menubar.edit \
  -text "Edit" -menu .menubar.edit.menu
pack .menubar.edit -side left

menu .menubar.edit.menu

.menubar.edit.menu add command \
    -label "Undo"
```

```
# Create a faked main area.
label .main -text "Main Area"

pack .menubar -side top \
    -fill x -expand true
pack .main -pady 100 -padx 200
```

This example, shown in Figure 4.6, uses a `label` widget as a faked main area. Most windowed applications have some sort of main area, and the menu bar is expected to span the top of this main area. In your applications, you're likely to fill this in with whatever widgets are necessary for your programs.

The `-fill x` option to the `pack` command for the menu bar ensures that the menu bar will stretch to fit. (See the section on the main window later in this chapter for more on this topic.)

Keyboard Shortcuts and Accelerators

The Windows and Motif style guides both specify a set of *keyboard shortcuts* (also called *mnemonics*) and *accelerator keys* for the standard menus. Both are means to choose menu choices using the keyboard instead of the mouse.

A keyboard shortcut is an underlined part of the menu choice or `menubutton` text, such as the *F* in **File**. Normally, you press **Alt-F** to invoke this choice, just as if you clicked on the word *File* with the mouse. The keyboard shortcut is always part of the text displayed, for example, the *F* in *File*.

An accelerator is an alternate keyboard combination, usually a Control- or Shift-key combination, that also invokes the same action as the menu choice. For example, **Ctrl-C** usually invokes the Copy action, and **Ctrl-V** the Paste action. (*X* is cut, *C* is copy and *V* is paste; all three keys are right next to each other on the standard QWERTY keyboard.) Typically, the accelerator is not part of the text for the menu choice.

For keyboard shortcuts, to get an underline in the `menubutton` or on a menu choice, use the `-underline` option and specify the index of the character to underline, as described in Chapter 3. This option makes an underline appear below the text, but if you do it on a menu, Tk will automatically set up the keyboard binding as well.

For the accelerator, use the `-accelerator` option to display text for the accelerator on the right side of the menu choice. Both of these appear in the following code:

```
frame .menubar -relief raised \
  -borderwidth 2

menubutton .menubar.edit \
  -text "Edit" \
  -underline 0 \
  -menu .menubar.edit.menu
pack .menubar.edit -side left

menu .menubar.edit.menu

.menubar.edit.menu add command \
    -label "Cut" \
    -underline 2 \
    -accelerator "Ctrl+X"

.menubar.edit.menu add command \
    -label "Copy" \
    -underline 0 \
    -accelerator "Ctrl+C"

.menubar.edit.menu add command \
    -label "Paste" \
    -underline 0 \
    -accelerator "Ctrl+V"

  # Create a faked main area.
label .main -text "Main Area"

pack .menubar -side top \
  -fill x -expand true
pack .main -pady 100 -padx 200
```

You can see this menu in Figure 4.6.

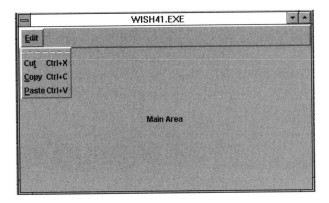

Figure 4.6 Keyboard shortcuts and accelerators on the **Edit** menu.

The -accelerator option stores a string for display only. No accelerator is really set up by this option. Unlike the keyboard shortcut that Tk will set up for menu choices, you must add a binding for the key combination.

N O T E

Binding Events to Call Tcl Scripts

A *binding* is a sort of Tcl proc that get executed when a certain keyboard or mouse event occurs, such as when the user presses the **Return** key in a widget.

Tk provides the powerful ability to bind a keyboard or mouse event to some action, such as **Ctrl-V** to a paste action. The original bindings in Tk come directly from X Window System keyboard and mouse events. Even so, the same bindings work on Windows.

You can bind the following event types in widgets to Tcl scripts, as shown in Table 4.1.

Table 4.1 Types of Events You Can Bind

Event Type	Meaning
Button	Mouse button press
ButtonPress	Mouse button press

Chapter 4 • Menus

ButtonRelease	Mouse button was pressed, now released
Key	Key on keyboard pressed
KeyPress	Key on keyboard pressed
KeyRelease	Key on keyboard pressed, now released
Enter	Mouse pointer enters window
Leave	Mouse pointer leaves window
Motion	Mouse moves through window
Expose	Redraw event on a window
Map	Window is mapped (packed) to the screen
Unmap	Window is unmapped (hidden)
FocusIn	Keyboard focus enters window.
FocusOut	Keyboard focus leaves window.
Gravity	Window "gravity" changes (UNIX-only)
Circulate	Window stacking order changes
Configure	Window position or size changes
Destroy	Window is destroyed
Property	An X Window property data is written to window (UNIX-only)
Visibility	Window visibility changes
Reparent	Window's parent is changed by window manager (UNIX-only)
Colormap	Window's colormap is mapped in or out

Few of these events are ever used in bindings, except for the mouse and keyboard events.

When you use the bind command, you can bind a particular event in a widget to a Tcl script. That is, you can bind a click on the left-most mouse button inside a menu choice to execute a particular Tcl script.

You can also make more general bindings, such as anytime **Ctrl-V** is pressed, execute the paste Tcl proc (presuming you write such a proc). To do this in Tcl, you can use the following as a template:

```
bind . <Control-v> { puts "paste" }
```

Note the use of a period (.) for the widget name. This binds the highest-level widget (and all its descendants). This allows us to bind all occurrences of **Ctrl-V** anywhere in the program. An alternative way is to use the tag all to bind the event to all widgets in the program:

```
bind all <Control-v> { puts "paste" }
```

The **Ctrl** key is a modifier. Tk recognizes a number of modifiers, shown in Table 4.2.

Table 4.2 Event Modifiers for Binding

Modifier	Meaning
Alt	**Alt** key
Control	**Ctrl** key
Shift	**Shift** key
Lock	**Caps lock** key
Meta	Usually **Alt** key
M	Same as meta
Button1	Mouse button one (normally left-most)
B1	Same as Button1
Button2	Mouse button two
B2	Same as Button2
Button3	Mouse button three
B3	Same as Button3
Button4	Mouse button four
B4	Same as Button4
Button5	Mouse button five
B5	Same as Button5
Mod1	Modifier 1
M1	Same as Mod1
Mod2	Modifier 2
M2	Same as Mod2

Mod3	Modifier 3
M3	Same as Mod3
Mod4	Modifier 4
M4	Same as Mod4
Mod5	Modifier 5
M5	Same as Mod5
Double	Used for double-clicks of mouse events
Triple	Used for triple-clicks of mouse events

If you don't understand what a modifier or event is really for, don't worry. Many of these events are obscure X Window System events and are rarely, if ever, used. See Appendix A for a listing of X Window System programming books if you're interested in finding out more about how the X Window System deals with events.

You can use these modifiers to control the event you are looking for, such as the infamous:

```
bind all <Control-Alt-Key-Delete> \
    { puts "DOS is over!" }
```

On Windows machines, your application will never see a **Ctrl-Alt-Delete** event, since DOS or Windows will grab the event.

N O T E

The basic syntax of bind is:

```
bind widget/tag <event> tcl_script
```

The *event* part appears between angle brackets, < and >. You can use a lot of detail if necessary. For example, holding down the **Shift** key and mouse button 1 would have an event syntax of <Shift-Button-1>. The number is the number of the button. For buttons, you can even abbreviate further. For example, you can signify **Button-1** with just <1>.

For keys, use the actual key value, such as **x** or **v**. For function keys and other special keys on the keyboard, you need the X Window System's **keysym** for that key. For example, **Delete**, **Return**, **Next** (instead of *Page Down*), and so on.

To bind an event to **Alt-a**, use `<Alt-Key-a>`.

Binding Mouse Events

Binding mouse events is just like binding keyboard keys. For example:

```
bind all <Button-3> {

    puts "Button-3 at %x %y"
}
```

WINDOWS

On UNIX, most users have three-button mice, but on Windows most mice have two buttons and the Macintosh is famous for its one-button mouse.

Because of this, you'll need to be careful with mouse button bindings, since the particular mouse button you're binding may not exist on the user's system.

The tricky part is that with a two-button mouse on Windows, Button 3 is actually the right-most mouse button. Button 2 doesn't exist.

Class Bindings

In addition to binding an event to a widget, you can bind it to a class of widgets, such as all button widgets. (The class name for such widgets is `Button`. You can find the class name for any type of widget in the on-line manual pages for the widget.)

Getting at Event Data in the Tcl Script

In your Tcl script for a particular event, you normally don't need access to data such as which button was pressed. If the script is bound to button 1, you know that button 1 was pressed.

Through a strange syntax, you can access this event data. If you script has any percent signs, %, in it, the Tcl interpreter will replace the percent sign (and the character following it), with data from the event. (Tcl actually makes a new script for your binding each time the binding gets invoked.) Table 4.3 lists the available % options.

Table 4.3 Percent Sign Options for Event Data in Bindings

Sequence	Use
%%	Used to place a real percent sign in the script.
%b	The button number for `ButtonPress` or `ButtonRelease` events.
%h	Height field for resizing (`Configure`) and redrawing (`Expose`) events.
%k	Keycode for key events, value depends on keyboard and operating system.
%w	Width field for resizing (`Configure`) and redrawing (`Expose`) events.
%x	x position (of mouse for button events, etc.).
%y	y position (of mouse for button events, etc.).
%A	(Uppercase), the ASCII value of the key pressed.
%K	**keysym** name for event, such as "delete" for **Delete** key.
%T	The event type.
%W	The window (widget) on which the event was reported.

There are many more percent sign options, which you can see in the on-line manual pages for the `bind` command. Most pertain only to UNIX and the X Window System.

The `%K` option is handy to figure out what name Tk uses for a particular key. The following binding can be used to see what Tcl thinks is on your keyboard:

```
bind all <Key> { puts "Key %K pressed." }
```

After typing this command, try typing keys on the keyboard, when the wish window is active. You'll find some interesting key names, like **Prior** for *Page Down*, **L1** for *F11* and so on. With key names, Tcl betrays its UNIX roots. Even so, bindings work fine on Windows as long as you use the names Tcl expects.

Bindings for Accelerators and Keyboard Shortcuts

Now that you know how to bind events, it's time to create a set of bindings for menu shortcuts and accelerators.

The **Edit** menu uses some common options, including the ones listed in Table 4.4, which the following code example will show how to set up.

Table 4.4 Some Edit Menu Choices

Choice	Shortcut	Accelerator	Old Accelerator
Cut	t	**Ctrl-X**	**Shift-Del**
Copy	C	**Ctrl-C**	**Ctrl-Ins**
Paste	P	**Ctrl-V**	**Shift-Ins**

The old accelerators come from earlier versions of Windows. Many Windows applications support both the old and the new (which come originally from the Macintosh.)

To set up the choices from Table 4.4 in Tcl, you need to display both the shortcut and the accelerator. Tk will automatically set up the key binding for the shortcut, if you use the -underline option. That's rather nice of Tk.

It is up to you, though, to set up the accelerator. The -accelerator option just sets up the text to display, not the binding.

The basic format follows:

```
proc cut_proc { } {
    # Place your code here...
    puts "Cut"
}
```

```
bind all <Control-Key-x> {

    cut_proc
}
```

I use a proc for each **Cut**, **Copy**, **Paste** and all other menu actions. Why? Because the -command option on the menu choice needs to call a Tcl script, and so does the binding on the keyboard accelerator. To avoid these two sets of code from getting out of sync, I ensure that both means to invoke the menu choice call the same Tcl script. The easiest way to do this is to create a proc for each menu choice and have both the binding and the -command option call the same proc.

Tk also automatically sets up a binding on **Alt-Key-E** to pull down the **Edit** menu. Sometimes, Tk is just really friendly.

To put all this together and create a partial **Edit** menu, you can use the following code:

```
proc cut_proc { } {
    # Place your code here...
    puts "Cut"
}

bind all <Control-Key-x> {

    cut_proc
}

proc copy_proc { } {
    # Place your code here...
    puts "Copy"
}

bind all <Control-Key-c> {

    copy_proc
}

proc paste_proc { } {
    # Place your code here...
```

```
    puts "Paste"
}

bind all <Control-Key-v> {

    paste_proc
}

frame .menubar \
  -relief raised -bd 2

menubutton .menubar.edit \
  -text "Edit" \
  -underline 0 \
  -menu .menubar.edit.menu

menu .menubar.edit.menu

.menubar.edit.menu add command \
  -label "Cut" \
  -underline 2 \
  -accelerator "Ctrl+X" \
  -command cut_proc

.menubar.edit.menu add command \
  -label "Copy" \
  -underline 0 \
  -accelerator "Ctrl+C" \
  -command copy_proc

.menubar.edit.menu add command \
  -label "Paste" \
  -underline 0 \
  -accelerator "Ctrl+V" \
  -command paste_proc

pack .menubar.edit -side left

  # Create a faked main area.
label .main -text "Main Area"
```

```
pack .menubar -side top \
  -fill x -expand true
pack .main -pady 100 -padx 200
```

With the preceding example, you should be able to create Windows-compliant menu bars.

There's a lot to the bind command. You'll probably want to look up the on-line manual information on bind if you're trying anything tricky.

Standard Menus

Both the Windows and Motif (on UNIX) style guides place a lot of emphasis on the menu bar. Every application should sport a menu bar, and the menus should follow a common theme. Motif is the de facto interface standard on UNIX and the X Window System.

The Macintosh also requires a menu bar, but it follows a slightly different style. The next section describes the Windows and Motif styles. Macintosh users will need to modify the discussion for their platform. (For example, the last choice in the Mac **File** menu is **Quit**, not **Exit**.)

To start with, both Windows and Motif follow the basic rules in the IBM Common User Access document (which describes how user interfaces should act), so both interfaces look virtually the same, with only a few minor differences. Both require a menu bar and mandate the following menu names, as listed in Table 4.5.

Table 4.5 Standard Menus

Menu Name	Keyboard Shortcut
File	F
Edit	E
View	V
Options	O
Help	H

Only the **File** menu is required. If the application allows editing, you should also include an **Edit** menu. Every application should provide help and a **Help** menu.

The File Menu

The **File** menu should always be the first menu on the menu bar. This menu has choices that, obviously, pertain to files, including loading, saving, and printing files. This assumes your application deals with files (which most do, including spreadsheets, word processors, and database managers).

The standard choices in the **File** menu are listed in Table 4.6.

Table 4.6 File Menu Choices

Menu Choice	Keyboard Shortcut	Purpose
New	N	Creates an empty new file for the user to act on
Open...	O	Opens a file that already exists
Save	S	Saves the current file to its current name
Save As...	A	Saves the current file to a different name
Print...	P	Prints the current file
Close	C	Closes window
Exit	X	Quits the application

Use common sense when building your menus. If your program has nothing to do with printing, for example, skip the **Print...** menu choice.

A few of the choices include ellipses. The ellipses tell the user that this menu choice will call up a dialog window, requiring further action from the user to complete the menu choice. (See Chapter 7 on dialog boxes.) In the case of **Open**, a file-selection dialog box should appear so that the user can choose a file.

For the **File** menu, if you use the **Open...** choice to open a file named **hello.tk**, the **Save** choice would save your work back to the file **hello.tk**.

For the **Save As...** menu choice, the ellipses implies a dialog box will appear. Again, this is a file-selection dialog box. This choice allows you to save the file under a different name.

The **Print...** menu choice can be **Print** or **Print...**, depending on whether a print dialog box appears or not (to perhaps choose the printer, the print quality, and paper size).

Use the **Close** menu choice when your application has multiple independent top-level windows (again, see Chapter 7). The **Close** choice then closes the window from which the user makes the menu choice. If you don't use multiple top-level windows, skip the **Close** choice.

The **Exit** choice is required for all applications. You can use the Tcl exit command for this purpose. In addition, if the user asks to exit but has modified a file without saving, your program should prompt the user to save the data before exiting. The main goal of all these interface guidelines is to help the user.

The Edit Menu

The **Edit** menu essentially provides a menu-driven cut, copy, and paste mechanism. The **Edit** menu should come second on the menu bar. Depending on the application, implementing **Undo** may be the toughest task for the whole program.

The standard **Edit** menu choices are listed in Table 4.7.

Table 4.7 Edit Menu Choices

Menu Choice	Shortcut	Accelerator	Purpose
Undo	U	**Ctrl-Z**	Undoes the last thing the user did
Redo	R	**Ctrl-Y**	Reverse last **Undo** operation
Cut	t	**Ctrl-X**	Removes the selected material and puts it in the clipboard

Continued

Table 4.7 continued

Menu Choice	Shortcut	Accelerator	Purpose
Copy	C	Ctrl-X	Copies selected material to clipboard
Paste	P	Ctrl-V	Pastes contents of clipboard to current location
Clear	l	Del	Clears selected material
Select All	none	Ctrl-A	Selects everything
Deselect All	none	none	Deselects all selected items

There are a lot of menu choices here. The key idea is to only use the ones that make sense for your application. **Undo**, **Cut**, **Copy**, and **Paste** are the most commonly used choices.

With **Undo**, you may also want to modify the text displayed (the -label option for the menu choice). For example, the undo choice in many applications may read **Undo Typing** or **Undo Paste**. If you can tell the user more information about what will be undone, you can help the user see what is allowed for **Undo** and what isn't. To dynamically change this text, you need to get at the menu choice.

To modify the first (zeroth) entry in a menu, use the entryconfigure option. If the menu is named *.menubar.edit.menu*, you can use the following Tcl command to modify the text of the first menu choice:

```
.menubar.edit.menu \
    entryconfigure 0 \
    -text "Undo Paste"
```

WARNING

If you use a tear-off menu, entry 0 is the tear-off dashed line. The **Undo** choice would then be entry number 1.

Cut removes the selected (highlighted) material and places that material (text, spreadsheet cells, whatever) into the clipboard. See Chapter 5 for more on Tcl clipboard commands.

Copy copies the selected material to the clipboard, but doesn't remove the material from where it was originally.

Paste pastes the contents of the clipboard at the current location (usually where an insertion cursor is). Everything after *Paste* is an optional choice.

Clear, an optional choice, removes the selected material but doesn't copy the material to the clipboard—potentially a dangerous operation. The **Clear** choice is supposed to leave a gap where the old material was. The **Delete** choice is also optional.

The View Menu

The **View** menu controls "views" of the data. That is, the **View** menu allows the user to adjust what is seen in the main window of your application. Some examples of this include choosing how to sort the data (by name, by size, by date, and so on), if the data should be sorted at all, and how much detail to show (file name only or file name, size, and owner, etc.). An outlining application, for example, could use the **View** menu to control how many levels of the outline are visible at one time.

View menus are highly dependent on what your application actually does. A spreadsheet **View** menu will look a lot different than the **View** menu on an SQL query-by-forms application.

The Options Menu

The **Options** menu is essentially a miscellaneous menu. Into this menu go various choices that allow the user to customize the application, such as choosing the that the application uses. As with the **View** menu, the **Options** menu is highly dependent on what your application actually does.

The Help Menu

These days, few users actually read manuals anymore. Because of this, it is essential to provide on-line help in some format or other. Users expect to see a

Help menu. Once users see windows and pull-down menus, their expectation of user-friendliness go way up. Adding a good on-line help system is an effective way to improve productivity with software you create.

The choices on the **Help** menu are really up to you. What makes the most sense for your application? Some common choices that you probably want to take advantage of do exist. These are shown in Table 4.8.

Table 4.8 Help Menu Choices

Menu Choice	Keyboard Shortcut
Contents	C
Index	I
Tutorial	T
About Application	A

If your application doesn't provide a certain type of help, such as an on-line tutorial, you should skip that menu choice, obviously. The **Contents** choice should provide a high-level table of contents for all the on-line help.

The **About** choice is the most fun. This lists information about your application. If your application is named *WunderWord*, this menu choice should read *About WunderWord*. Typically, this choice will call up a dialog box that shows a neato bitmap logo for your software, the version number, and copyright information. You'll often see customer support numbers in this dialog box window as well.

Placing the Help Menu

Although many Windows applications cheat on this, the **Help** menu button should really appear on the far right edge of the menu bar. (If the interface is in a language that uses right-to-left text, such as Hebrew and some dialects of Arabic, you should swap the order of the items on the menu bar.)

To get the **Help** menubutton to appear on the far right edge of the menu bar, use the -side right option for the pack command:

```
pack .menubar.help -side right
```

For all the other menubuttons, use -side left when packing. You'll also want to pack the **Help** menubutton last.

The Main Window

In addition to a standard menu bar, just about every windowed application sports some sort of main area. In a word processing application, for example, this main area contains the document and a scrollbar. You can also add a toolbar of bit map buttons just beneath the menu bar. See Chapter 9 for more on bit maps and toolbars.

The basic layout of most applications includes a menu bar at the top, a main area for the application and a status area at the bottom. Usually this status area is a label widget, sometimes in a frame, although you may want to include a text widget as well (see Chapter 5 for more on text widgets). In Tk, you can easily create all these elements. Use the following code as a guide:

```
frame .menubar -relief raised \
   -borderwidth 2

menubutton .menubar.file \
   -text "File" \
   -underline 0 \
    -menu .menubar.file.menu

menu .menubar.file.menu

.menubar.file.menu add command \
   -label "Save" \
   -underline 0

.menubar.file.menu add separator

.menubar.file.menu add command \
   -label "Exit" \
   -underline 0 \
   -command { exit }

menubutton .menubar.edit \
```

```
        -text "Edit" \
        -underline 0 \
        -menu .menubar.edit.menu

menu .menubar.edit.menu

.menubar.edit.menu add command \
    -label "Undo"
.menubar.edit.menu add separator

.menubar.edit.menu add command \
    -label "Cut" \
    -underline 2 \
    -accelerator "Ctrl+X"

.menubar.edit.menu add command \
    -label "Copy" \
    -underline 0 \
    -accelerator "Ctrl+C"

.menubar.edit.menu add command \
    -label "Paste" \
    -underline 0 \
    -accelerator "Ctrl+V"

menubutton .menubar.help \
    -text "Help" \
    -underline 0 \
    -menu .menubar.help.menu

menu .menubar.help.menu

.menubar.help.menu add command \
    -label "Contents" \
    -underline 0

.menubar.help.menu add separator

.menubar.help.menu add command \
    -label "About WunderWord" \
```

```
      -underline 0

  # Pack main menu bar items.
pack .menubar.file \
    .menubar.edit \
   -side left

  # Pack help menu.
pack .menubar.help -side right

  # Create a faked main area.
label .main -text "Main Area"

  # Status area.
label .status \
  -relief sunken \
  -borderwidth 2 \
  -text "Status/Message Area."

pack .menubar -side top \
  -fill x -expand true
pack .main -pady 100 -padx 200
pack .status -fill x \
  -anchor w
```

Figure 4.7 shows this sample main window.

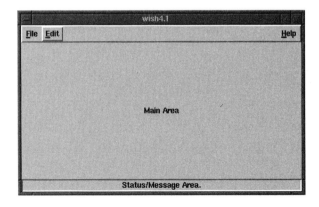

Figure 4.7 A typical main application window.

Option Menus

An option menu is a lot like a set of radiobuttons but in a more compact placement. This menu displays a current value, the value of the last choice picked. The user can display the option menu and then select a choice. The choice then appears in the menubutton associated with the option menu. An option menu is not like normal menus. It is more like a special widget that sets a variable value.

The command to create an option menu is tk_optionMenu:

```
tk_optionMenu w varname value1 value2 value3 ...
```

For example:

```
tk_optionMenu .option units \
        inches millimeters centimeters furlongs
set units inches

pack .option
```

This option menu, *.option*, uses the global variable *units* and allows the user to set it to the following values: inches, millimeters, centimeters, and furlongs (for supporters of old English measurements or horse racing fans).

Placing an option menu tends to be a problem since it changes size to match the current value. You also normally place a label next to the option menu to tell the user what the choice is for:

```
label .l1 \
  -text "Set units to:"
tk_optionMenu .option units \
        inches millimeters centimeters furlongs
set units inches

pack .l1 .option -side left
```

This example is show in Figure 4.8.

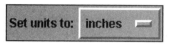

Figure 4.8 An option menu.

Since option menus are so like radiobuttons, at least in the end result, their use tends to overlap. Choose an option menu when you think it looks better or when screen space is tight, since an option menu takes up a lot less space than a set of radiobuttons for the same choices.

Pop-up Menus

A *pop-up menu* is a menu without a menubutton to call it up. Normally, you'll use the right-most mouse button (depending on the platform, it will be Button 1, 2, or 3) to call up a pop-up menu. Pop-up menus often contain shortcut options or allow you to change the properties of an item.

You create a pop-up menu the same way you'd create any other menu, with the menu command. When the proper moment comes (more on this later), you post the pop-up menu with the tk_popup command.

The syntax for tk_popup is:

```
tk_popup menu x y entry
```

The optional *entry* parameter specifies the index of which menu choice to activate.

The reason you need to post the menu yourself is because there is no menubutton widget to do the job for you.

A common way to post a pop-up menu is to create a binding on the right-most mouse button.

WINDOWS

On a two-button mouse in Windows, Tcl treats the right-most mouse button as Button 3, not 2, so you can bind Button 3 to call up pop-up menus and expect it to work on Windows and UNIX.

The main trick with pop-up menus is to get the pop-up to appear at the precise mouse location. Since the pop-up will appear in from a binding on <Button-3>, you can use the %x and %y syntax to get the current mouse position. Unfortunately, this position is in local coordinates, that is, local to the application window.

So, the next step is to get the global coordinates for the application window and then add this to the values in the %x and %y, as given by the Tk binding.

We can use the winfo command, described in more detail in Chapter 7, to retrieve the global (or root) coordinates of a widget, as shown next. The following command returns the global x coordinate for a given widget:

```
winfo rootx .widget
```

The rooty option works similarly:

```
winfo rooty .widget
```

The next step is to determine what widget to use. If the event occurs over a widget, we need to use that widget and get its global coordinates (of position 0, 0 in that widget). To do so, we use the %W syntax (see Table 4.3) to get the widget in which the event occurred.

To pull this together, we have the following binding for <Button-3>:

```
bind all <Button-3> {

  # Get global Y position of app.
  set gx [winfo rootx %W ]

  # Add to local mouse position.
  set mx \
    [expr %x + $gx]

  # Get global Y position of app.
  set gy [winfo rooty %W ]
```

```
puts "X $mx gx $gx gy $gy"

# Add to local mouse position.
set my [expr %y + $gy]

puts "Hit at $mx $my"

tk_popup .popup $mx $my
}
```

Note how this Tcl code adds the global *x* value of origin of the widget to the %x value of the mouse position within the widget.

The pop-up menu, named *.popup*, will then appear at the current mouse position. We make this pop-up menu like any other menu:

```
menu .popup

.popup add command \
  -label "Popup Choice 1" \
  -command { puts "Popup1" }

.popup add separator

.popup add command \
  -label "Popup Choice 2" \
  -command { puts "Popup2" }
```

You don't pack menus. In this case, the tk_popup command will handle this task.

N O T E

When you create pop-up menus, you should be very careful because there's no indication to new users that a pop-up menu exists. You'll want to ensure that all the choices on the pop-up menu are also available elsewhere in the interface. The pop-up menu should be a shortcut feature for expert users, not an essential part of the application's interface.

Summary

This chapter covers a major component of all graphical applications: menus and the menu bar.

A menu bar is merely a `frame` widget configured horizontally. On this `frame` widget, you place `menubutton` widgets to pull-down menus.

A menu widget must be a child of the `menubutton` that pulls it down or the menu it cascades from.

You can add menu choices to a menu via the `add` option. Use the `bind` command to set up keyboard accelerators. Both Windows and UNIX have similar conventions for what menus and menu choices should appear on an application's menu bar.

To create an option menu, a different kind of menu, use the `tk_optionMenu` command with a variable name and a set of values. An option menu is not like normal menus.

For a pop-up menu, use the `tk_popup` command to make it appear.

Chapter 5 continues on working with graphical applications and covers text editing, Tcl string functions, and scrollbars.

Tcl/Tk Commands Introduced in this Chapter

```
bind
menu
menubutton
tk_optionMenu
tk_popup
winfo
```

Text Editing with Tcl and Tk

This chapter covers:

- The entry widget for single-line text entry
- The multiline text widget
- Scrolled text widgets
- The scrollbar widget
- Controlling scrollbars
- String-handling commands in Tcl
- Creating a Tcl text editor that executes commands

Entering Text

Just about every graphical program requires some form of text-entry widget that allows users to enter file names, values, and other data. Tk provides two main widgets for this purpose: entry and text.

The entry widget provides a one-line entry area and is more like a single-value entry field. The text widget can be scrolled with many lines of text entry and is more like a text editor.

Creating Entry Widgets

For the entry widget, the -width option determines how wide you want the entry widget to be in characters. Thus, a width of 30 specifies an entry widget that can show 30 characters at once. This is very useful in cases where you need to control the input, and when you simply want a larger entry area.

To create an entry widget, all you need is the following:

```
entry .ent1 -width 30
pack .ent1
```

In most cases, you'll want to specify more options.

The -textvariable option sets a variable to hold the data the user enters. You can use this to both set an initial value and to get at the contents of the user input later on.

NOTE The entry widget has no -command option, so the normal way you associate Tcl code with an entry widget is to set up a binding, often on the **Return** key. You also want to use the -textvariable option.

On its own, an entry widget provides no prompts to the user, so entry widgets are usually associated with label widgets. The label then provides the prompt.

To set up an entry widget with a binding on the **Return** key and an associated label prompt, you can base your code on the following:

```
label .label -text "Enter user name: "
entry .ent -width 30 -textvariable entry1
pack .label .ent -side left

bind .ent <Key-Return> {
    # Your code goes here...
    puts $entry1
}
```

You can see this widget combination in Figure 5.1.

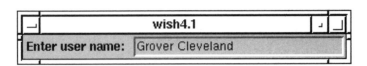

Figure 5.1 An entry widget with a label for a prompt.

Even if you don't set up the -textvariable option, you can still retrieve the text in the widget by using the get option:

```
widgetname get
```

For example, using the entry widget named .ent from the preceding example:

```
set var  [ .ent get ]
```

Password Entry

The -show option allows you to specify a character to show instead of the default (the contents of the widget). For example, the following label and entry can be used for a password entry, as shown in Figure 5.2.

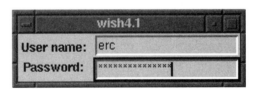

Figure 5.2 A password entry.

The code for this example follows:

```
frame .prompts -relief flat
label .prompts.user -text "User name: "
label .prompts.password \
  -text "Password: "
```

```
pack .prompts.user .prompts.password \
  -side top -fill x -expand true

frame .entries -relief flat
entry .entries.user -width 20 \
  -textvariable username
entry .entries.password \
  -width 20 \
  -show "*" \
  -textvariable password

pack .entries.user .entries.password \
  -side top -fill x -expand true

pack .prompts .entries -side left
```

Note that the label widgets for the prompts appear in one frame widget and the entry widgets appear in another frame. The reason for this is to line up the left edges of the entry widgets.

Of course, such placement won't be perfect, as the height of the labels is slightly less than the height of the entry widgets. With more than two rows, you'll start to notice the difference, especially if one text prompt becomes a lot larger than another.

What can you use to line these up? You can try the place command or various pack options. Start with what you can determine from the widgets. For example, two entry widgets using the same font with the same -width option will be the same size, so you can use these as the key widgets in the layout. If we lay them out from the right instead of the left, we have fixed-size height and width, at least for the entry widgets.

In that case, you can place each row in its own frame widget, instead of each column. Anchor the widgets to the right. For example, try the following code:

```
frame .row1 -relief flat
label .row1.prompt \
  -anchor e \
  -text "Please enter user name: "
```

```
entry .row1.user -width 20 \
  -textvariable username

pack .row1.user \
   -side right

pack .row1.prompt \
  -side left -expand true \
  -fill y -fill x -anchor e

frame .row2 -relief flat
label .row2.prompt \
-bg orange \
  -text "Password: " \
  -anchor e

entry .row2.password \
  -width 20 \
  -show "*" \
  -textvariable password

pack .row2.password \
    -side right

pack .row2.prompt \
  -side left -expand true \
  -fill y -fill x -anchor e

pack .row1 .row2 \
  -side top -fill x -expand true
```

You'll soon find that you can endlessly play with various layouts and still be close but not quite right. Look over the section on the packer in Chapter 3 for more on pack options to see how to get your layouts right.

Deleting All Text in an Entry Widget

The following command deletes all the text in an entry widget:

widgetname delete *0 end*

For example, using the same widget as before:

```
.ent delete 0 end
```

The delete option requires two parameters, the character index of where to start deleting and the index of the last character to delete. The special keyword end frees you from having to know how many characters are in the entry widget.

You'll likely call this option a lot. The user expects many entry fields to clear their input when the user enters a filename, username or other such entry. You can change the **Return** key binding from the preceding example to clear out the data using the following example:

```
bind .ent <Key-Return> {
    # Your code goes here...
    puts $entry1

    # Clear contents of widget.
    .ent delete 0 end
}
```

The Insertion Cursor

Each entry widget has an insertion cursor. This cursor appears in the gap between two characters. When you enter new text, Tk inserts the new text after the insertion cursor.

You can position the insertion cursor with the icursor option:

```
widgetname icursor position
```

For example, with an entry widget named *.ent*, you can move the insertion cursor to the start of the widget text with the following command:

```
.ent icursor 0
```

The position is the character index of where to place the insertion cursor. (Indices usually start with 0 in Tcl.) You can use a direct number or one of the entry widget's built-in positions, listed in Table 5.1.

Table 5.1 Special Insertion Positions for the Entry Widget

Position	Meaning
end	Just after the last character
insert	Just after the insertion cursor
sel.first	Start of selected text, if any is selected
sel.last	End of selected text, if any is selected

If you want to move the insertion cursor to the end of the text, use the following command:

```
.ent icursor end
```

The icursor option moves the insertion cursor, which controls where the user adds text. The user can always click the mouse at a different location to move the insertion cursor or use the left and right arrow keys. Inside a Tcl script, though, you're not limited by the position of the insertion cursor. You can insert text anywhere with the insert option:

```
widgetname insert start_position string
```

The *start_position* identifies where to start the insertion of the new string. This is an index to a character position, the same as that passed to the icursor option.

To insert the string "Inserted into the middle" into the text in an entry widget at, say, position 5, you can use the following command:

```
.ent insert 5 "Inserted into the middle"
```

If the text is too long for the widget's display, you'll see only part of the text, as shown in Figure 5.3.

Figure 5.3 An entry widget holding a lot of text.

Don't worry, the entry widget still holds the text, even if all of it is not visible at any time. You can use the left and right arrow keys to move the insertion cursor back and forth in the window.

Entry Widget Selections

The X Window System, so popular on UNIX, provides for the concept of a **selection**, a highlighted piece of data in some program on the screen. Only one program can own a given selection at a time, (you can name alternate selections, although almost every program uses the selection named PRIMARY).

Tk works well within the X environment and allows you to copy text from a terminal window and paste it into a Tcl entry or text widget. The reverse operation is also possible.

To set this up, you need to set the -exportselection option to true. You almost always want to do this, so that the entry widget works well in the surrounding window environment.

On UNIX, you can select text with the mouse and paste it without going through an intermediary, that is, the clipboard. Thus the -export-selection option is very important because the user can select data in the window and paste it into another window.

On Windows, you need to copy the data to the clipboard, unless you only use **wish**. See the section on cut, copy, and paste, later in this chapter for more on this.

N O T E

In the entry widget, the position sel.first is set to the first character in the selection, and sel.last to the end of the selection. You can use these positions with the delete option and so on.

151

In addition, the selection option allows you to control the contents of the selection. For example, the selection clear option clears the selection, obviously. For this, you need the widget name:

```
widgetname selection clear
```

For example:

```
.ent1 selection clear
```

Note that this clears the text highlighting, not the highlighted text itself.

The selection present option returns 1 if a selection is active in the widget. For example:

```
% .ent1 selection present
0
```

Scrolling in the Entry Widget

You can control scrolling in the entry widget with the xview option. The xview scroll option moves the text back and forth in the window, presuming the text goes beyond the entry window.

The following command scrolls the visible text back to show previous text by 10 units, an amount based on the average character size:

```
.ent1 xview scroll -10 units
```

To scroll the text forward to the end, use positive numbers.

Describing this scrolling is tough, since moving forward causes the text to move to the left, so that text that was off to the right now becomes visible. The best way to figure this out is to try the example commands.

N O T E

There's a lot more to the entry widget. You'll want to look up the on-line manual information for entry.

With the entry widget, you can make a **File Open** dialog box, you can ask for user names and passwords. In fact, you can allow users to enter most of the data items required in your program. Sometimes a single line of text is not enough. For those cases, you can use the text widget.

Multiline Text Widgets

While the entry widget provides only one line of text, the text widget allows for many, many lines in a scrolled widget. This is useful for text editing, file viewing, electronic mail messages and all sorts of fun things, including using the simple Tcl editor created in the following example, which shows a text widget and a scrollbar (more on that in the section on scrollbars later in this chapter) inside a frame widget:

```
frame .tx

text .tx.text \
    -yscrollcommand ".tx.scrl set"
scrollbar .tx.scrl -command ".tx.text yview"

# Pack scrollbar first.
pack .tx.scrl -side right -fill y
pack .tx.text -side left
pack .tx -side top
```

These commands create a window like the one shown in Figure 5.4.

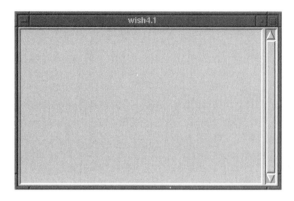

Figure 5.4 A text widget and a scrollbar.

The `scrollbar` needs to be connected to the `text` widget. When the user moves the `scrollbar`, the `text` widget needs to update as well. The `text` widget needs to be connected to the `scrollbar`, so that when the `text` widget moves its text (via Tcl commands or on user input), the `scrollbar` gets updated as well.

The `text` widget and the `scrollbar` are linked by their widget names via the `-ycommand` and `-command` options, respectively. This is how you connect a `scrollbar` to a `text` widget. For more on this, see the section in this chapter on connecting the text widget to the scrollbar.

Controlling the Text Widget Display

The `-height` option controls the height of the text widget, in characters. The `-width` sets the width of the text widget, again in characters. In most cases, the defaults work fine.

The `-wrap` option takes a value of none, for no wrapping, `char`, for character-by-character wrapping, or `word`, for wrapping only on word boundaries.

Controlling Spacing Between Lines

The text widget provides a number of confusing options for controlling the spacing between lines, as shown in Table 5.2.

Table 5.2 Text Widget Line-Spacing Options

Option	Meaning
-spacing1 *value*	Adds additional space above each line
-spacing2 *value*	Adds additional space between all lines but wrapped lines (assumed to be single lines for this spacing)
-spacing3 *value*	Adds spacing after each line

Deleting Text

Like with the entry widget, you can delete text with the delete option:

widgetname delete *start_index end_index*

The delete option deletes the text from the *start_index* to just before, but not including, the *end_index*. If you omit the *end_index*, delete just deletes one character.

The start and end positions are a bit more complicated than for the entry widget. For the text widget, you need to define a starting index, which allows a great deal of flexibility at the price of complexity.

Defining Positions in the Text

Tk calls a position within a text widget an **index**. The whole point of indices is to allow you to use symbolic names for the text to delete, much like the sel.first and sel.end positions for the entry widget, which indicate the starting and ending positions of the selection. The syntax for a text widget index is:

base modifiers

Table 5.3 lists the available values for the base part of the index.

Table 5.3 Base Values for Text Widget Indices

Value	Meaning
line.char	Character *char* (starting at 0) on line *line* (starting at 1)
@x,y	The character under the mouse at local position *x*, *y* (in pixels)
end	The character just after the last newline
markname	The character just after the mark markname
tagname.first	The first character in the given tag
tagename.last	The character just after the last in the given tag
windowname	The position of the embedded window of that name

These indices are so complicated because Tk allows you to define arbitrary positions within the text widget, called **tags**, **marks** and **embedded windows**. Although they are complicated, these neat features provide the basics of a full-blown hypertext system.

You can adjust the base part of an index with the modifiers, given in Table 5.4.

Table 5.4 Text Index Modifiers

Modifier	Meaning
+ *value* chars	Adjust the base index forward by *value* characters
- *value* chars	Adjust the base index backward by *value* characters
+ *value* lines	Adjust the base index forward by *value* lines
- *value* lines	Adjust the base index forward by *value* lines
linestart	Adjust index to first character on the line
lineend	Adjust index to last character on the line (the newline character)
wordstart	Adjust index to first character in word
wordend	Adjust index to just after the last character in word

To delete all the characters in the text widget *.tx.text*, you can use the following command:

```
.tx.text delete 1.0 end
```

The 1.0 specifies the first line (1) and the first character (0) in that line.

NOTE

Lines start counting with 1, characters in a line with 0. The rationale for lines starting with 1 is to maintain compatibility with a number of UNIX commands that also count lines starting with 1. Most other counts in Tcl start with 0.

You can use the index option to convert an index of one type into the *line.char* form that is easiest to understand:

```
widgetname index index_to_convert
```

This converts the *index_to_convert* and returns the same position, but in *line.char* format.

Text indices are kind of hard in theory but much easier in practice. You'll also need these indices for most other *text* widget commands, such as for inserting text.

Inserting Text

The basic form of the insert option is:

```
widgetname insert index characters
```

For example, to insert the string "In Xanadu did Kublai Khan a stately pleasure dome decree" into the beginning of a text widget, use the following command:

```
.tx.text insert 1.0 \
 "In Xanadu did Kublai Khan a
 stately pleasure dome decree."
```

You can also complicate the insert command with a list of tags, using the following syntax:

```
widgetname insert index characters taglist
```

This associates the tags in *taglist* with the new characters to be inserted. If you omit the *taglist*, the new characters will get any tags that are present on both ends of the insertion point.

You can add even more tags with repeated characters and *taglist* options:

```
widgetname insert index characters1 taglist1 characters2 taglist2 ...
```

You can repeat the pattern as long as you desire.

Searching Through the Text

The search option allow you to search for the position in the text that a given pattern can be found. The basic syntax follows:

```
widgetname search options pattern start_index end_index
```

The *end_index* is optional. Table 5.5 lists the options, which are all optional.

Table 5.5 Text Widget Search Options

Option	Meaning
-forward	Search in forward direction, the default
-backward	Search backward
-exact	Characters must match pattern exactly, the default
-regexp	Use pattern as a regular expression (see Chapter 2).
-nocase	Ignore case when searching
-count *variable*	If a match is found, place the number of characters into varname
--	Stops options

The -- option seems kind of strange at first glance. Tcl interprets all items starting with a dash, -, as an option. That's a problem, if you want to search for an item that starts with a dash (sort of like deleting a file named "-i" on UNIX). The double dash, --, stops all parsing for options and allows the pattern to start with a -.

Retrieving Text

You can retrieve the text with the get option, which uses the following syntax:

```
widgetname get start_index end_index
```

The *end_index* is optional.

The get option retrieves all the text from the *start_index* to the *end_index* (or a single character if you omit the *end_index*). To get all the text, use the following command, keeping with an example text widget named *.tx.text*:

```
% .tx.text get 1.0 end
In Xanadu did Kublai Khan a
  stately pleasure dome decree.
```

Marks, Tags and Embedded Windows

The text widget complicates Tk once you start getting into the concepts of marks, tags, and embedded windows. These items allow you to turn a plain old text widget into a hypertext browser or to support compound documents but you have to do a lot of work on your own.

The next sections introduce the theory behind marks, tags and embedded windows. After that, you'll see how to apply the theory and create hypertext links or embedded graphics.

Marks

A **mark** marks a position in the text with a symbolic name. This position appears in the gap between two characters. Thus marks are invisible. You can use marks as an index position in the text widget, as shown in Table 5.3.

A special mark named insert identifies the position of the insertion cursor. Moving this mark moves the insertion point. You can move the insertion cursor by using the mark set option with a mark named insert and specifying a new position. For example:

```
.tx.text mark set insert 2.7
```

A special mark named `current` identifies the current mouse position when it is translated to an index value in the `text` widget. This position is not updated while a mouse button is held down.

To create a mark, use the `mark set` option:

```
widgetname mark set markname index
```

The *index* indicates the position to set the mark. If the given *markname* already exists, this command moves the mark to a new position.

To get rid of a mark, use the `mark unset` option:

```
widgetname mark unset markname
```

You can unset a number of marks at once:

```
widgetname mark unset markname1 markname2 ...
```

You can query the names of all marks in a text widget with the `mark names` option:

```
widgetname mark names
```

Using Tags to Control Fonts

Unlike a mark, a tag has a beginning and an end. **Tags** associate special attributes or behavior with a section of text. For example, you can tag a section of text and then make the tagged text appear underlined or in a different font. (This is how you get multiple fonts in a `text` widget.)

Furthermore, you can bind events within a tagged area. For example, if you create a tagged area as a hypertext link, you can make the link appear underlined. You can also bind the button-1 event to the tag and execute Tcl code to jump to the link when the user presses the button-1 (usually the leftmost mouse button) over the tagged area. You can build a hypertext system with the `text` widget, but you must do it by hand.

A common use for tags is simply to display some text in a different font.

You can create a tag with the `tag add` option:

```
widgetname tag add tagname start_index end_index
```

You determine the *tagname*. For example, the following command adds a tag named *underline1* to the widget named *.tx.text*. This new tag starts on line 2 at the start of the word in column 1 (character position 0) and goes to the end of the word. The Tcl command follows:

```
.tx.text tag add underline1 \
    {2.1 wordstart} {2.1 wordend}
```

If you omit the *end_index*, the tag spans a single character.

If you want the same tag, say, for a font change, to apply to many areas in the text, you can pass multiple start and end indices:

> *widgetname tag add tagname* \
> *start_index1 end_index1* \
> *start_index2 end_index2* \
>
> *...*

Controlling Display Attributes with Tags

Once you create a tag, you can control the display attributes with the `tag configure` option:

```
widgetname tag configure tagname option value
```

For example, to set our *underline1* tag to underline the text, we can use the following command:

```
.tx.text tag configure \
  underline1 -underline 1
```

You can see the text underlined in Figure 5.5.

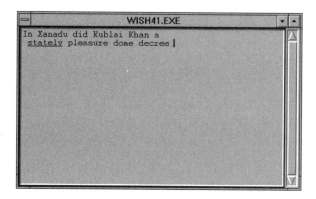

Figure 5.5 A text widget tag with underlined text.

Table 5.6 lists the options you can pass with tag configure. You can pass more than one option at a time.

Table 5.6 Tag Configuration Options

Option	Meaning
-background *color*	Set background color for tag
-bgstipple *bitmap*	Uses bitmap as a background stipple (brush pattern)
-borderwidth *pixels*	Sets border width of tagged area
-fgstipple *bitmap*	Uses bitmap as a foreground stipple (brush pattern)
-font *fontname*	Set font for tag
-foreground *color*	Set foreground color for tag
-justify *justify*	Justifies the line left, right or center
-lmargin1 *pixels*	Adds *pixels* to left margin for first line of tag only
-lmargin2 *pixels*	Adds *pixels* to left margin for all remaining lines of tag

continued

Table 5.6 continued

-offset *pixels*	Offsets the text baseline vertically by *pixels*
-overstrike *boolean*	Turns on (1) or off (0) overstrike mode
-relief *relief*	Sets relief to flat, groove, raised, ridge, or sunken
-rmargin *pixels*	Adds *pixels* to right margin; applies only when wrapping
-spacing1 *pixels*	Set spacing, see Table 5.2
-spacing2 *pixels*	Set spacing, see Table 5.2
-spacing3 *pixels*	Set spacing, see Table 5.2
-tabs *tablist*	Set tab stops within tag
-underline *boolean*	Turn on (1) or off (0) underlining of tag
-wrap *mode*	Controls wrap mode, one of none, char, or word

Binding Events to Tags

You can bind events that occur within a tag to execute a Tcl script, but, inside a tag, you can bind only mouse and keyboard events to a tag. These include Enter, Leave, ButtonPress, ButtonRelease, (mouse) Motion, KeyPress, and KeyRelease events.

You can bind events inside tags to actions using the tag bind option and the following syntax:

```
widgetname tag bind tagname event tcl_script
```

For example, when the user presses the left-most mouse button down, you can make a tag jump to a hypertext link. To set up such a binding, use the following template as an example:

```
.tx.text tag bind underline1 <Button-1> {

  # Pretend to jump.
  puts "Jumping."

}
```

Of course, it's up to you to add the actual hypertext behavior. Press the left-most mouse button over the underlined tag and you should see the following text printed: *Jumping.*

In addition to jumping to a hypertext link, many Web browsers, such as Mosaic or Netscape Navigator, display the jump location in a widget at the bottom of the window. This allows you to see where a hypertext link (think *tag*) will go. Normally, this appears when you move the mouse over the particular tag (hypertext link). To do something like this in Tcl, you can start with a label widget to display the jump-to location:

```
label .status \
    -text "Status Area"
pack .status -side bottom -anchor w
```

Next, you'll need to bind both the Enter and Leave events. On Enter, we need to extract the jump address (the Web's Universal Resource Locator) and set the text in the label widget to that value. The following code shows only how to set up the binding, not how to work with URLs (that exercise is left for the reader):

```
.tx.text tag bind underline1 <Enter> {

    # Display link.
    .status configure \
        -text "Over link."
}
```

We normally would bind the Leave event to clear the text in the label widget. In this case, though, we'll set this event to display a message. The purpose of this message is to allow you to experiment with the tag bindings and better see how the Enter and Leave events operate.

```
.tx.text tag bind underline1 <Leave> {

    # Clear display of link.
    .status configure \
        -text "No longer over link."
}
```

Now, move the mouse over the underlined tag. The text in the *.status* label should change. Move the mouse away. The text should change again.

You could also change the background color of the tagged area to provide even more indication to the user which tag is the "active" one. For example:

```
.tx.text tag bind underline1 <Enter> {

   # Change color in text widget.
   .tx.text tag configure \
      underline1 -background lightsteelblue

   # Display link.
   .status configure \
      -text "Over link."
}


.tx.text tag bind underline1 <Leave> {


   # Restore color in text widget.
   .tx.text tag configure \
      underline1 -background lightgray

   # Clear display of link.
   .status configure \
      -text "No longer over link."
}

.tx.text configure \
  -background lightgray
```

Now, when you move the mouse cursor into the tag, you should see a visual indicator that the tag is "active."

Deleting Tags

To delete a tag, use `tag delete`:

```
widgetname tag delete tagname
```

If you don't want to delete a tag, but just want to stop it from applying to a particular index, you can use the `tag remove` option:

```
widgetname tag remove tagname index
```

You can include multiple indices with this option.

You can query what tags exist with `tag names`:

```
widgetname tag names index
```

The *index* is optional. If omitted, you'll get the list of all tag names. if you use an *index*, you'll only get back the tags active at that position in the text.

Embedded Windows

While tags allow you to place special formatting on a section of text, **embedded windows** allow you to place a whole window at a position (index) in the text. Normally, such a *window* is a Tk widget.

If you think about creating a World-Wide Web browser in Tk, you can use embedded windows to display graphic images that appear in Web pages, especially since Tk labels can display GIF and other image formats.

Creating Embedded Windows

You can create an embedded window at a particular location, an index, within a text widget, using the `window create` option:

```
widgetname window create index option value ...
```

The *index* identifies where the new window is to be placed.

Table 5.7 lists the options you can use to configure the new embedded window at creation time or later with the `configure window` command.

Table 5.7 Text Widget Embedded Window Options

Option	Usage
`-align` *where*	Set *where* to `top`, `center`, `bottom`, or `baseline`, if the embedded window is shorter than a line of text
`-create` *tcl_script*	Execute *tcl_script* to create the embedded window; won't work with `-window`
-padx *pixels*	Extra space on each side of embedded window
-pady *pixels*	Extra space on each side of embedded window
-stretch *boolean*	If true (returns 1), stretch embedded window vertically to fit line of text
-window *widgetname*	Gives the widget name to display

For example, we can embed a window inside the `text` widget. In this case, we'll use a `button` widget, but you can use any widget you want:

```
button .tx.text.embed1 \
  -text "Emebedded Button"

.tx.text window create \
    {1.0 lineend} \
    -window .tx.text.embed1
```

WARNING

Don't pack the widget you intend to embed. The `text` widget takes care of this for you.

Figure 5.6 shows this embedded `button` widget in the `text` widget.

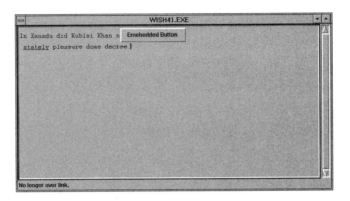

Figure 5.6 An embedded button widget.

Look at Chapter 9 for more on setting a `button` or `label` widget to hold a bitmap image, which is the most common use for embedding widgets in a text widget, since tags already provide a lot of the functionalities of buttons.

You could also use embedded widgets to create a data entry form often used in **HyperText Markup Language** (HTML) documents, the *linga franca* of the Web. To do this, you can create a `frame` and then create a `label` and `entry` widget within the `frame`. Embed the `frame` widget within the `text` widget:

```
frame .tx.text.embed2

label .tx.text.embed2.lbl \
   -text "Enter name: "
entry .tx.text.embed2.ent \
   -width 30 \
   -textvariable name
pack .tx.text.embed2.lbl \
   .tx.text.embed2.ent -side left

.tx.text window create \
   {2.0 linestart} \
   -window .tx.text.embed2
```

You need to `pack` subwidgets within the widget you embed. For example, *.tx.text.embed2.lbl* and *.tx.text.embed2.ent*. Again, don't `pack` the widget you intend to embed, that is, *.tx.text.embed2*.

N O T E

You can modify an embedded window with the `window configure` command, which uses the following syntax:

```
widgetname window configure index option value
```

You can use `window configure` with multiple options at the same time.

If you want to know the names of all embedded windows, the `window names` command returns the name of each embedded window in the widget:

```
widgetname window names
```

Making Hypertext Links in the Text

The neat part behind the confusion that surrounds marks, tags, and embedded windows is that you can use these tools to quickly create a hypertext system.

For example, a program called **tkWWW**, shown in Figure 5.7, uses the `text` widget (and a lot of customized code), to create a World-Wide Web browser. The `text` widget provides the basics for a hypertext system. Tags can outline links, and embedded windows can provide graphics.

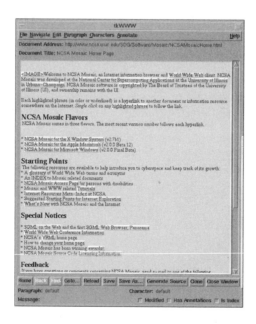

Figure 5.7 The tkWWW Web browser.

To do this, you'll want to set up a tag for each hypertext link. You'll then need to bind the tags to Enter, Leave, and Button-1 events. You can also use tags for the more mundane text formatting commands found in most hypertext systems, such as the World-Wide Web.

Disabling Widgets

In hypertext systems, you typically don't want the user to edit the document being displayed, but the text widget by default allows the user to edit the widget's contents. To get around this, you can disable most widgets, including the text widget, with the -state option. You can set the -state option to one of normal or disabled.

Try the following on the text widget created earlier in the section on multiline text widgets:

```
.tx.text configure -state disabled
```

Cut, Copy, and Paste with the Text Widget

Taking a step away from the hypertext examples, any real work with a text widget requires use of the clipboard. That is, if you want to make a usable interface. You can make the Tk text widget support cut, copy, and paste operations using a few simple Tk commands, including clipboard and selection.

The Clipboard

The clipboard provides a landing spot for data exchange. You can copy the selected text (or data in whatever form) to the clipboard from one application and paste it from the clipboard into another application.

The Clipboard and the Selection

The clipboard exists in limbo. You can't see its contents (without a clipboard-viewing program at least). The selection, however, is usually visible, unless the user scrolls out of the way or covers up a window.

All the standard operations of cut, copy, and paste involve the clipboard for data storage and the selection. For a copy operation, the selected text is copied into the clipboard. A paste reverses this and copies the clipboard text to the text widget (and overwrites any selection).

Getting the Selected Text

There are two main ways to get at the selected text. First, in a text widget, you can access the special tag Tk sets up for the selection. You can also use the more general selection command.

Accessing the Selection Tag

In a text widget, if the selection is in the widget, a special tag named sel (much like that for the entry widget) will indicate the span of the selection.

The Selection Command

While the special sel tag can prove useful, I normally stick to the more general selection command. This allows you to create a more general cut, copy, and paste mechanism, where you don't have to worry about which widget the selection resides at any time.

To get the current selection, use the following command:

```
set var [selection get]
```

The selection get command returns the current selection. By default, the data is in text format. You can use the -type option to request the data in a different format. The default value is STRING for text-string format.

UNIX

These types come from the X Window System's concept of selections. In X, you can play a game of twenty questions with the current selection. The idea is that you may want more than the actual selected data. You may want to know what window the data resides in. You may want the length of the data, as well as the actual contents of the data. The X Window System handles this with the concept of the **target type** of data you ask for.

For example, you can ask the application that owns the selection for the window ID of the window in which the selection appears (-type CLIENT_WINDOW). You can ask for the data as an integer (-type INTEGER), although this often causes an error.

You can ask for the length of the selected data (normally the number of characters in the selected text, but for other data formats this is undefined) with the -type LENGTH option. You can ask for the character position within the data where the selected text resides with the -type CHARACTER_POSITION option.

To find out what available types the application that owns the selection supports use the -type TARGETS option. This returns the name of all the target types supported. Note that different applications support different target types.

For example, try the following commands:

```
% selection get
These types come from the X Window System's concept
% selection get -type CLIENT_WINDOW
0x80000e
% selection get -type INTEGER
PRIMARY selection doesn't exist or form "INTEGER" not defined
% selection get -type LENGTH
0x13
% selection get -type CHARACTER_POSITION
PRIMARY selection doesn't exist or form "CHARACTER_POSITION"
not defined
% selection get -type TARGETS
STRING TEXT COMPOUND_TEXT LENGTH
LIST_LENGTH TIMESTAMP HOSTNAME
IP_ADDRESS USER CLASS NAME CLIENT_WINDOW
```

In virtually all cases, you use the -type STRING option, the default, or skip the -type option altogether. See Appendix A for a list of books on the X Window System that will explain selections in the UNIX environment.

WINDOWS

If you try the preceding commands on Windows, you're likely to get errors. Even so, Tk applications will work with selections and work very well with the clipboard, which is where UNIX is weakest.

In addition to different data target types, there are also different selections. The default selection is called the PRIMARY selection. This is the one that almost every application uses. On UNIX, you'll also see SECONDARY and CLIPBOARD selections. You can also define your own, using any name you want. The rules that apply to the PRIMARY selection apply to all: Only one application at a time may own any *particular* selection. Your application may own the PRIMARY selection, but another application may own SECONDARY.

You can use the -selection option to indicate the selection you want:

```
selection get -selection PRIMARY
```

The main problem with multiple selections is finding programs to exchange data with. Virtually all UNIX programs support the default PRIMARY selection. Very few support the FRAMROD selection.

Only in rare circumstances will you need a different selection, unless you're retrieving data from the clipboard, in which case you'll use the CLIP-BOARD selection.

UNIX

The on-line documentation for the selection command lists a host of other options, most of which are useful only in the UNIX environment.

Clearing the Selection

To clear the current selection, use the selection clear command:

```
selection clear
```

NOTE

Again, you can use the -selection option if you want to specify a different selection than PRIMARY.

This only clears the fact that something was selected. It does not delete the selected data.

Checking Who Owns the Selection

To check if your application owns the selection, use the selection own command:

```
selection own
```

If your application owns the selection, the selection own command will return the name of the widget that owns the selection. Otherwise, selection own returns a NULL string.

To see if your application owns the selection, you can use the following code:

```
if { [selection own] != "" } {

    # Have selection.

} else {
    # Don't have selection.
}
```

The selection is just the first part of cut, copy, and paste operations. The remaining part is working with the clipboard.

Putting Text in the Clipboard

The clipboard append command places data in the clipboard.

```
clipboard append data
```

This *data* is appended to whatever data was already in the clipboard. Because of this, you may want to clear the data out first. (See below.)

If the *data* starts with a hyphen, -, you'll want to use the - - option prior to the *data*, for example:

```
clipboard append -- ---
```

NOTE

This command appends three dashes, - - -, to the clipboard. Without the - - option, Tk would treat the data as an option, a bad option at that.

Clearing Text in the Clipboard

The clipboard clear command clears the data in the clipboard and asserts ownership:

```
clipboard clear
```

Retrieving Data from the Clipboard

To retrieve data from the clipboard, you need to use the selection get command with a -selection CLIPBOARD option. The following commands clears the clipboard, appends text, and then retrieves it:

```
% clipboard clear
% clipboard append "Hello Clipboard"
% selection get -selection CLIPBOARD
Hello Clipboard
```

Whew. With these commands, you can now put together the cut, copy, and paste operations discussed at the beginning of this section.

Copy

The copy operation is the easiest. What you need to do is:

- Check if any text is selected.
- If so, get the selected text.
- Clear the clipboard.
- Place the selected text in the clipboard.

All of these tasks can be accomplished with just the selection and clipboard commands, as shown in the clip_copy procedure:

```
proc clip_copy { } {

  # Check if any text is selected.
  if { [selection own] != "" } {

    # Clear the clipboard.
    clipboard clear
```

```
# Append the selected text to the clipboard.
clipboard append [selection get]
}

}
```

Cut

The cut operation is essentially the same as a copy, with an extra deletion:

- Check if any text is selected.
- If so, get the selected text.
- Clear the clipboard.
- Place the selected text in the clipboard.
- Delete the selected text.

To implement this, we could call the clip_copy procedure, shown earlier, and then delete the selected text. For this operation, we need the name of the widget that owns the selection, so that the data can be deleted, which leads to slightly different code:

```
proc clip_cut { } {

# Check if any text is selected.
set owner [selection own]

if { $owner != "" } {
   # Clear the clipboard.
   clipboard clear

   # Append the selected text to the clipboard.
   clipboard append [selection get]
```

```
# Delete the selected text.
$owner delete sel.first sel.last
}

}
```

In the clip_cut procedure, the sel tag is used to create the indices for the starting and ending positions of the selection.

Paste

The paste operation reverses (sort of) the copy operation:

- Get the text from the clipboard.
- Check if any text is selected.
- If so, delete the selected text.
- Insert the clipboard text at the current insertion position.

To implement this, you can use the following code example.

In the code, there are two main cases to deal with. If the user selected data in the window, the paste operation will replace the selected data with the contents of the clipboard. Otherwise, paste will merely insert the data at the current insertion point. Both alternatives require the name of the widget you want to paste in.

The following code implements a paste operation on a given widget:

```
proc clip_paste { widgetname } {

    # Get the text from the clipboard.
    set clip [selection get \
        -selection CLIPBOARD ]

    # Check if any text is selected.
    set owner [selection own]

    if { $owner == $widgetname } {

        # Save the index where the selection starts.
```

```
    set idx [$owner index sel.first]

    # Delete the selected text.
    $owner delete sel.first sel.last

    # Paste in the clipboard data.
    $owner insert $idx $clip

} else {

    # If no text is selected, insert at
    # insertion point within widget.
    $widgetname insert insert $clip
}

}
```

We'll use these procedures later, in the section on a Tcl-based text editor later in this chapter.

Text Widget Efficiency

Each character in a text widget requires about 2 or 3 bytes of memory. With modern computers (and modern memory-eating operating system requirements), you should be able to display a large amount of text before running into memory problems.

Connecting the Text Widget to a Scrollbar

The scrollbar widget, used in the preceding examples, provides a number of options you may want to exercise. You'll typically create a scrollbar with an associated widget, such as the text widget:

```
# Text-editing area
frame .tx

text .tx.text \
    -yscrollcommand ".tx.scrl set"
```

```
scrollbar .tx.scrl \
  -command ".tx.text yview"

# Pack scrollbar first.
pack .tx.scrl -side right -fill y
pack .tx.text -side left
pack .tx
```

When the user moves the scrollbar thumb, the scrollbar executes its -command Tcl script. When the scrollbar executes its -command script, it appends the current position within the scrollbar to the Tcl script, along with the particular xview (if horizontal) or yview (vertical) command.

Typically, the -command script is tied to a listbox (see Chapter 6) or the text widget's yview command, which expects the hidden value parameters the scrollbar passes to it.

To get a closer look at this, we can intercept the -command script. For example, try the following commands, slightly different from the ones presented earlier:

```
# Text-editing area
frame .tx

text .tx.text \
   -yscrollcommand ".tx.scrl set"

scrollbar .tx.scrl \
  -command { watch_scroll }

 # Pack scrollbar first.
pack .tx.scrl -side right -fill y
pack .tx.text -side left
pack .tx
```

We then need a watch_scroll procedure, which can print out the current value of the scrollbar and then still call the text widget's yview command:

```
proc watch_scroll { args } {

    puts ".tx.text yview $args"
```

```
# Call text widget to actually scroll it.
eval .tx.text yview $args
```

}

Now, try moving the scrollbar about. You should see something like the following:

```
.tx.text yview moveto 0.451561
.tx.text yview moveto 0.458679
.tx.text yview moveto 0.465796
.tx.text yview moveto 0.476473
.tx.text yview moveto 0.490707
```

If you click in the scrollbar's trough, you'll see something like:

```
.tx.text yview scroll -1 pages
.tx.text yview scroll -1 pages
.tx.text yview scroll 1 pages
```

If you click in the arrow buttons at the top or the bottom, you'll see something like:

```
.tx.text yview scroll -1 units
.tx.text yview scroll -1 units
.tx.text yview scroll 1 units
```

All of these are commands passed to the text widget's yview option.

NOTE

For horizontal scrollbars, you'll want to tie the -command option to the text widget's xview command, rather than the yview command.

To make a horizontal scrollbar, use the -orient option. Note that text widgets provide much more support for a vertical scrollbar than for an horizontal one.

To get text to scroll horizontally, you must also set the -wrap option for the text widget to none. You can try the following code:

```
# Text-editing area
frame .tx

text .tx.text \
  -yscrollcommand { .tx.scrl set } \
  -xscrollcommand { .tx.scrl_h set } \
  -width 30 \
  -wrap none

scrollbar .tx.scrl \
  -command { watch_scroll }

scrollbar .tx.scrl_h \
  -orient horizontal \
  -command watch_h_scroll

 # Pack scrollbars first.
pack .tx.scrl -side right -fill y
pack .tx.scrl_h -side bottom \
  -fill x
pack .tx.text -side left
pack .tx

proc watch_h_scroll { args } {

   puts ".tx.text xview $args"

   eval ".tx.text xview $args"
}
```

When you pack a text widget and a scrollbar, you'll need to pack the scrollbar first. This is because the text widget normally wants all available space. So to avoid crowding, pack the scrollbar first so it gets its fair share of the space.

N O T E

You can look up the on-line documentation on the text widget for more on this very complicated widget.

Tcl String-Handling Commands

In addition to the text and entry widgets that display strings on the screen, Tcl provides a large number of string-handling commands, which come in handy when you start retrieving strings from widgets and need to parse the string in some way.

The next section covers the most important string-handling commands. You can use them when you need to extract a substring from a string or closely examine the data held in a string. (And much, much more.)

Extracting Substrings

To get the length of a string, use the string length command:

```
% set str1 "1234567890"
1234567890
% string length $str1
10
```

NOTE Remember to use the $ with variable names, so the string commands don't interpret the variable name as a string itself.

To get the character at a particular position, use the string index command, which uses the following format:

```
string index $stringvar char_position
```

The *char_position* starts counting at 0. For example:

```
% string index $str1 4
5
```

To extract a range of characters, use the string range command, which uses the following format:

```
string range $stringvar first last
```

For example:

```
% string range $str1 2 5
3456
```

To get the index of the start or end of a word, use the string wordstart and string wordend commands:

```
string wordend $stringvar index
string wordstart $stringvar index
```

To get the hang of this, you should try an example:

```
% set str1 "In Xanadu did Kublai Khan"
In Xanadu did Kublai Khan
% string wordend $str1 4
9
% string wordstart $str1 4
3
```

Comparing Strings

The string compare command compares two strings.

```
string compare $string1 $string2
```

It returns -1, 0, or 1. If both strings are the same, string compare returns 0. if *string1* is less than *string2*, using the comparison of the ASCII characters in the string, then string compare returns -1. Otherwise, string compare returns 1, indicating that *string2* is greater than *string1* in terms of ASCII sort order.

```
% set string1 "ABCDEF"
ABCDEF
% set string2 "abcdef"
abcdef
% string compare $string1 $string2
-1
```

```
% string compare $string2 $string1
1
```

Searching in Strings

The string match command returns 1 if the given pattern matches the string:

```
string match pattern $stringvar
```

The pattern can contain a * as a wildcard to match anything (or nothing), a ? to match any one character, patterns in square brackets, such as [a-z] or an escaped character with a backslash. Tcl introduces yet another pattern-matching scheme (in addition to the glob and regexp methods described in Chapter 2) to mimic the UNIX C- shell, **csh**.

The string first command searches a string for the first occurrence of the characters in another string and returns the index position within the string of the first match:

```
string first characters_to_match $string_to_check
```

For example:

```
% string first "not" "I am not a crook."
5
```

If there is no match, string first returns -1.

The string last command works the same, but it returns the last match:

```
string last characters_to_match $string_to_check
```

Changing Case

The string tolower command returns a string with all characters lowercase. It does not modify the original string.

```
% string tolower "aaaBBBaaa"
aaabbbaaa
```

Similarly, the `string toupper` command returns a string with all characters uppercase.

```
% string toupper "aaaBBBaaa"
AAABBBAAA
```

Trimming Strings

The `string trimleft` command trims a set of characters from the start of the string. By default, `string trimleft` trims all leading white space from the string, returning the new string. Again, the original string is not modified.

```
string trimleft $stringvar characters
```

With the optional characters, you can specify which characters to trim. For example, to trim all leading *es*:

```
% string trimleft "eeeeStart of string" "e"
Start of string
```

If you skip the *characters* argument, `string trimleft` trims all leading white space characters: spaces, tabs, returns, new lines, and so on.

The `string trimright` command works the same, but from the end of the string working in.

Finally, the `string trim` command works from both ends: front and back. If you need to perform even more complicated string manipulation, there's even more in the on-line manuals for the `string` command.

A Tcl-Based Text Editor

One of the most troublesome aspects of writing Tcl applications on the Windows platform is the lack of a good environment. On UNIX, you create Tcl scripts inside an **xterm** shell window and can use the selection to copy and paste into the **wish** command prompt.

On Windows, the Console window created by **wish** supports only limited editing capabilities. The fact of the matter is that Tcl on Windows does not yet work as well as it does on UNIX (although things are getting better with each release).

You may find the text widget's default bindings of **Ctrl-y** for pasting, **Ctrl-w** for cutting, and **Alt-w** for copying helpful, especially on Windows.

NOTE

To help alleviate this problem, you can use the Tcl text widget to create a Tcl-oriented editor. Furthermore, you can add in Tcl commands to evaluate either the selected text or the whole contents of the text widget. With this, development on Windows becomes a much more positive experience. (This example also pulls together all the lessons in this chapter into one Tcl script.)

The key to making this work lies in being able to execute the text typed in.

Executing Tcl Scripts within Tcl

Remember the mantra that everything in Tcl is text, even Tcl commands. Because of this, you can create new Tcl scripts from within a Tcl script and execute them. The key to this is the eval command.

The eval command concatenates all its arguments together and then passes these to the Tcl interpreter. For example:

```
eval { puts "In eval." }
```

In a Tcl editor, you could create a button widget that, when invoked, will call eval on the selected text in a given text widget. Another button widget may call eval on all of the text in the given text widget.

With eval, you can make Tcl scripts that modify themselves. This is not always a good idea and can easily lead to problems. Because of that, you'll want to perform extra testing on any script in which you use eval.

WARNING

Creating the Script

To create a Tcl-based editor, you can start with the menu bar. This simple editor won't read in any files (but you can jump ahead to Chapter 6 for that topic, if you'd like), so the **File** menu will only have an **Exit** choice.

The **Edit** menu will allow for **Cut**, **Copy**, and **Paste**, as covered earlier.

Beneath the menu bar, a frame will hold the text widget, along with a scrollbar. Beneath that, another frame will hold three buttons, one to execute the selected text, one to execute all the text and one to clear (delete) all the text, allowing you to start over, as shown in Figure 5.8. Note how many extra widgets are required to support the one basic text widget where all the action lies. You'll find you need to create a lot of supporting widgets in most graphical applications.

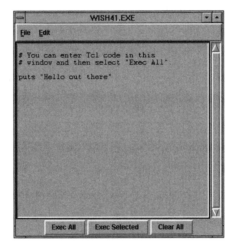

Figure 5.8 A Tcl editor/executor program.

For this program, we need the clip_cut, clip_copy, and clip_paste procedures created earlier in the section on cut, copy, and paste. We also need to create some new procedures.

To execute the selected text within a given widget, you can use the following procedure:

```
proc exec_sel { widgetname } {

  if { [selection own] != "" } {

    # Have selection.
    set sel [selection get]
```

```
    # Execute selection
    if { $sel != "" } {
      eval $sel
    }
  }
}
```

To execute all the text in a given widget, you can use the following:

```
proc exec_all { widgetname } {

    # Get all text
    set all \
        [$widgetname get 1.0 end]

    # Execute selection
    eval $all
}
```

To clear all the text in a given widget, you can simply delete from the start-ing location to the end, as shown here:

```
proc clear_all { widgetname } {

  $widgetname delete 1.0 end
}
```

The widgets used for this editor require a lot of options but not very compli-cated Tcl scripts, as you can see here:

```
# Menubar
frame .menubar \
  -relief raised -bd 2

 # File menu.
menubutton .menubar.file \
  -text "File" \
  -menu .menubar.file.menu \
  -underline 0
```

```
menu .menubar.file.menu

.menubar.file.menu add command \
  -label "Exit" \
  -underline 1 \
  -command { exit }

# Edit menu.
menubutton .menubar.edit \
  -text "Edit" \
  -menu .menubar.edit.menu \
  -underline 0

menu .menubar.edit.menu

.menubar.edit.menu add command \
  -label "Cut" \
  -command clip_cut \
  -accelerator "Ctrl+X" \
  -underline 2

.menubar.edit.menu add command \
  -label "Copy" \
  -command clip_copy \
  -accelerator "Ctrl+C" \
  -underline 0

.menubar.edit.menu add command \
  -label "Paste" \
  -command { clip_paste .tx.text } \
  -accelerator "Ctrl+P" \
  -underline 0

pack .menubar.file .menubar.edit \
  -side left

# Text-editing area
frame .tx

text .tx.text \
```

```
    -yscrollcommand {.tx.scrl set}

scrollbar .tx.scrl \
  -command ".tx.text yview"

# Pack scrollbar first.
pack .tx.scrl -side right -fill y
pack .tx.text -side left

# Toolbar at bottom.
frame .toolbar

button .toolbar.execall \
  -text "Exec All" \
  -command { exec_all .tx.text }

button .toolbar.execsel \
  -text "Exec Selected" \
  -command { exec_sel .tx.text }

button .toolbar.clear \
  -text "Clear All" \
  -command { clear_all .tx.text }

pack .toolbar.execall \
  .toolbar.execsel \
  .toolbar.clear \
  -side left

# Procedures
proc clip_paste { widgetname } {


  # Get the text from the clipboard.
  set clip [selection get \
      -selection CLIPBOARD ]

  # Check if any text is selected.
  set owner [selection own]

  if { $owner == $widgetname } {
```

```
        # Save the index where the selection starts.
        set idx [$owner index sel.first]

        # Delete the selected text.
        $owner delete sel.first sel.last

        # Paste in the clipboard data.
        $owner insert $idx $clip

    } else {

        # If no text is selected, insert at
        # insertion point within widget.
        $widgetname insert insert $clip
    }
}

proc clip_cut { } {

    # Check if any text is selected.
    set owner [selection own]

    if { $owner != "" } {
        # Clear the clipboard.
        clipboard clear

        # Append the selected text to the clipboard.
        clipboard append [selection get]

        # Delete the selected text.
        $owner delete sel.first sel.last
    }

}

proc clip_copy { } {

    # Check if any text is selected.
    if { [selection own] != "" } {

        # Clear the clipboard.
```

```
    clipboard clear

    # Append the selected text to the clipboard.
    clipboard append [selection get]
  }

}

# Accelerators.
bind all <Control-Key-x> {
    clip_cut
}

bind all <Control-Key-c> {
    clip_copy
}
bind all <Control-Key-v> {
    clip_paste .tx.text
}

  # Pack the highest-level widgets.
pack .menubar -side top \
  -fill x -expand true

pack .tx
pack .toolbar -side bottom
```

Try out the preceding script, especially if you work on the Windows platform. You should have a better editor to work in, and you should be able to paste data from other text-editing programs, such as **Notepad** or your favorite Windows text editor. Even Microsoft Word works with this.

If you get ambitious, you may want to extend this editor, and add things such as a file open and save dialog boxes. See Chapters 6 and 7 for more on this subject.

Summary

This chapter covered text widgets and commands related to working with text.

The `entry` widget provides a single-line text entry area. When you need a larger text area, you can use the multiline `text` widget.

In addition to text editing, the handy `text` widget allows you to tag areas of text and modify display attributes, (e.g., switch to an italic font). With tags, you can also bind events within the tag to execute Tcl code. This allows you to easily create a Hypertext system out of the `text` widget.

Continuing on this vein, you can embed widgets within the `text` widget to display graphic images, for example.

The `scrollbar` widget allows the user to scroll about the text displayed in a `text` widget.

The `string` command, with zillions of options, allows you to manipulate and extract from strings.

The `eval` command evaluates its arguments as a Tcl script, executing the script.

Finally, if you're getting tired of the poor text-input capabilities that Tcl provides on Windows with its Console window, you now have enough Tcl and Tk commands to create a viable Tcl editor and execute the code you type in. You can also copy and paste from other applications, such as your favorite editor.

Continuing on the scrolling theme, Chapter 6 covers scrolled `listbox` widgets and Tcl list-handling commands. It also discusses Tcl `file` and directory commands, including how to read a file into a text widget.

Tcl/Tk Commands Covered in this Chapter

```
clipboard
entry
eval
scrollbar
selection
string
text
```

## CHAPTER 6

Lists, Files, and Directories

This chapter covers:

- Tcl list variables and commands
- Special lists that hold command-line arguments
- The listbox widget
- Creating multicolumn listboxes
- Accessing files
- Scanning directories
- Building a file and directory browser

Lists

After the complications of the text widget, you'll find the listbox widget and list variables in general an easy undertaking. This chapter covers Tcl lists, then delves into a listbox widget for displaying lists. After that, this chapter shows how to access files and directories on both Windows and UNIX.

A **list** in Tcl is just a collection of elements, such as 1 2 3 4 5 six. All the elements are text, as is everything in Tcl.

A list variable is just a plain Tcl variable. The only fact that makes it a list is the fact that you store a number of elements in it. You can use the list commands described in this chapter on any regular Tcl variable. Unlike arrays, which use a special syntax, lists are normal Tcl variables and use normal Tcl syntax.

Building Lists

The list command builds a list out of all its arguments, returning this new list. It may modify the arguments if you have items such as backslashes in the list:

```
% set 11 [list arg1 arg2 arg3]
arg1 arg2 arg3
% puts $11
arg1 arg2 arg3
set 12 [list {arg1} {{arg2} {arg3}} ]
arg1 {{arg2} {arg3}}
% puts $12
arg1 {{arg2} {arg3}}
```

You can also use the concat command to build a list:

```
set 11 [concat arg1 arg2 arg3]
```

The concat command simply concatenates its arguments together, placing a space character between each item. The list command, on the other hand, will build up a proper list. That is, if one of the arguments to list is a multi-item element, the list command will ensure that it becomes a single element in the new list (a list may hold lists).

For example, compare the following:

```
% list {1 2 3} 4 "five six"
{1 2 3} 4 {five six}
% concat {1 2 3} 4 "five six"
1 2 3 4 five six
```

Notice the differing output.

Inserting Elements into a List

Use the linsert command to insert items into a list:

```
linsert listvar index element
```

You can pass more than one *element* to insert. These elements are inserted at a given *index* position. You can use the special position named end for appending to a list. Note that linsert does not modify the original list.

Try the following examples:

```
% set l1 { dog cat }
 dog cat
% set l2 [linsert $l1 end platypus]
 dog cat platypus
% puts $l2
 dog cat platypus
```

You can also add data to the list itself:

```
% set l2 [linsert $l2 1 wolverine]
 dog wolverine cat platypus
% puts $l2
 dog wolverine cat platypus
```

To get the number of items in a list, use the llength command:

```
llength listvar
```

Appending Elements to a List

The lappend command appends a number of items (as many as you want) onto the end of a list, using the following syntax:

```
lappesnd listvar item1 item2 item3 ...
```

The is much like the append command (with no *l*), but items are assumed to be added to a list.

You can replace elements in a list with the lreplace command:

```
lreplace listvar first_index last_index newdata1 newdata2 ...
```

The lreplace command replaces all the items in the list from the *first_index* to the *last_index*, using all remaining parameters as the data items to fill in the list.

If no new data is provided, then the list elements in the range are merely deleted.

Pulling Out Elements from a List

To pull out a given element from a list, use the *lindex* command:

```
lindex listvar index
```

Pass 0 for the first element of a list, end for the last. Try the following commands:

```
% set ll { 1 2 3 4 5 6 7 8 nine }
 1 2 3 4 5 6 7 8 nine
% lindex $ll end
nine
% lindex $ll 0
1
% lindex $ll 5
6
```

To pull out a sublist, use the lrange command:

```
lrange listvar first_index last_index
```

You must provide both the *first_index* and the *last_index*. For example:

```
% set ll { 1 2 3 4 5 6 7 8 nine }
 1 2 3 4 5 6 7 8 nine
% lrange $ll 2 5
3 4 5 6
% lrange $ll 6 end
7 8 nine
```

Breaking Up Lists

You can break up lists with the `split` command and build them back together with the `join` command.

The `split` command looks for a set of special split characters given in its arguments and splits the value into multiple list elements. The syntax is:

```
split string split_chars
```

For example, if you have an XBase database and a set of comma-delimited data, you can use `split` to separate the elements, as shown here:

```
% set data "Eric Johnson, St. Paul, cat owner"
Eric Johnson, St. Paul, cat owner
% split $data ,
{Eric Johnson} { St. Paul} { cat owner}
```

In this example, the split character is a comma. Note that the list elements get the leading space that appeared after the comma. (To strip this out, you can use the `string trimleft` command introduced in Chapter 5.)

You can undo the effect of `split` with `join`, which takes the following syntax:

```
join listvar separator
```

What the `join` command does is connect together all the list elements in the list and place the separator character between each item. Note that since `join` takes the *listvar* as one argument, if you have separate data items, you must enclose them in curly braces or double quotation marks.

To undo the `split` example, you can use the following command:

```
% join {{Eric Johnson} { St. Paul} { cat owner}} ,
Eric Johnson, St. Paul, cat owner
```

Note the extra curly braces to make the data into one argument to the `join` command.

Searching Through Lists

The lsearch command searches through a list and takes the following syntax:

```
lsearch mode listvar pattern
```

The *mode* controls the type of search, familiar from the string searches described in Chapter 2. It can be one of -exact, -glob, or -regexp. See the section on regex expressions in Chapter 2 for more on the modes. You can omit the *mode*, which defaults to -glob.

Sorting Lists

The lsort command returns a sorted list, generated from its input list. You can modify the method used to sort, as listed in Table 6.1.

Table 6.1 Sort Methods

Method	Meaning
ascii	Use ASCII string comparisons to sort.
integer	Convert values to integers and sort in numerical order.
real	Convert values to floating-point numbers and sort in numerical order.
command *tcl_script*	Use the *tcl_script* to compare items.
increasing	Sort in increasing order, with the smallest items first.
decreasing	Sort in decreasing order, with the largest items first.

The default options are -ascii and -increasing.

With the -command option, your *tcl_script* should accept the two values to compare and should return a value based on the comparison. A return value of 0 means the items are considered equal. A return value less than 0 means that the first element is less than the second. A return value of greater than 0 means that the first element is greater than the second.

If you want to perform a fancy sort, see the on-line manual information on lsort.

Special Lists for Accessing the Command Line

Tcl provides some special variables that contain the arguments passed on the DOS or UNIX command line. Familiar to most C programmers, these arguments mimic the argc, argv, and environment parameters passed to the C main function but with a twist.

Table 6.2 lists these special variables for accessing command-line and environment data.

Table 6.2 Command-Line Variables

Variable	Type	Holds
argc	integer	Number of command-line arguments in argv.
argv	list	Command-line arguments, but not command itself.
argv0	string	Name of file passed to wish or tclsh.
env	array	Holds UNIX or Windows environment variables.

See Chapter 2 in the section on special arrays for environment variables for more on the env variable.

If you invoke a Tcl script with the following arguments, 1 2 3 4 5 6 seven, the special arg variables will hold the values shown in Table 6.3. The following command shows an example of the syntax:

```
wish pr_argv.tcl 1 2 3 4 5 6 seven
```

Table 6.3 Contents of `arg` Variables for `args 1 2 3 4 5 6 seven`

Variable	Holds
argc	7
argv	1 2 3 4 5 6 seven
argv0	pr_argv.tcl

The `argc` value holds the number of command-line arguments, in this case, *seven*. `argv` holds the arguments passed to the Tcl script, `1 2 3 4 5 6 seven`.

Unlike the UNIX and DOS tradition, `argv` does not hold the full command line (which would include **wish** and **pr_argv.tcl**). Instead, it just holds all the *arguments* to the Tcl script you're executing.

The **pr_argv.tcl** script mentioned in the preceding example merely prints out all the command-line arguments. The script follows:

```
puts "Number of arguments is: $argc"
puts "Full command line is: $argv"

for {set i 0} {$i < $argc} {incr i} {

    set curr_arg [lindex $argv $i]

    puts "Arg $i is: $curr_arg"
}
exit
```

When you run this script with some command-line arguments, you'll see the following output:

```
% wish pr_argv.tcl 1 2 3 4 5 6 seven

Number of arguments is: 7
Full command line is: 1 2 3 4 5 6 seven
Arg 0 is: 1
Arg 1 is: 2
```

```
Arg 2 is: 3
Arg 3 is: 4
Arg 4 is: 5
Arg 5 is: 6
Arg 6 is: seven
```

WINDOWS

On Windows, you typically don't run commands from a command-line (DOS) shell, especially for Windows programs such as **wish**. You can, however, add Tk scripts to the Program Manager. You just need to use wish and the script to run as the command name, and set up the working directory properly. Figure 6.1 shows a property dialog box from the Windows Program Manager for running a Tcl script named **dirview.tk**.

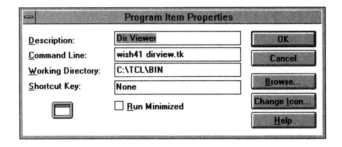

Figure 6.1 Setting up a Program Manager item for a Tcl script.

N O T E

Note also that Windows does not have a console window, so any text output to the screen with puts will likely generate an error. You need a fully graphical application.

Well, after all this work on lists, it's time to use them in a widget.

Listbox Widgets

The listbox widget provides a list of items from which the user can select. You can configure the list for multiple or single selection.

Create a listbox with the listbox command, such as the following one:

```
listbox .list -height 10
pack .list
```

The -selectmode option controls how items may be selected in the list. Table 6.4. shows the possibilities.

Table 6.4 Listbox Selection Modes

Mode	Meaning
single	Only one item may be selected at a time.
browse	Only one item may be selected, but you can select by dragging.
multiple	Multiple items may be selected.
extended	Multiple items may be selected.

With a -selectmode of multiple, clicking mouse button 1 over an item toggles whether it is selected. Many items may be selected at once.

With a -selectmode of extended, clicking mouse button 1 with the **Shift** key down extends the existing selected items by including all items in between the mouse position and the previously selected item. Clicking mouse button 1 with the **Control** key down toggles whether the item under the mouse is selected or not. **Shift-Up Arrow** and **Shift-Down Arrow** also extend the current selection.

The -height option controls the desired height of the widget, in lines. The -width option similarly controls the width, in units of an average character width.

Like the text widget, you want to set the -exportselection option to true, which allows the selected list item to be copied and pasted elsewhere.

N O T E There is no -command option for a listbox widget. You therefore need to connect a list to either a binding, like a double-click or a button widget and then use the selection get option to extract the selected items.

To add new items to a listbox, use insert:

```
widgetname insert index element
```

You need to do this to fill in the original values in the listbox. In most cases, you want to append items, or insert them at the end. You can use a special index value of end for this purpose:

```
widgetname insert end element
```

For example:

```
listbox .list -height 10
.list insert end "Minnesota"
.list insert end "Alabama"
.list insert end "Oregon"
.list insert end "New York"
.list insert end "Maryland"
.list insert end "Georgia"
pack .list
```

See the following section on list indices for more options when creating the index.

Connecting a Listbox to a Scrollbar

Virtually all listboxes have an associated scrollbar widget. You connect a listbox to a scrollbar much the same as for the text widget, shown in Chapter 5. An example follows:

```
listbox .list \
    -height 10 \
    -yscrollcommand ".scrb set"

.list insert end "Minnesota"
.list insert end "Alabama"
.list insert end "Oregon"
.list insert end "New York"
.list insert end "Maryland"
```

```
.list insert end "Georgia"
.list insert end "Ohio"
.list insert end "Alaska"
.list insert end "Washington"
.list insert end "Virginia"
.list insert end "North Dakota"
.list insert end "Iowa"
.list insert end "Texas"

scrollbar .scrb \
  -command ".list yview"
pack .scrb -side right -fill y
pack .list -side left
```

You can see this scrolled listbox in Figure 6.2.

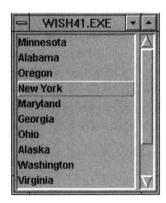

Figure 6.2 A scrolled listbox.

Listbox Indices

Like the text widget, the listbox widget allows you to specify an item by its index within the listbox. You can use the item number, with 0 for the first item, or you can use a more symbolic place, called an *anchor*.

Table 6.5 lists the possible anchor values.

Table 6.5 List Item Indices

Index	Meaning
number	Item number, starting with 0.
end	Last item in list
@*x,y*	Item under local *x, y* position.
active	Item with location cursor.
anchorname	Item at given anchor.

List Anchors

You can convert other forms of indices into the standard numeric format with the index option:

```
widgetname index index_to_convert
```

This command returns a new index generated from the *index_to_convert*. The new index is in numeric format.

Armed with these indices and anchors, you can identify an individual item in a list or a range of items.

Accessing Listbox Items

To get the number of items in a listbox, use size:

```
widgetname size
```

This returns the number of items in the list.

To delete items in a list, use delete:

```
widgetname delete first last
```

This command deletes all items from the *first* index to the *last*. You may omit the *last* index, in which case, only one item gets deleted.

To retrieve a listbox item, use get:

```
widgetname get first last
```

If you ask for only one item (and skip the *last* index), you will get the item (the string displayed). If you ask for a range of items, you'll get a Tcl list of the items in the range.

The activate option activates an item in the list, identified by its index:

```
widgetname activate index
```

Finding Out which Items Are Selected

You can find out which listbox items are selected by using the curselection option, which has the following syntax:

```
widgetname curselection
```

This command returns a list of all the indices of the selected items, not the selected items themselves. For example, if the item at list index 5 is selected, the curselection option will return 5, not the text of the item.

NOTE

If you have a -selectmode of single, then curselection can only return one item, the index of the selected item. To then retrieve the selected item, you can use the following procedure:

```
proc list_selected { widgetname } {

    set i [$widgetname curselection]

    set item [$widgetname get $i]

    return "$item"
}
```

Use selection clear to clear the selection in the list:

```
widgetname selection clear first last
```

This clears all selections between the first and the last indices. The last index is optional.

To see if an item is selected, use `selection includes`:

```
widgetname selection includes index
```

This command returns 1 if the selection includes the given index.

To select items in the list, use `selection set`:

```
widgetname selection set first last
```

Again, the *last* index is optional.

Making an Item Visible

To make a list item visible, you can use the `see` option:

```
widgetname see index
```

This option takes the index of the item you want to make visible.

Listbox Examples

The following Tcl script creates a `listbox` and allows you to select items from it. The `listbox` holds a form of command history, from which you can select a previous command. Double-clicking on a list element re-executes that command. If you single-click on a list element, the element appears selected. You can use the middle mouse button (on a three-button mouse) to paste the selected item in the `entry` widget. This allows you to edit a previous command. Pressing the **Return** key in the `entry` widget also executes the command and appends it to the `listbox`. The Tcl code follows:

```
# History list.
frame .hist

listbox .hist.list \
   -height 10 \
```

```
    -width 30 \
    -selectmode single \
    -yscrollcommand ".hist.scrb set"

scrollbar .hist.scrb \
  -command ".hist.list yview"
pack .hist.list .hist.scrb \
    -side left -fill x -fill y

 # Command-entry.
frame .cmd
entry .cmd.entry -width 30 \
   -textvariable entry_var

label .cmd.label -text "Command: "
pack .cmd.label .cmd.entry \
  -side top -anchor w

pack .hist -side top -fill x
pack .cmd -side bottom -fill x

 # Execute a command
 proc exec_cmd { cmd } {

  # Execute command.
puts "Eval on ([subst $cmd])"

   eval [subst $cmd]

  # Add it to list
  .hist.list insert end "$cmd"

  # Clear entry.
  .cmd.entry delete 0 end
}

 # Return selected list item.
proc list_selected { widgetname } {

   # Default return value.
   set item ""
```

```
    set i [$widgetname curselection]

    if { $i != "" } {
        set item [$widgetname get $i]
    }
  return "$item"
}


bind .hist.list <Double-Button-1> {

  # Get selected item.
  set cmd [list_selected .hist.list]

  # Execute command.
  exec_cmd $cmd
}


bind .cmd.entry <Key-Return> {

    exec_cmd $entry_var
}
```

You can see this command-history script in Figure 6.3.

Figure 6.3 Using a listbox for a command history.

NOTE

Since the exec_cmd procedure executes commands from within the context of a procedure, most variables won't be accessible, because the global statement was not executed first.

A Multicolumn List

A common problem with listboxes is creating two or more separate lists and having them all work off a single scrollbar. For example, lists of files, sizes, and modification dates often use three columns in a list. In Tk, the way to do this is to use separate listboxes and then tie them together to the same scrollbar.

To set up multiple listboxes like this, you create the listboxes the same way as always but set each listbox's -yscrollcommand option to the same command on the same scrollbar, as shown here:

```
listbox .frame.list1 \
  -borderwidth 1 \
  -relief raised \
  -selectmode single \
  -yscrollcommand ".frame.scroll set"

listbox .frame.list2 \
  -borderwidth 1 \
  -relief raised \
  -selectmode single \
  -yscrollcommand ".frame.scroll set"
```

The key to making this work is in the scrollbar's -command. Normally, each scrollbar is tied to a single listbox (or text) widget. What you need to do is tie this scrollbar to a number of listboxes. The tricky part, as shown in the watch_scroll procedure in the last chapter, is that the scrollbar appends data onto the Tcl command it executes. And, we don't know exactly what data this is until the scrollbar moves. (The amount of this data has also changed between versions of Tk.)

To take care of this problem, create a procedure called multi_scroll, as shown in the following example:

```
# The scroll_list holds a list of
# the widgets to scroll. The args
# hold all the remaining arguments, which
# come from the scrollbar. All these
# are passed to each widget in the
# scroll_list.
#
proc multi_scroll { scroll_list args } {

  # Get info on list of args.
  set len [llength $scroll_list]

  for {set i 0} {$i < $len} {incr i} {
      set temp_list [lindex $scroll_list $i]

      # Uncomment next line for debugging.
      puts "Command: $temp_list yview $args"

      eval $temp_list yview $args
  }

}
```

The key to this procedure is that the *scroll_list* argument must be a list, the list of all the widget names we want to scroll at once. The list requirement comes from the special args argument. This special argument holds a variable-length list of all the remaining arguments. The problem is that it holds all the remaining arguments. Our problem is that we don't know how many lists will be tied together. That's one variable-length list of values (the names of the listbox widgets to scroll together). Also, the scrollbar appends an unknown amount of data to the arguments, which makes another variable-length list. The procedure in the preceding example uses the special args argument for this second list.

For the first variable-length list of listbox widgets to scroll, the multi_scroll procedure requires that it be called with a list. So, you need to use the following method when creating the scrollbar:

```
scrollbar .frame.scroll \
    -command \
```

```
{ multi_scroll {.frame.list1 .frame.list2} }
```

Note that the two listbox widget names appear within curly braces, to make the two items into one list (and one argument to multi_scroll).

The full source for this example follows:

```
# Tcl script that creates multiple listboxes
# with one scrollbar.
#

#
# This proc scrolls a number of listboxes
# all together from one scrollbar.
#
# The scroll_list holds a list of
# the widgets to scroll. The args
# hold all the remaining arguments, which
# come from the scrollbar. All these
# are passed to each widget in the
# scroll_list.
#
proc multi_scroll { scroll_list args } {

  # Get info on list of args.
  set len [llength $scroll_list]

  for {set i 0} {$i < $len} {incr i} {
      set temp_list [lindex $scroll_list $i]

      # Uncomment next line for debugging.
      puts "Command: $temp_list yview $args"

      eval $temp_list yview $args
  }

}

#
# Fill in list with various data.
```

```
#
proc FillList { listvar } {

  for {set i 0} {$i < 40} {incr i} {

    set str [format "Item %d" $i]

    # Curly braces make str into one item.
    eval $listvar insert end {$str}
  }
}

# Use a frame around all lists.
frame .frame -relief groove -borderwidth 3

listbox .frame.list1 \
  -borderwidth 1 \
  -relief raised \
  -selectmode single \
  -yscrollcommand ".frame.scroll set"

listbox .frame.list2 \
  -borderwidth 1 \
  -relief raised \
  -selectmode single \
  -yscrollcommand ".frame.scroll set"

listbox .frame.list3 \
  -borderwidth 1 \
  -relief raised \
  -selectmode single \
  -yscrollcommand ".frame.scroll set"

 # Fill lists with data.
FillList .frame.list1
FillList .frame.list2
FillList .frame.list3

pack .frame.list1 .frame.list2 \
    .frame.list3 -side left
```

```
scrollbar .frame.scroll \
    -command \
    { multi_scroll {.frame.list1 .frame.list2.frame.list3} }
```

```
pack .frame.scroll -side right -fill y
```

```
pack .frame
```

This program creates three listbox widgets, as shown in Figure 6.4. All the lists should scroll together.

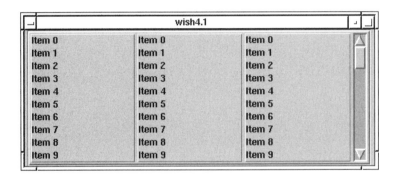

Figure 6.4 Multiple listboxes with one scrollbar.

Accessing Files

Most applications read, modify, and write files. Tcl provides a number of commands to help perform these mundane tasks.

To read a file, you need to open it and then read data from the file. When done, you need to close the file. Writing to a file works the same way, but you write data instead of reading, obviously. If the file doesn't exist, the open command, with the right parameters, will create it.

For both operations, you first need to open the file with the open command:

```
open filename access permissions
```

The *filename* must be a valid filename on your system, otherwise an error will result. See Chapter 8 for more on errors and handling them.

PORTABILITY

In addition, Tcl has a bit of a problem with the Windows idea of file names. Windows uses a backslash, \, to separate directories. UNIX uses a forward slash, /. In fact, Tcl treats the backslash as a line continuation marker, so you normally need to *escape* the backslash by using two. For example, specify the directory \USERS\ERC instead as \\USERS\\ERC. The \\ construction tells the Tcl interpreter to ignore other meanings for the backslash and insert one real backslash (not a line continuation marker) into the text.

You can also use UNIX-style file names on Windows. For example, the following commands both change to the same directory:

```
cd /tcl/bin
cd \\tcl\\bin
```

File names entered on a Windows system are likely to contain back-slashes.

WINDOWS

The DOS file system, called FAT for File Allocation Table, only allows file names in the form of a maximum of eight characters, a single period, and a maximum three-character file extension. Any files stored under Windows 3.1 must follow these conventions. The same goes for Windows NT using a FAT file system (the NT file system, NTFS, allows longer file names). Windows 95 also allows longer file names.

The *access* argument to open must have an *r* (for read), *w* (for write), or *a* (append). Table 6.6 shows further modifications of this.

Table 6.6 File Access Codes for the Open Command

Code	Meaning
r	Open file for reading only. File must exist.
r+	Open file for reading and writing. File must exist.
w	Open file for writing, destroying any existing data.

continued

Table 6.6 continued

Code	Meaning
w+	Open file for reading and writing; destroying any existing data.
a	Open file for writing. File must exist. New data is appended to the end.
a+	Open file for reading and writing. New data is appended to the end. The file does not have to exist.

WARNING

If you're used to programming in the C language, the access codes given in Table 6.6 are slightly different from what you're used to.

If you don't like the values in Table 6.6, above, you can use an alternate set of access codes. In this format, you must include one of the following flags: RDONLY (read only), WRONLY (write only), or RDWR (read and write). You can also add in other flags, providing a list of options. The other available flags are listed in Table 6.7.

Table 6.7 Flags for Access Codes

Flag	Meaning
APPEND	Start at end of file.
CREAT	Create file if it doesn't exist.
EXCL	With CREAT, returns an error if the file exists.
NOCTTY	Prevents file from becoming controlling terminal (for terminal devices).
NONBLOCK	Prevents process from blocking while opening file.
TRUNC	If file exists, truncate all data in it.

N O T E

If you open a file for both reading and writing, you must use the seek command for positioning in the file. See the following section for more information.

The *permissions* argument applies only to new files you create. The default permissions are 0666 (you knew Tcl was possessed, didn't you?), which means read, write and execute permissions for all users. The leading zero indicates this is an octal (base 8) number.

UNIX

The permissions follows the UNIX model for file permissions. See Appendix A for books on UNIX if this concerns you.

The open command returns a file ID, for use with read or puts commands. The main way to work with a file ID is to set it into a variable and then use this variable for all subsequent file operations.

PORTABILITY

The actual contents of a file ID shouldn't matter (and may well differ on Windows, UNIX, and Macintosh systems).

Built-In File IDs

Three file IDs always exist for all Tcl programs: stdin, for input from the terminal or Console window, stdout, for output to the Console window, and stderr, also for output to the Console window, but intended for error messages. These file IDs come from UNIX and C language conventions.

WINDOWS

You should avoid using Console input and output on Windows. Windows users expect to see graphical programs. UNIX users tend to be more lenient, but the whole point of writing graphical applications is to get beyond the limitations of the text-only programs of the past.

The Console window has proven essential for debugging Tcl applications, but you shouldn't burden the end user with the Console window. In addition, if you run a Tcl script from the Program Manager, the script will not likely have the Console window that **wish** creates when run without a script to execute. In this case, output to stdout (or just a puts command without a file ID), will generate an error.

To read in data from a file, first open the file and then use the read command, which takes many forms:

```
read $fileid
read -nonewline $fileid
read $fileid number_bytes
```

If you don't specify the number of bytes, read will pull in the entire file. The -nonewline option tells read to skip any final newline character at the end of the file, commonly put there by the text widget.

To write data to a file, use the familiar puts command with an expanded syntax:

```
puts -nonewline $fileid string
```

The -nonewline argument is optional. Up to now, we've skipped the *fileid* argument with puts. When you do this, puts writes its data to the terminal or Console window.

With puts, you need to know that Tcl uses buffered file output routines. For speed, any operating systems delay writing data to a file until enough has been buffered in main memory. This is because writing to disk is typically a very slow operation when compared to writing to memory. Once enough data is collected, the buffering routines automatically write the data to disk.

In most cases, this works well. But, it has the unfortunate side effect that after you call puts, your data may not yet be stored in the file. If this matters (in most cases it does not), you can use the flush command:

```
flush $fileid
```

The flush command will force all the buffers to write out to disk. This may take some time, and the flush command will not return until it finishes, which may introduce delays in your Tcl scripts.

When you're done with a file, close it with the close command:

```
close $fileid
```

The close command also flushes all buffers, so you normally don't need to call flush.

To read in all the data in a presumably small file and store it in the variable named *data*, use the following procedure:

```
proc read_file { filename } {

  # Default value.
  set data ""

  if { [file readable $filename] } {

    set fileid [open $filename "r"]

    set data [read $fileid]

    close $fileid
  }

  return $data
}
```

The problem with this procedure is that it reads the whole file at once. This may cause problems with a multimegabyte file.

To get around this, you may read in files in increments. For example, a common block size is 2 KB, or 2048 bytes. You can then create a while loop to read in the file in blocks of this size. Of course, few files are arranged to have an exact multiple of 2048 (or any other amount of) bytes. So, with each call to read, you need to test whether you're at the end of the file. The eof command, short for end of file, does this:

```
eof $fileid
```

The eof command returns 1 at the end of the file and 0 otherwise. To read all the bytes in a large file, a block at a time, you can use the following code snippet as a guide:

```
if { [file readable $filename] } {

  set fileid [open $filename "r"]
```

```
# Are we at the end of the file.
while { [eof $fileid] != 1 } {

    # Read one block.
    set data [read $fileid 2048]


    # Process data.

    # ...insert your code here...
}

close $fileid
}
```

NOTE If there are fewer bytes left in the file than you ask for, the read command will return only those bytes that are in the file. Thus, in the preceding example, at least one call to read will return less than 2048 bytes, unless the file is an exact multiple of 2048 bytes in size.

Reading a File Line By Line

A more common approach toward reading data from files is to read text files a line at a time. This is very common if you want to process each line, such as send it to the Tcl interpreter with the eval command. To read files this way, you can use the gets command:

```
gets $fileid varname
gets $fileid
```

There are two forms of gets, seemingly just to confuse you. The first form, and the one I recommend, stores the line read into the given variable. In this form, gets returns the number of bytes read in, or a -1 if the end of the file was reached.

In the second form, gets returns the characters read in, and an empty string if the end of the file was reached.

In both forms, gets removes the newline character that terminates the line.

So, to read in an entire file line by line, you can use the following code:

```
if { [file readable $filename] } {

  set fileid [open $filename "r"]

  # Are we at the end of the file.
  while { [gets $fileid data] >= 0 } {

    # Process data.

    # ...insert your code here...
    puts $data
  }

  close $fileid
}
```

Seeking Data in Files

In most cases, read and puts work sequentially through a file, but sometimes you need to access a particular location in a file. For this, you can use the seek command:

```
seek $fileid offset starting_location
```

What seek does is move the file pointer, the indicator that stores where you are in a file. The read and puts commands both work from the current position of the file pointer. When completed, read and puts both update the file pointer (to the end of the data read in or written, respectively). The seek command moves the file pointer to an arbitrary location, so that the next read or puts command uses this new position.

With seek, the *offset* argument is the number of bytes to move the file pointer. The optional *starting_location* can be one of start (for the beginning of the file), current (for the current position of the file pointer) or end (for the end of the file). The *starting_location* defaults to start.

If you want to `seek` to a position 4096 bytes into a file, use the following command:

```
seek $fileid 4096 start
```

This moves the file pointer 4096 bytes from the beginning of the file.

If you want to position the file pointer 4096 bytes from the end of the file (assuming the file is longer than 4096 bytes), use the following command:

```
seek $fileid -4096 end
```

Note the use of a negative number, since we want to move backwards relative to the end of the file. (Trying to go forward beyond the end of the file is not recommended and usually results in an error. Trying to go backward beyond the beginning of a file also results in an error.)

To seek into the file 10 bytes forward from the current position of the file pointer, use the following code:

```
seek $fileid 10 current
```

You'll usually use the seek command with the `file size` command (see Table 6.8, below), so that you know the size of the file.

If you aren't sure where the file pointer is located, use the `tell` command, which tells the current position:

```
set varname [tell $fileid]
```

Reading a File into a Text Widget

To read a text file and store its data into a `text` widget, you can use the following code, based on the `read_file` proc given previously:

```
proc read_file { filename } {

    # Default value.
    set data ""

    if { [file readable $filename] } {
```

```
   set fileid [open $filename "r"]

   set data [read $fileid]

   close $fileid
  }

  return $data
}

proc read_into_text { textwidget filename } {

   # Read in file.
   set data [read_file $filename]

   # Check if we have any.
   if {$data != "" } {

      # Delete all existing text in widget.
      $textwidget delete 1.0 end

      # Insert new text.
      $textwidget insert end $data
   }
}
```

If you think the file will be large, you may want to read in the file in blocks, as shown earlier (2048 bytes makes a good block size). In that case, use the text widget's insert end command with each block read.

Saving the Contents of a Text Widget to Disk

To store out all the text from a text widget to a disk file, you can use the following example code:

```
proc write_file { filename data } {

   set fileid [open $filename "w"]

   puts $fileid $data
```

```
    close $fileid

}
```

```
proc save_text { textwidget filename } {

    set data [$textwidget get 1.0 end]

    write_file $filename $data
}
```

Of course, you may want to check for errors. See Chapter 8 for more on this topic.

N O T E If the first letter of the filename passed to open is a | character (often called a *pipe* character), then open assumes the file name is a command to execute and to connect via a pipe. See Chapter 10 for more on pipes and launching programs from within Tcl scripts. For now, don't use the | character in file names.

WINDOWS Tcl's file commands are built around the idea that a forward slash, /, separates the directories in a full path name. Windows uses a backslash, \, and the Macintosh a colon, :, to separate directories. Tcl is not yet able to work as well with the file names on Windows as it does on UNIX. Luckily, you can use the forward slash in Tcl scripts on Windows in most cases.

Table 6.8 lists the file commands in Tcl.

Table 6.8 File Commands

Command	Usage
file atime *filename*	Returns time file was last accessed, as integer
file dirname *filename*	Returns all characters in file name, up to the last slash, or a period, if there are no slashes
file executable *filename*	Returns 1 if the file is marked as an executable
file exists *filename*	Returns 1 if the file name exists, 0 otherwise

file extension *filename*	Returns the file extension, e.g., ".txt"
file isdirectory *filename*	Returns 1 if the file name is a directory
file isfile *filename*	Returns 1 if the file name is not a directory
file lstat *filename*	Same as file stat, but follows symbolic links
file mtime *filename*	Returns time file was last modified, as integer
file owned *filename*	Returns 1 if the file name is owned by the current user
file readable *filename*	Returns 1 if the file name is readable, 0 otherwise
file readlink *filename*	Returns the file a given symbolic link points to
file rootname *filename*	Returns the base part of the file name, up to the first period (.)
file size *filename*	Returns the size of the file, in bytes
file stat *filename varname*	Invokes the stat() system call
file tail *filename*	Returns all the characters in file name after the last forward slash
file type *filename*	Returns `blockSpecial`, `characterSpecial`, `directory`, `file`, `fifo`, `link` or `socket`
file writable *filename*	Returns 1 if the filename is writable, 0 otherwise

Many of these file commands have to do with file permissions. Windows 3.1 doesn't support much of this, but Windows NT and UNIX do.

With the `file stat` command, the variable *varname* filled with data is an array. The following array elements are filled in: `atime`, `ctime`, `dev`, `gid`, `ino`, `mode`, `mtime`, `nlink`, `size`, `type`, and `uid`. (See the on-line manual information on the `file` command for more.)

In addition to file operations, Tcl provides a number of disk directory-scanning commands.

Scanning Directories

To list the files in a directory, Tcl uses the `glob` command, not the familiar **ls** or **DIR** commands, as shown in Table 6.9.

Table 6.9 File-Listing Commands

System	Command
UNIX	ls
DOS	DIR
Tcl	glob

With Tcl, you can always use the exec command to run the UNIX **ls** program (provided your script is running on UNIX). But, in most cases, glob will work fine. The glob command takes the following syntax:

```
glob -nocomplain pattern
```

The *pattern* is any valid glob-style search pattern, as discussed in Chapter 2 in the section on the switch command. The -nocomplain option tells glob not to generate an error if the return list is empty, that is, if no files were found. You'll almost always want to use this option.

To list all the files in a directory, you can use the following code:

```
set files [glob -nocomplain *]

if { $files != "" } {

    foreach filename $files {
        puts $filename
    }

}
```

You can sort the list returned by glob using the lsort command:

```
set files [glob -nocomplain *]

if { $files != "" } {

    set sorted [lsort $files]
```

```
foreach filename $sorted {
    puts $filename
}
```

}

This results in easier to read output.

You can also use glob to return only some files, based on the search pattern. For example, you can use a pattern of *.txt to return all file names ending in .txt, such as **chap03.txt** and **report.txt**.

Changing Directories

In addition to listing directories, you may need to change to a different working directory and then scan the files located there.

The pwd command returns the current working directory:

```
% pwd
/home/erc/tcl
```

On Windows, this looks more like:

```
tcl> pwd
C:\ERC\TCL
```

WINDOWS

The cd command allows you to change the current working directory:

```
% cd /home/erc
% pwd
/home/erc
```

You can go up one level in the directory hierarchy by using the shorthand name .. for the parent directory:

```
cd ..
```

This works on Windows and UNIX.

The cd command accepts the standard UNIX usage for directory names. A tilde character specifies the user's home directory, as in:

```
% cd ~
% pwd
/home/erc
```

On this system, home directories are located in /home. This location may vary on different UNIX systems.

If you use a tilde with a user's name, such as ~kevin, cd takes you to that user's home directory:

```
% cd ~kevin
% pwd
/home/kevin
```

Windows 3.1 doesn't support user names while Windows NT does, so don't depend on these commands working on Windows.

A Tcl Directory Browser

We can build on the commands introduced in this chapter to build a Tcl directory browser. If you've ever tried this in another programming language, such as C, you'll appreciate how easy Tcl makes this.

For this browser, we'll have a list of subdirectories in the current directory, and a list of files. The file list will really show two listbox widgets connected to the same scrollbar. The first listbox will show the file name, the second its size.

The listboxes will appear in frames, with a label on top to show what the is held in the list. Note the use of nested frame widgets to get things to line up.

When you run this script on UNIX, you'll see a window similar to that shown in Figure 6.5.

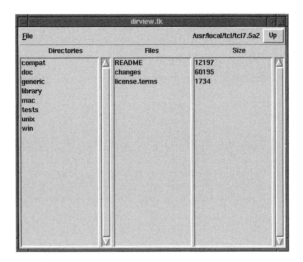

Figure 6.5 The **dirview.tk** script on UNIX.

If you run it on Windows, you'll see something more like that in Figure 6.6.

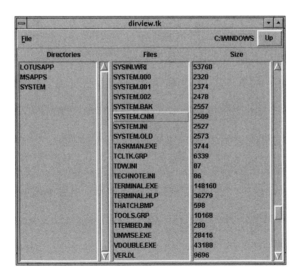

Figure 6.6 The **dirview.tk** script on Windows.

The **dirview.tk** script follows:

```
# Tcl/Tk Directory Viewer

# File menu
frame .menubar -bd 1 \
 -relief raised

menubutton .menubar.file \
  -text "File" \
  -underline 0 \
  -menu .menubar.file.menu

menu .menubar.file.menu

.menubar.file.menu add command \
  -label "Exit" \
  -underline 1 \
  -command exit

 # Cheat and place a button on menubar.
button .menubar.up \
  -text "Up" \
  -command go_up

 # Place a label here, too.
label .menubar.curdir -text "Dir"

pack .menubar.file -side left

pack .menubar.up \
   .menubar.curdir -side right

 # Frame for everything under menubar.
frame .main -bd 0

frame .main.dir -bd 1

label .main.dir.label -text "Directories"
```

```
frame .main.dir.f -bd 0

listbox .main.dir.f.list \
  -height 20 \
  -selectmode single \
  -yscrollcommand ".main.dir.f.scrb set"

scrollbar .main.dir.f.scrb \
  -command ".main.dir.f.list yview"

pack .main.dir.f.list .main.dir.f.scrb \
  -side left -fill y

pack .main.dir.label \
  -side top -fill x
pack .main.dir.f -side bottom

 # Frame for file names.
frame .main.files -bd 0

label .main.files.files \
  -text "Files"

listbox .main.files.file_list \
  -height 20 \
  -selectmode single \
  -yscrollcommand ".main.sizes.f.scrb set"

pack .main.files.files \
  -side top -fill x

pack .main.files.file_list \
  -side bottom

 # File size area.
frame .main.sizes -bd 0

label .main.sizes.size -text "Size"

frame .main.sizes.f
```

```
listbox .main.sizes.f.size_list \
  -height 20 \
  -selectmode single \
   -yscrollcommand ".main.sizes.f.scrb set"

scrollbar .main.sizes.f.scrb \
 -command { multi_scroll \
    {.main.files.file_list .main.sizes.f.size_list} }

pack .main.sizes.f.size_list \
  -side left

pack .main.sizes.f.scrb -side right \
 -fill y

pack .main.sizes.size \
  -side top -fill x

pack .main.sizes.f -side bottom

pack .main.dir .main.files .main.sizes \
   -side left

# Pack top-level widgets.

pack .menubar -side top \
   -fill x -expand true

pack .main -side left

 # Procedures

proc multi_scroll { scroll_list args } {

 # Get info on list of args.
 set len [llength $scroll_list]

 for {set i 0} {$i < $len} {incr i} {
    set temp_list [lindex $scroll_list $i]

     # Uncomment next line for debugging.
```

```
    # puts "Command: $temp_list yview $args"

    eval $temp_list yview $args
}

}

# Fill lists with filenames

proc read_dir { dirlist filelist sizelist } {

    # Clear listboxes
    $dirlist delete 0 end
    $filelist delete 0 end
    $sizelist delete 0 end

    set unsorted [glob -nocomplain *]

    if {$unsorted != "" } {

        set files [lsort $unsorted]

        # Separate out directories

        foreach filename $files {

            if { [file isdirectory $filename] != 0 } {
                # Is a directory.

                $dirlist insert end "$filename"
            } else {
                # Is a file.
                $filelist insert end "$filename"

                # Fill in size
                set sz [file size $filename]

                $sizelist insert end $sz
            }
        }
```

```
  }

  # Now, store current dir in label.
  .menubar.curdir configure \
    -text [pwd]
}

# Go up one directory.
proc go_up { } {

  # Go up one.
  cd ..

  # Read directory.
  read_dir .main.dir.f.list \
    .main.files.file_list .main.sizes.f.size_list
}

# Change dir on double-click.
bind .main.dir.f.list <Double-Button-1> {

    # Get selected list item
    set diritem [.main.dir.f.list curselection]

    set dir [.main.dir.f.list get $diritem]

    # Change directories
    cd $dir

    # Fill lists
    read_dir .main.dir.f.list \
        .main.files.file_list .main.sizes.f.size_list
}

read_dir .main.dir.f.list \
        .main.files.file_list .main.sizes.f.size_list

# end of dirview.tk
```

The read_dir procedure reads a directory and separates its elements into
files and subdirectories, each going to a separate list. For normal files, the

file size command returns the size and that value goes into another list. Both the file name and file size lists are tied to the same scrollbar, so that the proper size value will be synchronized with its corresponding file name.

The **dirview.tk** script cheats in a few regards. First, it places button and label widgets on the menu bar (to go up one directory and to display the current directory). That's a no-no. You should only place menubutton widgets on a menu bar. In a test program, it's OK to cheat a little.

Summary

This chapter introduced Tcl's lists, which are normal Tcl variables (unlike arrays shown in Chapter 2). Tcl provides a number of list-handling commands, such as lsort to sort a list, lindex to extract an element from a list and list to build lists.

To display a list on the screen, you can use the listbox widget. Normally tied together with a scrollbar, the listbox can be configured with a -selectmode of single, multiple, browse, or extended.

Tcl provides a number of file commands, such as open, read, and close. To write data to a file, use the puts command, which defaults to writing to the terminal or Console window if you don't specify a file ID.

The glob command lists the files in a directory that matches a pattern, including the all-inclusive * pattern. The cd command changes to a different working directory and the pwd command returns the current working directory.

Chapter 7 shows how to make dialog windows, such as a file open dialog box, as well as creating other top-level application windows.

Tcl/Tk Commands Introduced in this Chapter

cd	lappend	lsort
close	lindex	open
concat	linsert	puts
eof	list	pwd
file	listbox	read
flush	lrange	seek
glob	lreplace	split
join	lsearch	tell

CHAPTER 7

Dialog Windows

This chapter covers:

- Dialog windows
- Modal and nonmodal dialog windows
- Convenience dialog windows
- Creating top-level application windows
- Positioning dialog windows
- Handling the close window manager option
- Building your own convenience dialog windows
- Error dialog windows
- Drop-down lists

Dialog Windows

In user interface terminology, a **dialog window** is a window that appears to gather information from the user for a particular purpose. For example, most applications include print dialog windows to control printing options, file open dialog windows to select a file to load, and error dialog windows to alert the user to serious problems.

Tk provides the means to create all these types of dialog windows and more. This chapter covers dialog windows as well as all sorts of other types of top-level windows, including application windows and pop-up windows.

Modal and Nonmodal Dialog Windows

The first question you must answer when creating a dialog window is whether to make it modal or nonmodal. A **modal** dialog window requires that the user interact with it right now. A **nonmodal** dialog window just sits there; if the user wants to interact with it, the user will.

While a lot of application developers make frequent use of modal dialog windows, I tend to shy away from them. A major point of graphical user interfaces is to put the user in control, and modal dialog windows take away a measure of that control. The user should be able to choose when to respond and what to respond to. If you can avoid making a dialog window modal, do so.

There is a place for modal dialog windows. When used with care—and not overused—you can put modal dialog windows to good use. If there's something the user absolutely has to respond to or something in which it makes no sense to continue until the user responds, consider using a modal dialog window if you run out of alternatives.

Coming from a background in factory automation, I'm always extremely careful about having a program decide whether the user must respond. If your plant is burning down, you shouldn't be stopped by a modal dialog window demanding you complete a file name properly, for example.

NOTE

If you do need to create a modal dialog window, you can use the tkwait command to make the dialog window modal. The tkwait command waits until one of three conditions happens: a variable's value changes, a widget becomes visible on the screen, or a widget gets destroyed. The three forms follow:

```
tkwait variable varname
tkwait visibility widgetname
tkwait window widgetname
```

Normally, you'll only use the `variable` and `window` (destroyed) forms of `tkwait`. The `visibility` form is intended for use with the `grab` command, something that is required for very few applications and is inherently unportable in all of its subtleties. (If you're interested, you can look up the online manual information on `grab`. Generally, you won't need this command.)

In most cases, you'll create a dialog window using the `toplevel` widget command. You'll place `button`, `label`, and `message` widgets inside the `toplevel` widget.

To make `tkwait` work, you need to either have the all button widgets' `-command` option `destroy` the `toplevel` widget or have each `button` set a chosen variable to a different value. Which method you choose determines which form of `tkwait` to use.

Next, call `tkwait` with the name of the `toplevel` widget.

The `tkwait` command allows you to build a modal dialog window by hand (see the section on building your own dialog windows later in this chapter for more on this). You often don't even have to do this much work, if you need only a simple convenience dialog window.

Convenience Dialog Windows

Tk provides the ability to create simple dialog windows as a convenience. Such a dialog window displays a text message, a bitmap, and a number of buttons, such as the warning dialog window shown in Figure 7.1.

Figure 7.1 A warning dialog window.

These convenience dialog windows include question dialog windows, which ask the user a yes/no type of question, warning dialog windows, which alert the user to a problem, error dialogs alerting the user to a more serious problem, and information dialog windows, which inform the user of some new data (e.g., new mail has arrived).

Tk comes with a handy routine to create modal convenience dialog windows, the tk_dialog command, which uses the following syntax:

```
tk_dialog widgetname title text bitmap default_button label1 label2 ...
```

The *widgetname* should be only one level below the top-most (.) widget, such as *.dialog* or *.error* but not *.toplevel.frame* or something like that. The *title* appears in the window's title bar. The *text* shows up in a message widget.

The *bitmap* identifies one of Tk's built-in bitmap shapes, based loosely on the Windows and Motif standard shapes for errors and warnings. The bitmap may be one of the *bitmap* names shown in Figure 7.2. (There are more options than this, as shown in Chapter 9 in the section on bitmaps.)

Figure 7.2 Tk's built-in bitmaps.

Some of these bitmaps aren't appropriate for convenience dialog windows. For example, a progress dialog window, which normally would use the hourglass bitmap, should really have pause and resume buttons, which makes the use of tkwait (which is called in tk_dialog) problematic.

The *default_button* argument to tk_dialog specifies the index (starting at 0) of the button widget to mark as the default button, the button that gets executed when the user presses the **Return** key. This button also gets a special highlighted border, which tk_dialog places automatically.

The *label* arguments to tk_dialog are the text you want to appear in the buttons. tk_dialog will create as many buttons as you provide labels.

The return value of tk_dialog is the index (starting at 0) of the button the user picked.

For example, to make a warning dialog window, as shown in Figure 7.1, you can use the following command:

```
set result [tk_dialog .dlg "Warning" \
    "This is a warning dialog." warning 0 OK Cancel]
```

This dialog window diverges a bit from the Windows interface style guide, but it is good enough for most uses. The tk_dialog routine is written in Tcl, so you can build your own if you'd like (see the section on building your own convenience dialog windows later in this chapter for more on this).

Many dialog windows require a lot more interaction with the user and many more widgets than are allowed in dialog windows created by tk_dialog. For these more advanced dialog windows, you'll need to build them yourself.

Building Your Own Dialog Windows

You'll need to build file open, print, and other dialog windows necessary for your application. As with most tasks in Tcl, this isn't very difficult.

To create your own dialog windows, you need to create a toplevel window and then set up the proper window manager options to make this widget into a dialog window. Then, you need to fill in the toplevel widget with whatever widgets you want inside the dialog window, usually including listboxes and entry widgets.

Creating Top-Level Application Windows

To create a top-level window, you need to make a toplevel widget. You can use this widget as both a top-level application window or as a dialog window. Some applications require multiple top-level windows, beyond the top-level widget (.). Each top-level window has a window title bar and can be moved about the screen by the user.

Most applications require only one such window but some require more. To create such a window, use the toplevel command:

```
toplevel .top
```

Once created, you can fill in the toplevel widget with any of the standard Tk widgets we've been using so far. For example:

```
toplevel .top
label .top.label \
   -text "This is a top-level window"
```

```
button .top.button \
  -text "Push Me" \
  -command { puts ouch }

pack .top.label .top.button \
  -side left
```

NOTE You don't pack a toplevel widget. Much like the main widget named ., when the child widgets get packed, you'll see the new toplevel widget. You can also use the -width and -height options if you want to specify a particular size for the new toplevel widget.

You can see this toplevel widget in Figure 7.3.

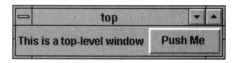

Figure 7.3 A simple toplevel widget.

You can fill in your toplevel widget with any Tk widgets you desire. The toplevel acts a lot like the frame widget, only the toplevel widget has a title bar and can be moved about the screen.

To specify that a toplevel widget is a dialog window, you can use the -class option:

```
toplevel .dlg -class Dialog
```

There are a number of other options you may want to set to turn a toplevel widget into a dialog window.

Setting Window Manager Options

The main options you need to set lie with the window manager. Under the X Window System on UNIX, the **window manager** program owns the window title bars. The window manager creates these windows (for title bars are windows themselves) and places the text therein. To control the title bar, you need to send specially formatted messages to the window manager.

On Windows, however, the title bar is considered part of the application's window. Luckily, Tcl hides most of these platform differences.

To set a title into the title bar, you need to use the `wm title` command:

```
wm title widgetname titlestring
```

The `wm` command contains a zillion options for communicating with the window manager or configuring your own windows. For a dialog window, you are supposed to register the fact that the dialog window is a **transient** window for the main application window. On doing this in Tk, however, you'll sometimes lose the title bar completely.

This should depend on the window manager program in use on UNIX. The **fvwm** window manager, common on Linux, for example, removes the title bars for these top-level widgets (by default; this is configurable). The **mwm** window manager, however, does not.

To mark a `toplevel` widget as a transient window (really a dialog window), use the following syntax:

```
wm transient dialogname main_window
```

The *main_window* is almost always the top-level . widget. The *dialogname* is the name of your dialog window to mark as transient.

Positioning Dialog Windows

You can position a dialog window with the `wm geometry` command:

```
wm geometry widgetname geometry_spec
```

This command takes a widget name and a *geometry_spec*. The *geometry_spec* uses a rather strange X Window System format of *width*X*height*+*x*+*y*. You can omit the size (*width*X*height*) or position (+*x*+*y*) if you want. An easier way to set the size is to use the `-width` and `-height` options on the `toplevel` widget.

To create a dialog window and position it, you can use the following commands as an example:

```
toplevel .dlg -class Dialog
wm title .dlg "This is a dialog"
wm transient .dlg .
wm geometry .dlg +200+300

button .dlg.b -text "Button"
pack .dlg.b -side left
```

These commands create a dialog window and position it at 200 pixels from the left and 300 pixels down from the top.

In X, the geometry specifications also allow you to figure positions from any edge of the screen, with odd origin values for each of the four corners, as shown in Table 7.1.

Table 7.1 Specifying the corner of the display.

Geometry	Location
+0+0	Upper left corner
-0+0	Upper right corner
+0-0	Lower left corner
-0-0	Lower right corner

Try the following commands:

```
wm geometry .dlg -0-0
wm geometry .dlg -0+0
wm geometry .dlg +0+0
wm geometry .dlg +0-0
```

You may want to center your dialog window within the main application window or on the screen. To get the screen size, you can use the following commands:

```
set width  [winfo screenwidth  .]
set height [winfo screenheight .]
```

For example:

```
% set width  [winfo screenwidth  .]
1024
% set height [winfo screenheight .]
768
```

The following procedure positions a dialog window in approximately the center of the screen:

```
proc dialog_position { dlg } {

    set width  [winfo screenwidth  .]
    set height [winfo screenheight .]

    set x [expr ($width/2)  - 100]
    set y [expr ($height/2) - 100]

    wm geometry $dlg +$x+$y
}
```

Positioning the Main Widget

You can also position the main application widget with the wm geometry command, but you also may need to lie to the window manager and claim the user picked the position for the window. If you try the wm geometry command and nothing happens, try the following command first and then execute the wm geometry command:

```
wm positionfrom . user
```

The reason for this is that many window manager programs don't honor positions specified by the program (the default). Instead, your program has to claim the user actively chose the location.

Handling the Close Window Manager Option

Most window managers provide for a window menu, and usually this menu has a choice labeled **Close** or **Quit**. Typically, when the user chooses this option, Tk terminates your program, sometimes not very gracefully.

There is a way to get around this. Now, when the user asks for a window to close, you should close it, even if it means stopping the application. The user should be in charge, after all. But you may want to confirm with the user. You may need to prompt the user to save a file before quitting, or you may merely want to execute some clean-up code before abrupt termination.

To do all this, you need to set up a protocol handler to handle the WM_DELETE_WINDOW protocol (this is an X Window System term). For this, call the wm protocol command, which uses the following syntax:

```
wm protocol widgetname protocol tcl_script
```

The *widgetname* should be a toplevel widget, as well as the . widget. (So, you'll need to call this for all top-level widgets.) The *protocol* is WM_DELETE_WINDOW and you provide the *tcl_script*.

To query the user to confirm quitting the program, you can use the following code, which sets up the procedure handle_close to handle all dialog and main window close messages:

```
proc handle_close { widgetname } {

    if { $widgetname == "." } {
      # Prompt before quitting.
      set result [tk_dialog .dlg "Exit" \
        "Do you really want to exit program?" \
        question \
        0 "Exit" "Don't Exit" ]
        # Delete widget depending on result...
    } else {
      # Destroy dialog.
```

```
    destroy $widgetname
  }
}
```

```
wm protocol . WM_DELETE_WINDOW { handle_close . }
```

The handle_close procedure destroys any dialog windows sent to it. This is based on the idea that what the user says goes. But if the user asks to close the widget named ., the handle_close procedure prompts the user with a dialog window such as the one shown in Figure 7.4.

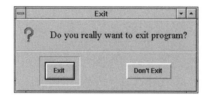

Figure 7.4 Querying the user whether to quit.

You'll want to set something like the handle_close procedure for all toplevel widgets you create.

Now we have enough tools to start building dialog windows.

Building Your Own Convenience Dialog Windows

You can build your own convenience dialog windows if you would rather not use tk_dialog. In addition, chances are your application requires some complicated dialog window, going far beyond the simple convenience dialog windows provided by tk_dialog.

A good approach is to divide the problem. If you don't know in advance how many widgets you need to place into a dialog window, or whether it should be modal, you can set up procedures at the beginning and the end, leaving the middle to be different for each dialog window.

For example, the following dialog window procedure makes a toplevel widget and optionally marks it as a transient (dialog) window:

```
# Creates (empty) dialog.
proc dialog { widgetname title trans } {

    toplevel $widgetname -class Dialog
    wm title $widgetname $title

    # Only mark as transient on demand.
    if { $trans } {
        wm transient $widgetname  .
    }

    # Handle wm Close choice.
    wm protocol $widgetname \
        WM_DELETE_WINDOW "handle_close $widgetname "
}
```

One way of separating the top part of the dialog, usually holding a message and a number of entry widgets from the bottom, which holds the **OK**, **Cancel**, and other buttons, is to use a frame widget for the top and another frame for the bottom. This also makes the widgets easier to lay out.

Furthermore, we can assume all of the widgets needed in the dialog window will go into the top area. We can create routines to build up the bottom frame widget, populated only with buttons such as **OK** and **Cancel**. Then pack in the top frame and all is complete.

The following code will create the bottom area. The dialog_button procedure creates and packs one button. The dialog_bottom procedure builds all the buttons for the whole bottom area.

```
# Builds a button on a dialog.
proc dialog_button { widgetname msg count } {

    button $widgetname \
     -text $msg \
     -command "global dlg_button; set dlg_button $count"
```

```
    pack $widgetname -side left \
      -padx 20 -pady 10

    return $widgetname
}
```

```
# Create frame for bottom area of dialog.
proc dialog_bottom { widgetname args } {

    frame $widgetname.b -bd 2 -relief raised

    set i 0
    foreach msg $args {

        dialog_button $widgetname.b.$i $msg $i

        incr i
    }

    pack $widgetname.b -side bottom -fill x
}
```

N O T E   The use of quotation marks around the -command Tcl script is essential. We need the values $var and $count to be parsed now, not later (when the variables will no longer exist). We need the values held in each. You have to be careful about this when working with Tcl procedures.

The following procedure then makes a dialog window modal and positions it near the center of the screen:

```
proc dialog_wait { dlg } {
    global dlg_button

    # Position dialog.
    dialog_position $dlg

    tkwait variable dlg_button
```

```
    destroy $dlg

    return $dlg_button
```

```
}
```

Error Dialog Windows

We can pull all this together and build an error dialog window from scratch. For the error dialog window , we'll have a message widget and a label displaying a bitmap. We could have just as easily created a label and an entry widget, or a frame holding a number of scrolled listbox widgets.

Try out the following Tcl code, which uses the procedures created earlier:

```
global ret_value

dialog .errdlg "Error" 1

frame .errdlg.t -bd 2 -relief raised

label .errdlg.t.bit -bitmap error

message .errdlg.t.msg \
   -width 4c \
   -text "When in danger\
     or in doubt,\
     run in circles,\
     scream and shout."

pack .errdlg.t.bit .errdlg.t.msg \
   -side left

pack .errdlg.t -side top -fill x

 # Create bottom area.
dialog_bottom .errdlg OK Cancel
```

```
# Wait on user response.
dialog_wait .errdlg
```

File Open and Save Dialog Windows

To make file dialog windows, all you need to do is place listbox widgets in a frame and then put them in the top frame of the dialog window. Look in Chapter 13 for Tcl commands to scan a disk directory and place all the file names into a listbox widget.

Drop-Down Lists

More common in the Windows environment, drop-down lists are also part of Motif 2.0 and the Common Desktop Environment on UNIX. Tk doesn't support drop-down lists—at least not directly, but you can build one on your own.

First of all, an option menu using the tk_optionMenu command may do the trick for you. See Chapter 4 for more on this. You could save yourself some work.

The main problem with an option menu is the lack of space. An option menu doesn't scroll, so you're limited by the screen size, but if you use a listbox widget, you can scroll the choices and conceivably present thousands of choices.

You can put the listbox in a toplevel widget to make the listbox appear as though it is floating on the screen. In this case, we want the toplevel widget to have no window manager title bar at all, much like a menu. While you could try playing with the menu widget itself, you can also use another option to the wm command:

```
wm overrideredirect widgetname 1
```

The overrideredirect (that's "override redirect") option specifies that the given window not be given any decorations, such as the title bar, from the window manager. Under the X Window System, this is what menus use. To turn this option off, use:

```
wm overrideredirect widgetname 0
```

For the entry part of the widget, we can use a label prompt, an entry widget, and then a button to call up the list. To follow the Windows style, you should place a down-pointing arrow bitmap in the button. Such bitmaps in buttons are covered in Chapter 10. For now, we'll use a simple button showing text, "...", to signify that more options are available.

When we put all this together, we have an entry area that looks like what is shown in Figure 7.5.

Figure 7.5   The drop-down list entry area.

This can be created with the following example code:

```
label .prompt -text "Font: "

entry .fontname \
  -textvariable fontname \
  -width 24

button .pop -text "..." \
  -command { drop_list }


pack .prompt .fontname .pop \
  -side left
```

The code to create the drop-down list is a bit more complex. First, we have to determine the position of the list, which should be beneath the button and entry widgets. We can use the entry widget's position.

To convert the entry widget's position to global coordinates, you can use the winfo rootx and winfo rooty commands:

```
set x [winfo rootx .fontname]
set y [winfo rooty .fontname]
```

We can then create the drop-down list in the drop_list procedure:

```
proc drop_list { } {

    # Determine position.
    set x [winfo rootx .fontname]
    set y [winfo rooty .fontname]

    toplevel .popup
    wm overrideredirect .popup 1

    wm geometry .popup +$x+$y

    # Make list.
    listbox .popup.list \
        -height 5 -width 24 \
        -selectmode single \
        -yscrollcommand ".popup.scrb set"

    # Add in some font names.
    .popup.list insert end "Arial"
    .popup.list insert end "Bookman"
    .popup.list insert end "Courier"
    .popup.list insert end "Helvetica"
    .popup.list insert end "Kanji Mincho"
    .popup.list insert end "Times Roman"
    .popup.list insert end "New Century Schoolbook"
    .popup.list insert end "Lucida"
    .popup.list insert end "Charter"
    .popup.list insert end "Symbol"
    .popup.list insert end "Wingdings"

    scrollbar .popup.scrb \
        -command ".popup.list yview"

    pack .popup.scrb -side right -fill y
    pack .popup.list -side left


    bind .popup.list <Double-Button-1> {
```

```
global fontname
set item [.popup.list curselection]
set fontname [.popup.list get $item]

# Close window.
destroy .popup
    }
}
```

All together, this makes a workable drop-down list. When pulled down, this list looks like what is shown in Figure 7.6.

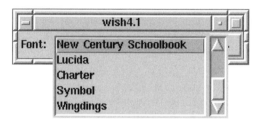

Figure 7.6 A drop-down list with the list pulled down.

There are a number of other means to create drop-down lists. If you don't like the behavior of the widgets shown earlier, you can experiment to see if you get the behavior and look you want.

Summary

This chapter introduced the toplevel widget, used to make dialog windows and other top-level application windows.

To make a dialog window into a modal dialog window, you can use the tkwait command. The tkwait command waits until one of three things happens: a variable's value changes, a widget becomes visible on the screen, or a widget gets destroyed.

The tk_dialog command creates modal convenience dialog windows, such as error, warning, and information dialog windows.

The `wm geometry` command allows you to position any top-level widget.

The `wm protocol` command allows you to trap the `WM_DELETE_WINDOW` message, which is really the **Close** choice on the window menu.

You can build drop-down lists using `wm overrideredirect` to make the `toplevel` widget not have any window manager decorations.

Tcl/Tk Commands Introduced in this Chapter

```
tk_dialog
tkwait
toplevel
winfo
wm
```

SECTION II

Advanced Applications

Now that you've tackled the basics, this section delves into some more advanced issues for creating cross-platform graphical applications with Tcl and the Tk toolkit.

Chapter 8 starts out by addressing the toughest issue of all: how to debug applications. It discusses a number of techniques to help find out what is wrong with your scripts and how to fix them.

The Tcl canvas widget, covered in Chapter 9, allows you to create drawing items such as lines and arcs. You can go much further with the canvas widget and include text items and embed any Tk widget into the canvas. You'll find the canvas great for creating hypertext Web page browsers, graphical file managers, and a host of other purposes. This chapter also delves into bitmaps and images, including Tk support for GIF imagery.

Since Tcl is a scripting language, you'll often want to launch UNIX or Windows applications from within your scripts. Chapter 10 shows how to do this and covers some common pitfalls when trying to execute other applications from Tcl.

While Tcl and Tk provide a rich set of commands, you'll often want to extend this set to new commands, especially if you embed the Tcl interpreter into your applications as a sort of macro language. Chapter 11 shows how to embed the Tcl interpreter and Chapter 12 covers adding new commands to that interpreter.

Finally, Chapter 13 wraps up the discussion by concentrating on miscellaneous commands to help round out robust applications.

CHAPTER 8

Tcl Tricks and Traps: Handling Errors and Debugging

This chapter covers:

- Handling errors
- Handling errors with tkerror
- Catching errors with catch
- Using tkerror to help debug your applications
- Tracing the execution of Tcl scripts for debugging
- Finding out more about the state of the Tcl interpreter

Handling Errors

Errors, unfortunately, are a fact of life. If you want your Tcl scripts to be robust, you must deal with errors. You need to announce some errors to the user; others can be dealt with silently inside your scripts.

Of course, we'd all prefer to eliminate all errors from the scripts during the development phase. This chapter discusses errors in Tcl, how to handle them, how to defeat them, and how to debug your code.

Most Tcl errors are reported immediately to the terminal or console window, but a number of errors come from what is called **background code**. This code is executed for an event binding or in a number of other situations where you set up a procedure in advance and the code is executed later, but it is not part of the standard flow of control in the Tcl script.

260

Handling Background Errors with `tkerror`

When any Tk procedure detects an error in a script called from `bind` or any other source of background processing, it executes a procedure called `tkerror`. Since you can redefine any procedure in Tcl with the `proc` command, you can override `tkerror` with your own routine.

The default `tkerror` displays a dialog box and provides a stack trace of the error, as shown in Figure 8.1.

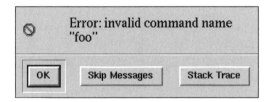

Figure 8.1 The result of the default `tkerror` procedure.

This is very useful when developing your application, because it helps you root out problems. The stack trace is especially helpful, but it's not good for end users because, chances are, they won't know Tcl. So, robust applications should override `tkerror`.

The `tkerror` procedure takes one argument, the error message, to display:

```
proc tkerror { errmsg } {

 # Your code goes here.

}
```

Now, you'll want to create a tkerror procedure that does more than this. For example, you may want to display an error dialog box, to let the user know what happened; but before you can do this, you need to know more about the error information available through Tcl.

Reporting Errors in Your Code

If you detect an error in a procedure, you can use the expanded form of return to return an error code and assorted information about the error. From Chapter 2, the return command allows the following arguments:

```
return -code code -errorinfo info -errorcode code string
```

Going through the options one at a time, Table 8.1 shows the values allowed for the -code option.

Table 8.1 The -code Value from the Return Command

Code	Meaning
ok	Normal procedure return
error	Error return; same as error command
return	Causes calling procedure to return as well
break	Acts like the break command, jumps out of innermost loop
continue	Acts like continue command, jumps to top of innermost loop
number	Returns this number as the completion code

If a number of errors build up while processing inside your tkerror routine, tkerror will get called for each one. If this is a problem, you should return a -code of break from tkerror, which breaks this loop.

You can fill in stack trace information in the -errorinfo value. This value gets set into the global variable named *errorInfo*. This is used by the default tkerror procedure and should show the text of the actual lines of Tcl code where the error was detected.

The value set into the -errorcode option gets stored in the global variable *errorCode*. If you omit it, the value is set to NONE.

The *errorCode* variable contains a list of error codes formatted a special way, as shown in Table 8.2. The first element in the list specifies how to interpret the data following.

Table 8.2 Data Stored in the errorCode Global List Variable

errorCode	Meaning
ARITH DIVZERO *message*	Arithmetic divide by zero error
ARITH DOMAIN *message*	Arithmetic argument outside domain of a function error
ARITH OVERFLOW *message*	Floating-point overflow
ARITH UNKNOWN *message*	Unknown arithmetic error
CHILDKILLED *pid signal message*	Child process killed by a signal
CHILDSTATUS *pid code*	Child process exited with nonzero code
CHILDSUSP *pid signal message*	Child process suspended by a signal
NONE	No information available. Do not pass go
POSIX *error message*	Error in POSIX kernel call

Setting Error Data

You can use the error command to store data in the global error variables. Don't set values in these variables directly. The Tcl interpreter assumes you'll follow the proper conventions, and it's always best to follow the established conventions. The error command uses the following syntax:

```
error message info code
```

The *message* is the text of the error message to return to the application. The *info* argument will get appended to the data in the global variable *errorInfo* (this is a list that gets appended to). The *code* argument will get placed in the *errorCode* global variable. See Table 8.2 for the format of the data. Both the *info* and *code* arguments are optional.

Many of these error values make a lot more sense if you're writing Tcl functions in C, as you'll see in Chapter 12. The math errors, for example, generally occur within the C function that implements a math procedure, rather than in Tcl code.

Building a New tkerror Procedure

Whew. With all this information on errors, you can now build a new version of tkerror that displays more data to the user. For example:

```
proc tkerror { errmsg } {

  global errorInfo errorCode

  set msg \
    [format "Error: %s\nResult: %s." \
       $errmsg $errorCode]

  # Alert user to error.
  tk_dialog .dlg "Error" $msg error 0 OK

}
```

WARNING

It's very important that a routine called on errors doesn't generate errors itself. Can you find all the places in the preceding example where tkerror might fail? Just creating button widgets in the dialog box might fail with out-of-memory or out-of-color-cell errors.

To test this tkerror procedure, try binding the following event:

```
bind all <Control-Key-e> {

  error "This is a sample error."
}
```

Then, type a **Ctrl-E** in the **wish** window. Remember, tkerror is called for background errors. You'll see a dialog box such as the one in Figure 8.2.

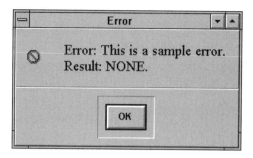

Figure 8.2 The new tkerror procedure.

To test other kinds of errors, you can bind **Ctrl-M** (for math) to generate another error, as shown here:

```
bind all <Control-Key-m> {

    set v [ expr acos(-3) ]
}
```

If you now type a **Ctrl-M**, you'll see the error message shown in Figure 8.3.

Figure 8.3 A math error trapped by our tkerror procedure.

The use of bound **Ctrl** key combinations is just a convenience to generate the type of background error tkerror reports. There's nothing special about **Ctrl-E** or **Ctrl-M**.

NOTE

Catching Errors with Catch

If a script causes errors, or you think it might, you can use catch to capture any errors from the script and continue processing normally. For example, many applications allow users to provide some form of customization file. With Tcl, it makes sense to keep this file in Tcl format, using the Tcl syntax (because you already have a file parser—the Tcl interpreter). But when you execute this file, you don't want a bad command in the user's customization file to stop the whole program. So, you can use catch. The syntax is:

```
catch tcl_script varname
```

The catch command executes the given *tcl_script*, capturing any errors that occur. catch returns 0 on success, and a return code (from the -code option to the return command) if any errors occurred, as listed in Table 8.1.

The optional *varname*, if present, is used to store any values returned by the script (the normal return value) or an error message, if one is given.

The Great Unknown

You can define a procedure called unknown to trap calls to procedures that don't exist, that is, they have not been defined with the proc command.

Whenever the Tcl interpreter encounters an unknown command, it will try to execute the procedure named unknown. If you haven't defined such a procedure, Tcl generates an error. To stop these errors from appearing to the user, you probably want to define the unknown procedure. For example, try the following:

```
% ouch these are bogus arguments
invalid command name "ouch"

% proc unknown { commandname args } {

  # Your code here...
  puts "Unknown: $commandname $args"

}

% ouch these are bogus arguments
Unknown: ouch these are bogus arguments
```

In this example, the first attempt at the nonexistent ouch command resulted in an error. The second attempt, after defining the procedure, invoked the unknown procedure. The unknown procedure takes two arguments. The *commandname* is the name of the unknown procedure. The args contain all the arguments that were passed to this procedure. The default unknown procedure tries to load up the Tcl code for the missing procedure. See the online manuals for more on this.

Debugging Tcl Applications

Tcl and Tk provide a number of hooks to help you debug your applications. First of all, since Tcl is a much simpler and a much higher-level language than C or C++, there's typically a lot less code to debug. A text editor in Tcl uses a lot less code than one written in C or C++. With less code, your debugging task becomes a lot easier.

Furthermore, due to the short cycle of edit/run, edit/run (rather than edit/compile/link, edit/compile/link for C and C++), you can test out code and code snippets much more quickly. I've found the following techniques handy when debugging Tcl scripts, some old, some new:

- Use the simple puts command to print out a message, both that a procedure gets executed and also the value of variables you think you're having a problem with.

- Replace the procedure you find problematic, or suspect to be so. With Tcl, you can replace any procedure with the proc command. You can use this to gradually create a working procedure out of a nonworking one.

- Use the stack trace from the default tkerror procedure. While often not exact, this provides something close to the line that caused the error.

- Use the trace command to see how a variable is getting written to.

Debugging with tkerror

You can use the default tkerror procedure and dialog box shown in Figure 8.1, to help you debug your scripts. By default, tkerror presents you the option of seeing a stack trace for the error, as shown in Figure 8.4.

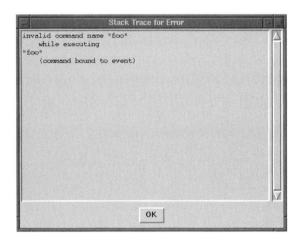

Figure 8.4 The stack trace feature of `tkerror`.

You can use this stack trace to identify the line that caused the problem. This won't always be the line that is truly at fault, but it can help you get there.

Tracing the Execution of Tcl Scripts for Debugging

You can use the `trace` command to execute a Tcl script whenever a variable changes. With global variables, the routine you suspect of causing a problem may be innocent; it may be that another procedure is causing the problem and writing bad data to the variable.

The `tkerror` command takes the following syntax:

```
trace variable varname operations tcl_script
```

The *operations* argument can be one or more of the values listed in Table 8.3.

Table 8.3 The Available Operations for the Trace Command

Operation	Meaning
r	Execute *tcl_script* whenever *varname* is read.
w	Execute *tcl_script* whenever *varname* is written to.
u	Execute *tcl_script* whenever *varname* is unset.

A variable that is nonglobal, that is, local to a procedure, gets automatically unset when the procedure returns.

N O T E

The *tcl_script* gets invoked with the following arguments:

tcl_script varname elementname operation

The *varname* is the variable that is changed. If *varname* is an array, *elementname* holds the array element name that was changed (unless you're tracing the whole array).

The upvar command may access a variable under a different name. So, the name you see in your *tcl_script* may not always be the one you're looking for.

N O T E

Furthermore, you may need to use upvar or uplevel to get at the value if your *tcl_script* is a procedure.

The following code sets up a tracing procedure and traces changes to the variable:

```tcl
proc trace_testvar { varname elementname operation } {

    upvar $varname var1

    puts "Tracing $operation: $varname with value $var1."

}


# Set up trace.
trace variable testvar {rwu} trace_testvar

# Use testvar: writing.
set testvar {Sample Value}

# Reading.
set x $testvar
```

To turn off a trace on a variable, use the `trace vdelete` command:

```
trace vdelete varname operations tcl_script
```

The *varname*, *operations*, and *tcl_script* all must match the values originally passed to the `trace variable` command.

269

```
See the online manuals for more information about trace.
```

Finding Out More about the State of the Tcl Interpreter

You can use the `info` command to get information on the state of the Tcl interpreter. This can be useful if you think some procedure has been over-written with a new version or otherwise question what the Tcl interpreter thinks is going on.

Table 8.4 lists the many variants of the `info` command.

Table 8.4 The Tcl `info` Command

Command	Use
info args *procedure*	Returns the arguments, in order, for *procedure*
info body *procedure*	Returns the body (code) of the given *procedure*
info cmdcount	Returns number of commands executed by the interpreter
info commands	Returns names of all Tcl commands
info commands *pattern*	Returns names of all Tcl commands that match *pattern*
info complete *command*	Returns 0 if *command* needs more input, 1 otherwise
info default *procedure* *argument varname*	If *argument* in *procedure* has a default value, returns 1 and places value in *varname*; returns 0 otherwise
info exists *varname*	Returns 1 if *varname* exists in current procedure; 0 otherwise

continued

Table 8.4 continued

Command	Use
info globals	Returns list of all global variables
info globals *pattern*	Returns list of all global variables matching *pattern*.
info level	Returns stack level number (0 is top level)
info level *number*	Returns parameters of current call at that stack level
info library	Returns Tcl library directory (held in *tcl_library* global variable)
info locals	Returns all current local (inside procedure) variables
info locals *pattern*	Returns all current local (inside procedure) variables that match *pattern*
info nameofexecutable	Returns full pathname of executable
info patchlevel	Returns current patch (revision) level of interpreter, same as *tcl_patchLevel* global variable
info procs	Returns name of all Tcl procedures
info procs *pattern*	Returns name of all Tcl procedures that match *pattern*
info script	Returns name of innermost script file being executed, or NULL string if none
info sharedlibextension	Returns shared library extension, such as .dll or .so
info tclversion	Returns same data as global *tcl_version* variable
info vars	Returns name of all currently active variables (local and global)
info vars *pattern*	Returns name of all currently active variables (local and global) that match *pattern*

For example, you can try the following commands to see how extensive the Tcl language is, especially with Tk added in the picture:

```
% info nameofexecutable
/usr/local/tcl/bin/wish4.1
% info tclversion
7.5
% info vars
tcl_rcFileName tkPriv.:0 tcl_interactive tcl_version
argv argv0 tk_library tk_version errorCode auto_path
errorInfo tk_strictMotif tkPriv env tcl_patchLevel
argc tk_patchLevel tcl_library tcl_platform

% info commands
tkCheckRadioInvoke menubutton tell subst open eof
tkTraverseToMenu pwd bindtags glob list
tkTextKeySelect tkScaleControlPress tkMenuUnpost
listbox pid exec tkTextSetCursor tkScrollButtonUp
pack time unknown clipboard eval
tkTextClipboardKeysyms tkScrollByPages lrange
tk_popup checkbutton lsearch tkTextTranspose
gets tkMbEnter canvas case lappend proc message
place bind break llength tkButtonInvoke
auto_execok tkScaleActivate tkMenuButtonDown
return tkListboxBeginSelect linsert error
tkTextScrollPages tkPostOverPoint tkTraverseWithinMenu
tkButtonDown catch tkwait raise info split
tkTextKeyExtend tkListboxSelectAll
tkMenuFirstEntry tkTextSelectTo array if
tkMenuInvoke auto_mkindex concat join lreplace
tkListboxUpDown option source global
tkScrollButtonDown switch tkScrollToPos tkMbLeave
tkEntrySeeInsert auto_reset toplevel update
tkScrollButton2Down tkScrollByUnits tkScrollDrag
tkScaleEndDrag tkFirstMenu wm tkTextPrevPara
tkEntryInsert close for cd auto_load scale label
focus file append tkListboxBeginExtend
tkButtonEnter format tkEntryKeySelect tkScrollEndDrag
tkEntrySetCursor radiobutton image button read set scan
tkMenuFindName tkListboxDataExtend trace tkEntryTranspose
seek tkTextUpDownLine tkTextButton1 tkListboxExtendUpDown
```

```
lower while tkEntryMouseSelect destroy after flush
tkScaleButtonDown tkListboxBeginToggle winfo tkMbMotion
scrollbar grab menu continue uplevel tkCancelRepeat
. selection tkEntryAutoScan tkButtonUp tkButtonLeave
foreach rename tkMenuLeave tkMenuMotion tkListboxCancel
tkListboxAutoScan tkListboxMotion entry fileevent send
frame regexp tkMbPost tkScaleButton2Down tkMenuNextEntry
tkMenuLeftRight text tkScrollSelect tkSaveGrabInfo
tkEntryBackspace tkEntryButton1 upvar tkTextNextPara
tkMbButtonUp expr unset load regsub tkTextInsert
tkScreenChanged tkTextResetAnchor tkTextAutoScan
tkScrollStartDrag exit history interp
tkScaleIncrement puts incr lindex lsort
tkScaleDrag tkMenuFind tkMenuEscape
tkScrollTopBottom tkEntryClipboardKeysyms
tk bell string
```

CD-ROM

On the CD-ROM, you'll find a number of Tcl/Tk debugging programs in the **contrib/debug** directory, such as **tdebug** and **tkdebug**.

Summary

This chapter covered techniques for trouble-shooting your Tcl applications. You can create a tkerror procedure to trap background errors generated by Tk from things like event bindings. If you don't override tkerror, Tk will display its own error window.

You can use the catch command to catch any errors coming from a Tcl script. This is very useful if you load in a file of Tcl commands and this file contains errors.

The trace command allows you to trace modifications and accesses to a variable.

The info command tells you what is stored inside the Tcl interpreter itself.

Tcl/Tk Commands Introduced in this Chapter

```
error
info
return
trace
```

## CHAPTER 9

The Canvas Widget, Bitmaps, and Images

This chapter covers:

- The canvas widget
- Creating drawing items in the canvas widget
- Generating PostScript output
- Bitmaps
- Creating bitmaps From X bitmap files
- Images
- Creating images from GIF files
- Creating images from PPM files
- Displaying thumbnail images
- Toolbars

The Canvas Widget

Tcl, even with Tk, does not make a full-fledged drawing package. You're not going to create AutoCAD or a 3D solid modeling package in Tcl, although you may well want to embed Tcl as an application customization language in such an application.

Even though Tcl is a not a graphics drawing system, you can a do a lot with the `canvas` widget and with images and bitmaps, with a remarkably small number of commands.

The `canvas` widget gives you a canvas on which to place drawing items, including lines, rectangles, bitmaps, and even widgets. Once placed, the `canvas` widget takes care of drawing the items, sort of like a display list of structured graphics in 3D graphics systems. The structured graphics model means that you don't—directly—draw into the `canvas`. Instead, you place graphics items such as lines and ovals. When necessary, the `canvas` widget displays all items in the display list, going from the beginning to the end. That means the first item created is the first to be drawn. If a later item obscures the first item, you may never even see it. Thus, it's important to watch the order in which you create drawing items. Once created, you may move graphics drawing items, change their colors and so on.

To create a `canvas` widget, use the `canvas` command:

```
canvas .can
pack .can
```

You can control the size of the `canvas` widget with the `-width` and `-height` options:

```
canvas .can -width 300 -height 250
pack .can
```

Creating Drawing Items in the Canvas Widget

You can fill the `canvas` widget with a number of drawing items, such as lines and rectangles. To draw into a `canvas` widget, you create items and the `canvas` widget takes care of the rest.

The `canvas` widget uses the model of a display list for drawing. It maintains a list of items to display.

To create drawing items, use the `create` option:

```
widgetname create type x y options
```

When you create a drawing item, the command will return a number that you can use as an ID for the drawing item in subsequent commands.

Table 9.1 lists the available item types you can create and the necessary arguments for that type of item.

Table 9.1 Canvas Item Types

Type	Required Data
arc	*widgetname* create arc *x1 y1 x2 y2*
bitmap	*widgetname* create bitmap *x y*
image	*widgetname* create image *x y*
line	*widgetname* create line *x1 y1 x2 y2 ...*
oval	*widgetname* create oval *x1 y1 x2 y2*
polygon	*widgetname* create polygon *x1 y1 x2 y2 ...*
rectangle	*widgetname* create rectangle *x1 y1 x2 y2*
text	*widgetname* create text *x y*
window	*widgetname* create window *x y*

In addition to the required data, you may add a number of options to each of the item types.

Arc Drawing Items

An arc item can draw an arc, a pie slice, or a piece of a circle (chord), bounded by a rectangle, using the following basic command:

```
widgetname create arc x1 y1 x2 y2
```

The *x1*, *y1*, *x2*, and *y2* arguments are for the rectangle that bounds the arc and helps define its shape.

You can specify a number of options, as shown in Table 9.2.

Table 9.2 Arc Options

Option	Usage
-extent *degrees*	The span of the arc, in degrees
-fill *color*	If set, fills arc with given *color*; otherwise, arc is not filled
-outline *color*	If set, outlines arc with given *color*; otherwise, arc is not outlined
-start *degrees*	Controls angle where arc starts, in degrees
-stipple *bitmapname*	Fills arc by using *bitmapname* as a brush pattern
-style *type*	One of arc, chord, or pieslice (the default)
-tags *taglist*	Applies all the tags in *taglist* to the item
-width *outlinewidth*	Controls size of pen used to outline arc

For example, to create an arc, you can use the following command:

```
.can create arc 10 20 100 300 \
    -start 45 -extent 180 \
    -fill maroon -style pieslice
```

PORTABILITY

The way Windows and X draw items such as arcs is slightly different, which means you won't see exactly the same arc on both systems.

Bitmap Drawing Items

A bitmap item has a foreground and background color only. (For color images, use the image drawing item). Table 9.3 lists the available options.

Table 9.3 bitmap Options

Option	Usage
-anchor *position*	One of n, s, e, w, nw, ne, sw, se, or center
-background *color*	Controls background color
-bitmap *bitmapname*	Specifies which bitmap to display
-foreground *color*	Controls foreground color
-tags *taglist*	Applies all the tags in *taglist* to the item

You'll almost always need the -bitmap option. The command to create a bitmap item takes the following format:

```
widgetname create bitmap x y
```

You can use the following example as a guide:

```
.can create bitmap 200 20 -bitmap error
```

See the section on images and bitmaps later in this chapter for more on how to set up a bitmap.

Image Drawing Items

An image can hold a monochrome bitmap or a color image in a number of formats, including GIF and PPM (from the Portable Bitmap, or PBM, suite of image file utilities). Table 9.4 lists the relevant options.

Table 9.4 Image Options

Option	Usage
-anchor *position*	One of n, s, e, w, nw, ne, sw, se or center
-image *imagename*	Names the image to display
-tags *taglist*	Applies all the tags in *taglist* to the item

The command to create an image is almost the same as for a bitmap:

```
widgetname create image x y
```

See the section on images and bitmaps later in this chapter for more on how to set up an image.

Line Drawing Items

Lines are not the simple creatures you're used to, as reflected in the many options in Table 9.5.

Table 9.5 Line Options

Option	Usage
-arrow none	No arrowheads
-arrow first	Arrowhead on first point of line
-arrow last	Arrowhead on last point of line
-arrow both	Arrowhead on both first and last point of line
-arrowshape *shapelist*	List of three coordinates specifies how to draw arrow heads
-capstyle *style*	How to draw ends of line. One of butt, projecting, or round
-fill *color*	Controls line color; defaults to black; no option creates a transparent line
-joinstyle *style*	How to connect line segments, one of bevel, miter, or round
-smooth 1	Draw line as a curve, with a series of Bézier splines
-smooth 0	Draw line as a series of segments
-splinesteps *number*	Uses *number* segments to approximate each spline
-stipple *bitmapname*	Fills line by stippling given bitmap
-tags *taglist*	Applies all the tags in *taglist* to the item

The basic command takes the following format:

```
widgetname create line x1 y1 x2 y2 …
```

One really nice thing that Tk provides is arrowheads on either (or both) ends of the line. For example:

```
.can create line 100 10 100 100 -arrow both
```

You can use a line to go from point A to point B. Or, you can make a polyline, going from point A through point B through point C and so on. Just keep adding coordinates, as shown in the following staircase example:

```
.can create line \
   110 10 \
   110 20 \
   120 20 \
   120 30 \
   130 30 \
   130 40
```

You can convert the lines into splines with the -smooth option:

```
.can create line \
   150 10 \
   200 45 \
   150 195 \
   -smooth 1
```

Oval Drawing Items

The oval drawing item creates an oval or a circle item from a bounding rectangle. You can fill an oval with the -fill option. This, and other oval options appear in Table 9.6.

Table 9.6 Oval Options

Option	Usage
-fill *color*	If set, fills oval with given *color*; otherwise, oval is not filled
-outline *color*	If set, outlines oval with given *color*; otherwise, oval is not outlined
-stipple *bitmapname*	Fills oval by stippling given bitmap
-tags *taglist*	Applies all the tags in *taglist* to the item
-width *outlinewidth*	Controls size of pen used to draw outline

To create an oval, you can use the following command:

```
widgetname create oval x1 y1 x2 y2
```

To try some of the options, you can use the following:

```
.can create oval 160 150 220 250 \
    -fill limegreen \
    -outline limegreen \
    -stipple gray50
```

Note the use of both the fill color and the outline color to get both to appear the same color. Otherwise, you could draw the outline in a different color if you'd like.

NOTE

Polygon Drawing Items

The polygon drawing item allows you to create many-sided figures or a smooth, curved figure (using the polygon vertices as spline control points). Table 9.7 lists the allowed options.

Table 9.7 Polygon Options

Option	Usage
-fill *color*	If set, fills polygon with given *color*; otherwise, polygon is not filled
-outline *color*	If set, outlines polygon with given *color*; otherwise, polygon is not outlined
-smooth 1	Draws each line in the polygon as a curve, with a series of Bézier splines
-smooth 0	Draws each line as a series of segments
-splinesteps *number*	Uses *number* segments to approximate each spline.
-stipple *bitmapname*	Fills polygon by stippling given bitmap
-tags *taglist*	Applies all the tags in *taglist* to the item
-width *outlinewidth*	Controls size of pen used to draw outline

To create a `polygon` drawing item, use the following format:

```
widgetname create polygon x1 y1 x2 y2 ...
```

You can add as many vertices as you'd like, as shown here:

```
.can create polygon \
  220 10 \
  250 10 \
  250 30 \
  210 50 \
  220 80 \
  -fill orange
```

When working with event bindings, all points inside the `polygon`, whether it is filled or not, are considered to be inside the polygon. For `arcs`, `ovals`, and `rectangles`, the item must be filled for all points inside to be considered part of the item.

NOTE

Rectangle Drawing Items

The rectangle drawing item allows you to create, as you'd expect, a rectangle. Table 9.8 lists the relevant options.

Table 9.8 Rectangle Options

Option	**Usage**
-fill *color*	If set, fills rectangle with given *color*; otherwise, rectangle is not filled
-outline *color*	If set, outlines rectangle with given *color*; otherwise, rectangle is not outlined
-stipple *bitmapname*	Fills rectangle by stippling given bitmap
-tags *taglist*	Applies all the tags in *taglist* to the item
-width *outlinewidth*	Controls size of pen used to draw outline

The rectangle command follows the usual form:

```
widgetname create rectangle x1 y1 x2 y2
```

For example:

```
.can create rectangle \
  265 200 300 230
```

Text Drawing Items

The text item exists to place more than a display-only text string into the canvas. You can select text in a text drawing item. In your scripts, you can append, insert, and delete characters. As such, the text drawing item is a lot like the entry widget.

The basic `text` item command is as follows:

```
widgetname create text x y
```

The major options appear in Table 9.9.

Table 9.9 Text Options

Option	Usage
-anchor *position*	One of n, s, e, w, ne, nw, se, sw, or center
-fill *color*	If set, fills text with given *color*; otherwise, the default color is black
-font *fontname*	Names font to use for the text; see Chapter 3 for more on fonts
-justify *justification*	One of left, right, or center
-stipple *bitmapname*	Fills text by stippling given bitmap
-tags *taglist*	Applies all the tags in *taglist* to the item
-text *textstring*	Sets text to *textstring*
-width *linelength*	Controls maximum length of a line of text

You can create a `text` item with the following command:

```
.can create text 150 130 \
   -text "Tk Canvas Widget"
```

Embedded Window Drawing Items

Much like the `text` widget, you can embed any Tk widget inside the `canvas` widget, using the `window` drawing type. Just about every `window` drawing item requires the `-window` option, which lists the name of the widget to embed. The options appear in Table 9.10.

Table 9.10 Window Options

Option	Usage
-anchor *position*	One of n, s, e, w, ne, nw, se, sw, or center
-height *size*	Controls size of window
-tags *taglist*	Applies all the tags in *taglist* to the item
-width *size*	Controls size of window
-window *widgetname*	Embed *widgetname*

The command to embed a window is rather simple:

```
widgetname create window x y
```

In real life, this is a lot more complex, as the short example following shows:

```
button .can.b -text "Push Me" \
  -command { puts ouch }

# Don't pack the widgets you embed.

.can create window 260 185 \
  -window .can.b
```

Follow these rules when creating an embedded window:

- Don't pack the widgets you intend to embed
- Create the widget as a child of the canvas widget

See the section on embedded windows in Chapter 5 for more on the rules for embedding.

The result of all these commands is shown in Figure 9.1.

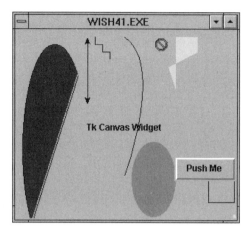

Figure 9.1 The canvas widget in action.

Coordinate Positions for Drawing Items

All of the drawing items require some coordinate arguments to specify where to place the item.

Unlike most windowing systems, all coordinates in the canvas widget are floating-point numbers. As usual, the origin is in the upper-left corner.

N O T E

You can modify a coordinate position with one of the letters Tk accepts for units. Table 9.11 lists the available units.

Table 9.11 Units for Coordinates in the Canvas Widget

Letter	Meaning
m	Millimeters
c	Centimeters
i	Inches
p	Points (used in publishing); one point is 1/72 of an inch.

For example, 1.234p means 1.234 points, and 5.67i means 5.67 in. If you omit a units letter, the units default to pixels (e.g., 7.89). The reason for the units is so that you can create a 2-in. square item on one screen and have it appear as 2 in. on all other systems, too.

WARNING

Graphical windowing systems such as Windows and X are notoriously bad at generating true distances. The problem is in the monitor's screen size. You can, for example, swap a 15-in. monitor for a 17-in. monitor on a PC and not make any software changes. Because of this, Windows or X have no way of knowing how large you monitor's screen is. Without this knowledge, Tk cannot generate a true distance. Thus, don't even pretend that 2.00i will really generate a true two-inch line. Assume the value will be off somewhat.

Scrolling the Canvas Widget

To create a scrolled canvas widget, you follow much the same rules as for the text and listbox widgets, as shown here:

```
canvas .can \
  -width 300 -height 250 \
  -xscrollcommand ".hscr set" \
  -yscrollcommand ".vscr set" \
  -confine false

scrollbar .hscr \
  -command ".can xview" \
  -orient horizontal

scrollbar .vscr -command ".can yview"

# Pack scrollbars first.
pack .vscr -side right -fill y
pack .hscr -side bottom -fill x

pack .can -side left -expand yes -fill both
```

In addition, you can use the -confine option to confine the canvas to the value set with the -scrollregion option. The -scrollregion option contains a list of four coordinates, which identify the left, top, right and bottom edges of the area on the canvas that can appear or be drawn into.

When making a scrolled canvas, set the -confine option to false, and then pack with the -expand yes and -fill both options.

NOTE

Naming Drawing Items

Each drawing item has a number that identifies it. You can use this number to refer to the drawing item for further manipulation. You can also provide a **tag name** for a canvas item. In fact, you can use the same tag name to identify a number of drawing items.

The special tag all, for example, is a special built-in tag name that refers to all of the drawing items.

A special tag named current applies to the top-most item underneath the mouse cursor. Tk automatically updates this special tag when the mouse moves. Most drawing item commands accept either the numerical ID for an item or a tag name. The tag name may refer to one item or many.

For example, to delete a drawing item, or items if a tag name identifies many items, use the delete option. The syntax follows:

```
widgetname delete tag ...
widgetname delete id ...
```

Manipulating Canvas Items

To change a drawing item, you use the itemconfigure option, in one of two forms:

```
widgetname itemconfigure tag options
widgetname itemconfigure id options
```

The *options* are any of the allowed options for each drawing item, as shown in Tables 9.2 and 9.10.

To move an item, you can also use one of two forms of the command:

```
widgetname move tag xoffset yoffset
widgetname move id xoffset yoffset
```

The *xoffset* and *yoffset* values must be valid coordinate amounts.

Transforming Canvas Items

With the `canvas` widget, you can scale, but not rotate, drawing items. To scale, use one of the following forms of the command:

```
widgetname scale tag xorigin yorigin xscale yscale
widgetname scale id xorigin yorigin xscale yscale
```

The *xscale* and *yscale* values contain the scaling factors. A scaling factor of 2.0 generates an item twice the size. A scaling factor of 1.0 generates no scaling. The *xorigin* and *yorigin* values are used for the origin of the scaling operation.

Binding Events to Canvas Drawing Items

Like for the `text` widget, described in Chapter 5, you can `bind` events to items in the `canvas` widget, as shown here:

```
canvas .can -width 300 -height 250
pack .can

.can create text 200 20 \
  -text "Move Me"


# Store initial positions.
.can bind 1 <Button-1> {

  global x y

  set x %x
  set y %y
}


.can bind 1 <B1-Motion> {
```

```
global x y

set newx %x
set newy %y

set distx [expr $newx - $x]
set disty [expr $newy - $y]

.can move 1 $distx $disty

# Store values for next time
set x $newx
set y $newy
}
```

These commands allow you to move a particular item about on the canvas by dragging with the left-most mouse button.

Generating PostScript Output

You can generate PostScript output for all or part of a canvas widget. This is great for printing your drawings. The basic format of the command is:

```
widgetname postscript options
```

Table 9.12 lists the basic options for generating PostScript output.

Table 9.12 Canvas Widget PostScript Options

Option	Usage
-colormode gray	Generate a grayscale image
-colormode color	Generate a color image
-colormode mono	Generate a monochrome image
-file *filename*	Output to a file; command then returns a NULL string
-height *size*	Specify how high an area in the canvas to output

continued

Table 9.12 continued

Option	Usage
-rotate 1	Specifies landscape mode
-rotate 0	Specifies portrait mode, the default
-width *size*	Specify how wide an area in the canvas to output
-x *coord*	Specifies starting X coordinate to output
-y *coord*	Specifies starting Y coordinate to output

Table 9.13 lists the options for controlling the output page.

Table 9.13 Canvas Widget PostScript Output Page Options

Option	Usage
-pageanchor *anchor*	Anchors the canvas output on the printed page
-pageheight *size*	Scales the output to *size* height on the page
-pagewidth *size*	Scales the output to *size* width on the page
-pagex *position*	Controls the positioning point on the page
-pagey *position*	Controls the positioning point on the page

See the online manual for more on the canvas widget.

Images and Bitmaps

Tk supports two types of images, called bitmap and photo. The bitmap type supports only images with a foreground and background color. The photo type supports GIF and PPM color images.

You create both kinds of images with the image create command. The next sections show first how to create bitmaps and then how to create images. After that, you'll find a number of commands for manipulating images.

Image Names

Every image requires a unique name (if you don't provide one, Tk will). To use an existing image, you need to know this name. To create one, you provide the new name. You also need the name to delete it.

Built-In Bitmaps

You can create a bitmap with the image create bitmap command, or you can use one of the built-in bitmaps supplied by Tk. To show all of Tk's built-in bitmaps and their names, you can use the following code:

```
proc bit_frame { widgetname label bitmap } {

    frame $widgetname
    label $widgetname.text -text $label
    label $widgetname.bitmap -bitmap $bitmap

    pack $widgetname.bitmap \
        $widgetname.text -side top

    pack $widgetname -side left
}


bit_frame .error error error
bit_frame .gray25 gray25 gray25
bit_frame .gray50 gray50 gray50
bit_frame .hourglass hourglass hourglass
bit_frame .info info info
bit_frame .questhead questhead questhead
bit_frame .question question question
bit_frame .warning warning warning
```

This leads to a window like that shown in Figure 9.2.

Figure 9.2 Tk's built in bitmaps.

Many widgets accept a -bitmap option with the name of the built-in bitmap to use, or the name of a bitmap file, if the file is in X bitmap format. If you use the -bitmap option, as shown in the preceding Tcl example, the widget displays the bitmap, rather than any text it may hold. You can use the -bitmap option with the button, checkbutton, label, radiobutton, and menubutton widgets; although you should not place a bitmap in a menubutton on the menu bar. You can also use the -bitmap option in menu choices created with the menu add command.

If the built-in bitmaps shown in Figure 9.2 don't appeal, you can create your own. You can either use the -bitmap option with a file name, or you can create a bitmap with the image command and use the -image option. If you use the -bitmap option, you need to follow a special syntax:

```
-bitmap built_in_name
-bitmap @filename
```

If you don't use a built-in bitmap, you must precede the *filename* with an @ character.

Creating Bitmaps from X Bitmap Files

For bitmap images, Tk supports the X Window System's bitmap file format. This format is quite simple in nature and a bitmap file looks like a snippet of C code:

```
#define warning_width 6
#define warning_height 19
static unsigned char warning_bits[] = {
 0x0c, 0x16, 0x2b, 0x15,
 0x2b, 0x15, 0x2b, 0x16,
 0x0a, 0x16, 0x0a, 0x16,
```

```
0x0a, 0x00, 0x00, 0x1e,
0x0a, 0x16, 0x0a};
```

To create a bitmap from a file of this type, you can use the `image create bitmap` command, which takes the following form:

```
image create bitmap name options
```

There are a number of options to control the new bitmap, as shown in Table 9.14.

Table 9.14 Bitmap Creation Options

Option	Usage
-background *color*	Sets image background color
-data *datastring*	Uses data in *datastring*, must be in X bitmap format
-file *filename*	Loads data from file
-foreground *color*	Sets image foreground color
-maskdata *datastring*	Specifies a bitmap to use as a mask; must be in X bitmap format
-maskfile *filename*	Specifies a bitmap to use as a mask; must be a file in X bitmap format

To create a bitmap image from raw bitmap data, you can use the following code:

```
set data "#define peace16_width 16
#define peace16_height 16
static unsigned char peace16_bits[] = {
    0xf0, 0x07, 0xb8, 0x0e,
    0x8c, 0x18, 0x86, 0x30,
    0x83, 0x60, 0x83, 0x60,
    0x81, 0x40, 0x81, 0x40,
    0x41, 0x41, 0x23, 0x62,
    0x13, 0x64, 0x0e, 0x38,
```

```
    0x0c, 0x18, 0x38, 0x0e,
    0xf0, 0x07, 0x00, 0x00};"
# Create bitmap.
image create bitmap peace16 -data $data
```

To then use this bitmap in a widget, such as a `label` widget, you can use the following code:

```
# Use bitmap in widget.
label .bit -image peace16
label .label \
    -text "16-by-16 pixel Peace Sign"
pack .bit .label
```

When you execute the above commands, you'll see a bitmap like the one shown in Figure 9.3.

Figure 9.3 Creating a bitmap label.

Note that we use a `-image` option (not a `-bitmap` option) since we created the bitmap with the `image` command and didn't use a built-in bitmap, like `error`.

To create a bitmap image from an X bitmap file, you can use the following code, which is almost exactly the same, except from the source of the data:

```
# Create bitmap.
image create bitmap peace16 \
    -file "peace16.xbm"

# Use bitmap in widget.
label .bit -image peace16
label .label \
    -text "16-by-16 pixel Peace Sign"
pack .bit .label
```

To make this work, you must have a file with the bitmap data, such as the one following (and in the preceding example, the file must be named **peace16.xbm**):

```
#define peace16_width 16
#define peace16_height 16
static unsigned char peace16_bits[] = {
    0xf0, 0x07, 0xb8, 0x0e,
    0x8c, 0x18, 0x86, 0x30,
    0x83, 0x60, 0x83, 0x60,
    0x81, 0x40, 0x81, 0x40,
    0x41, 0x41, 0x23, 0x62,
    0x13, 0x64, 0x0e, 0x38,
    0x0c, 0x18, 0x38, 0x0e,
    0xf0, 0x07, 0x00, 0x00};
```

The *datastring* specified from the `-data` option and the file specified from the `-file` option must be in the same format.

N O T E

Many of the example bitmaps that come with Tk use a **.bmp** file extension, short for bitmap. The problem is that these Tk bitmap files are really stored in X bitmap format, not the more recognizable Windows BMP format. If you try to use a BMP image in Tk (without custom programming) or treat a Tk **.bmp** file as a BMP image, you'll experience problems due to the differing image file formats.

WARNING

Following Internet convention, I name all my X bitmap files with a **.xbm** extension to avoid confusion.

Creating X Bitmap Files

You can create the files used for Tk bitmaps from the X Window program called **bitmap**. You can also use a number of image file conversion programs, including **PBM** (mentioned more below in the section on PPM images), **ImageMagick** or **xv** programs. These are UNIX utilities. Very few Windows or Macintosh programs create images in X bitmap format, but virtually every Web browser will read them.

Photo Images

Tk calls color images **photo** images. For this type, you can use images in CompuServe GIF format or the PPM from the Portable Bitmap (PBM) suite of image conversion programs. To create such an image, the basic syntax follows:

```
image create photo name options
```

Photo images are stored internally using 24 bits of color per pixel, which can use up a lot of memory. On low-color systems, Tk automatically dithers the images.

Table 9.15 lists the options when create a photo image.

Table 9.15 Photo Image Options

Option	Usage
-data *datastring*	Specifies image data is held in *datastring*
-format *type*	Specifies the image format: gif, ppm, or pgm
-file *filename*	Uses the given *filename* for the image data
-gamma *gammavalue*	Tells the image command to perform gamma correction with the given value, which defaults to 1 (no correction)
-height *size*	Controls the size of the image, in pixels
-palette *colorpalette*	Controls the color palette
-width *size*	Controls the size of the image, in pixels

Creating Images from GIF Files

To create an image from a GIF file named **mryuk.gif**, you can use the following commands:

```
image create photo mryuk -file mryuk.gif
```

You can then display this image in a `label` widget (or any other widget that accepts a `-image` option):

```
label .bit -image mryuk
pack .bit
```

With large images, you'll experience a noticeable delay when executing these commands. Figure 9.4 shows the completed widget.

Figure 9.4 Mr. Yuk in a Tk label widget.

Creating Images from PPM Files

In addition to GIF images, which are very popular for the Windows and Macintosh platforms (and are used heavily in World-Wide Web pages), you can create images from PPM and PGM data files. Both of these formats are internal formats used by the PBM, or portable bitmap, suite of freeware image conversion programs. To convert an image file from one format to another, PBM works by having you convert the image, say, in GIF format, to a PBM internal format, such as PPM, and then converting the data to the desired output format, such as Windows BMP format. The PPM and PGM formats hold the intermediary data.

The reason for this was to avoid having to write a GIF to BMP converter, then a GIF to Macintosh PICT converter, and then a BMP to Macintosh PICT converter, and so on. Instead, each program in the PBM suite converts to and from the PBM internal formats. This allows a very small number of programs to convert data from almost any image file format to any other.

To create an image in one of these formats, you use the same command as before, as shown here:

```
image create photo jah_lion -file jah_lion.ppm

label .ppm -image jah_lion
pack .ppm
```

You can see this Reggae icon in Figure 9.5.

Figure 9.5 Ya, mon, a PPM image in a label widget.

There are two main formats for PPM and PGM images: **raw** and **ASCII**. For the image command, your images must be in PPM and PGM raw data format.

NOTE

Commands on Images

Once a photo image is created, you can use the name of the image as a command, just like for widgets. The photo images support a number of options, including blank, copy, and write.

To blank an image, which makes it transparent, use blank:

imagename blank

To copy parts of an image, use the following:

imagename copy *sourceimagename*

With the `copy` option, you can control what part is copied and where it will appear in the image. Table 9.16. lists some of these options.

Table 9.16 Image Copy Options

Option	Usage
-from *x1 y1 x2 y2*	Copy the given area from the source image
-to *x1 y1 x2 y2*	Place the source data in the given area in the target image
-shrink	Shrink the target image data
-zoom *mag_x mag_y*	Magnify the width by a factor of *mag_x*, height by a factor of *mag_y*
-subsample *x y*	Shrinks image by skipping pixels; only uses every *x*th pixel in *x* direction and *y*th pixel in *y* direction

You can also use the common `configure` option to change values in an image.

You can write out an image with the `write` option:

```
imagename write filename options
```

Displaying Thumbnail Images

To provide a flavor of the `image` command and a number of its options, you can use Tk to create a neat GIF thumbnail image viewer with very little code, from the **picdir.tk** file:

```
# Sample image thumbnail-viewing program.

 #
 # Shrinks image for display
 # in a small button, maintaining
 # aspect ratio.
 #
 # im = image to shrink
```

```
# width = max size of shrunken image.
# height = max size of shrunken image.
#
proc shrink_image { im width height } {

    # Determine proper aspect ratio to get size.
    set w [image width $im]
    set h [image height $im]

    set iw [expr ($w * $height)/$h]
    set ih [expr ($h * $width)/$w]

    # If iw is too big, use ih.
    if { $iw >= $width } {
        set iw $width
    } else {
        set ih $height
    }

    # Create new, blank, small image.
    image create photo $im.small \
      -format gif \
      -width $iw -height $ih

    set samp_x [expr $w/$iw]
    set samp_y [expr $h/$ih]

    $im.small copy $im \
      -subsample $samp_x $samp_y \
      -to 0 0 $iw $ih

    return $im.small
}


#
# Returns 1 if GIF or PPM, 0 otherwise.
# filename = name of file to check.
#
proc identify_file { filename } {
```

```
  set ext [file extension $filename]

  switch $ext {
     .GIF { return 1 }
     .gif { return 1 }
     .PGM { return 1 }
     .pgm { return 1 }
     .PPM { return 1 }
     .ppm { return 1 }
  }

 return 0
}


#
# Creates toplevel window to show image in.
# name = toplevel name
# filename = image to display
#
proc show_image { name filename } {

    image create photo $name.im \
       -file $filename

    toplevel .$name
    button .$name.im \
      -image $name.im \
      -command "destroy .$name"

    pack .$name.im

    wm title .$name $filename
}


 # Initialize
global fcount x y
set fcount 0
set x 50
```

```
set y 50

#
# Displays small image in canvas.
# can = canvas widget
# filename = image to shrink
#
proc disp_file { can filename } {

  global fcount x y

  # Debugging info.
  puts "$filename"

   # Create frame, button and label for file.
  frame $can.$fcount
  label $can.$fcount.tx -text $filename

   # Create image for the file if image file.
  if { [identify_file $filename] == 1 } {

    # Create image.
    image create photo $fcount -file $filename

    # Shrink image.
    set small [shrink_image $fcount 100 60]

    button $can.$fcount.im -image $small \
      -command "show_image $fcount $filename" \
      -relief flat

    # Free memory
    image delete $fcount

  } else {

    # Use question mark bitmap
    button $can.$fcount.im \
      -bitmap question -relief flat
  }
```

```
    pack $can.$fcount.im $can.$fcount.tx -side top

    # Don't pack frame, embed it.

    $can create window $x $y -window $can.$fcount

    set x [expr $x + 110]

    if { $x > 800 } {

       set x 50
       set y [expr $y + 100]
    }

   set fcount [incr fcount]
}


 # Create canvas
canvas .can \
   -xscrollcommand ".hscr set" \
   -yscrollcommand ".vscr set" \
   -confine false

scrollbar .hscr \
   -command ".can xview" \
   -orient horizontal

scrollbar .vscr -command ".can yview"

 # Pack scrollbars first.
pack .vscr -side right -fill y
pack .hscr -side bottom -fill x

pack .can -side left \
   -expand yes -fill both

# Fill in files
set files [glob -nocomplain *]
```

```
if { $files != "" } {

    set sorted [lsort $files]

    foreach filename $sorted {
        disp_file .can $filename
    }

    # Configure scrollbar.
    set w 900
    set h [expr $y+80]
    .can configure \
        -scrollregion "0 0 $w $h"
}


# End of file picdir.tk
```

You can see the output of this script in Figure 9.6.

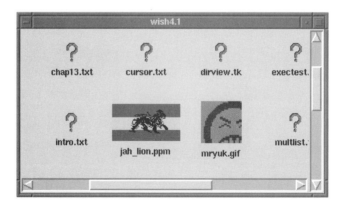

Figure 9.6 The **picdir.tk** script displaying thumbnail images.

The **picdir.tk** script, while small, is rather complex for a Tcl script. The shrink_image procedure creates a small image that is a shrunken version of a larger image passed to it. For best display, it tries to maintain the aspect ratio of the image.

The identify_file procedure is used for a simple test to see whether a file is a supported image file. It might be better to use the catch command described in the last chapter and try to load all files as images. If the `image create photo` command creates an error, then you may want to display an alternative image, such as the question bitmap.

The `show_image` procedure creates a `toplevel` widget and a `button` inside that to display the image. When you click on the **Image** button, the `toplevel` widget gets destroyed.

The `disp_file` procedure is the workhorse command. It displays a file as three widgets embedded inside a `canvas` widget, a `label` to hold the file name, a `button` to display the image, and a `frame` to hold the other two. The `disp_file` procedure embeds this `frame` widget in the `canvas` at a fixed distance so that each `frame` widget is separated.

There are a number of ways in which you may want to extend this script. First, it is terribly slow. Second, when the user clicks on text files, you could call up a scrolled `text` widget in a top-level window to edit the file. Clicking on a directory should scan that directory. You could add a `button` to go up to the parent directory, as well.

Furthermore, small images get tiled inside the display `button`. Images that aren't tiled do not appear as good as we'd all like for thumbnail images. See if you can change this as well by working with the image options.

Deleting Images

You can delete a named image with the `image delete` command:

```
image delete name
```

Images, especially photo images, use a lot of computer memory. You should always delete images you create.

NOTE

Querying Images

You can query the size or type of a given image. You can also check the available types of images and the images already defined.

To get the size of an image, use the `image width` and `image height` commands:

```
set w [image width name]
set h [image height name]
```

To get the type of an image, use the `image type` command:

```
set t [image type name]
```

To get a list of all available image types, use the `image types` command:

```
% image types
photo bitmap
```

Most Tk only systems support `bitmap` and `photo` image types.

Don't confuse the `image type` with the `image types` command.

WARNING

To get a list of all created images, use the `image names` command:

```
image names
```

The Main Window Revisited

Chapter 4 covers style guide issues and common layouts for most application windows. Virtually all graphical applications start with a menu bar at the top, a main area underneath, and a status area at the bottom. With bitmaps under our belt, we can now extend this to include a toolbar underneath the menu bar. Many applications, such as Microsoft Word, sport a bitmap toolbar that gets placed, by default, immediately underneath the menu bar.

Creating Toolbars

In Tk, a toolbar is merely a set of button widgets inside a frame and packed horizontally (with the -side left option). Each button widget provides a shortcut to perform a task from the menus. Thus, creating a toolbar is relatively easy.

Help on Toolbars

In addition to displaying a toolbar, it's also very common for graphical applications to provide short help on items inside the toolbar. Normally, this is done when the mouse enters the button in the toolbar. A short message appears in the status area (usually a label widget) that describes the toolbar button.

To implement short help on the toolbar, we can use the bind command to trap Enter events in each of the buttons. On the Enter event, the bind script should set the -text option for a label widget at the bottom of the window, used for the status area (see chapter 4 for more of a discussion on the status area).

For the help message, you have to remember to keep the text in a global variable, or else the bind script won't be able to access the value. One idea is to use an array variable to store the help messages. As the array element, you can key off the widget name. (Remember that inside the bind command, any instance of a %W is replaced with the widget name, so this name is easy to get.) You could also use double quote, ", substitution rather than curly braces, { and }.

If you use a global array named *help_msg* to store the help messages and a label widget named *.status* that displays the help message, your bind command will look something like the following:

```
bind widgetname <Enter> {
   global help_msg

   .status configure -text $help_msg(%W)
}
```

Summary

This chapter introduced the multi-faceted `canvas` widget. You can use the `canvas` as an area to draw on. In addition, you can place a lot of functionality within a `canvas` widget, turning it into something much more than a mere drawing canvas.

To draw in a `canvas` widget, you need to create drawing items, such as `arcs`, `rectangles`, and embedded `windows`. You can generate PostScript output from a `canvas` widget with the `postscript` option.

Tk provides a number of built-in bitmaps. You can also create your own from data stored in X bitmap format, using the `image create bitmap` command. You can create color images out of GIF or PPM data using the `image create photo` command. You can use monochrome bitmaps or color images inside a toolbar in your programs.

Tcl/Tk Commands Introduced in this Chapter

```
canvas
image
```

CHAPTER 10

Launching Applications from Tcl

This chapter covers:

- The exec command
- Tricks of combining eval with exec
- Redirecting input and output in commands
- Pipes
- Executing Tcl scripts from within Tcl
- Executing scripts after a time-out

Executing Commands

Tcl is a scripting language, and launching applications from within scripts is a very common task. Luckily, Tcl provides a number of handy utilities to help.

The primary means to launch applications from within Tcl is the exec command, which uses the following basic syntax:

```
exec command arguments
```

The *command* executed must be a valid command for your system. Any *arguments* will be passed on to the *command*. If you end the arguments with an ampersand, &, the *command* will get executed in the background.

UNIX and Windows support a radically different set of commands, which means that cross-platform scripts are tough to create if you use exec.

PORTABILITY

Tricks of Combining Eval with Exec

One very common problem with the exec command is that it may interpret its arguments differently than you intend. On a UNIX system (the concepts are the same under Windows, you'll just use different commands), the following Tcl command probably won't do what you expect:

```
set command {date "+%d %B, %y"}
exec $command
```

From your knowledge of the Tcl interpreter, the preceding command will try to execute a UNIX command by the name of date +%d %B, %y (note the embedded spaces). The real intention is to execute a command called **date** (the UNIX date acts differently than the DOS one, by the way) with +%d %B, %y as its arguments. To separate the command name from the arguments in a Tcl variable, you can use something more like the following commands:

```
set command {date "+%d %B, %y"}
eval exec $command
```

The use of eval allows for the variable *command* to be expanded to its component parts.

While the preceding example may seem contrived, many Tcl scripts will need to execute programs and pass arguments to those programs. To deal with all the associated problems of separating the arguments from the command and yet passing the whole command, arguments and all, in a variable to the exec command, you can use the following procedure to execute commands from Tcl:

```
proc exec_cmd { command } {

    # Check if command is a built-in procedure.
    set cmd [info commands $command]
```

```
# Now, check if cmd is a NULL string.
set length [string length $cmd]

if { $length > 0 } {
        # Execute Tcl procedure.
        eval $command
} else {
        # Execute command
        eval exec $command
}

}
```

The exec_cmd procedure first checks if the command is a Tcl procedure. If so, a simple use of eval will execute that command. If not, then exec_cmd passes command to the operating system with the eval exec $command statement.

On Windows 3.1, you'll likely see some special effects such as screen flashing when you run the exec_cmd procedure. Windows NT systems are more well-behaved when executing subprocesses.

WINDOWS

Standard Input, Output, and Error

Associated with your commands, UNIX includes the idea that all programs have at least three open files: stdin (input), stdout (output), and stderr (error output). At a UNIX terminal (or terminal window), stdin normally comes from your keyboard. Data you enter at the keyboard gets sent to the application as if it came from the file ID of stdin. (UNIX treats almost everything as a file.) The stdout and stderr file IDs are similarly tied to the terminal's display. Data output via stdout or stderr is sent to the terminal. For example, the Tcl puts command normally sends its output to stdout.

Error messages get sent to stderr, while normal output goes to stdout. This allows you to redirect the output of a command to a file while still seeing error messages on your screen.

N O T E

Redirecting Input and Output in Commands

Like the UNIX command line (and to a limited extent, the DOS command line), Tcl allows you to redirect the input and output for programs launched via the exec command.

Table 10.1 lists the various ways you can redirect input and output with exec.

Table 10.1 Redirecting Input and Output with exec

Syntax	Meaning
|	Output (stdout) of one command is piped to next
|&	Output (stdout and stderr) of one command is piped to next
< *filename*	*Filename* is read in and passed as the standard input to command
<@ *fileid*	Data from *fileid* is read in and passed as the standard input to command
<< *data*	The *data* is passed to the first command as its standard input
> *filename*	Output from last command gets sent to *filename*, not to screen
>> *filename*	Standard error output from last command gets appended to *filename*
>@ *fileid*	Output from last command gets sent to opened *fileid*, not to screen
>& *filename*	Both standard error and output from last command get sent to *filename*, not to screen
>>& *filename*	Both standard error and output from last command get appended to *filename*
>&@ *fileid*	Both standard error and output from last command get sent to opened *fileid*, not to screen
2> *filename*	Standard error output from last command gets sent to *filename*, not to screen

2>> *filename*	Standard error output from last command gets appended to *filename*
2>@ *fileid*	Standard error from last command gets sent to opened *fileid*, not to screen

PORTABILITY

While it is nice to be able to redirect the output and input of commands, you'll generally only use this capability on UNIX, where such commands are commonplace. On Windows or the Macintosh, you'll find fewer commands that print data to a Console window. In fact, Tcl on Windows has to go so far as to create its own console window for stdin, stdout and stderr, because Windows doesn't really have a command line as UNIX does.

To make your applications portable, you'll want to use I/O redirection sparingly.

Pipes

UNIX and DOS use the term **pipe** to describe sending the output of one command to the input of the next command in a sequence. For example, on UNIX, you can get a count of the number of files in a directory with the following compound command:

```
ls -1 | wc -l
```

This command line invokes two UNIX commands: **ls**, which lists the files in a directory, and **wc**, which is short for *word count*. The pipe symbol, |, causes the output of the **ls** command to get sent as the input to the **wc** command. The **ls** command gets a -1 as its argument, which specifies to list all the file names one per line. The -l argument to the **wc** command, in turn, tells **wc** to report only a line count, not character and word counts. The **wc** command gets the output of the **ls** command and counts the number of lines in that output.

Pipes allow you to combine together a number of UNIX commands to create a new command. In addition, you can use pipes inside a Tcl script to allow your script to capture the output of a command, or control the data sent to it as input.

To set up a pipe in Tcl, use the open command and a filename that starts with | and ends with the command to execute. For example:

```
set fileid [open "|ls" r]
```

The "filename" passed to open is really a command name. The preceding Tcl commands set up the *fileid* variable to reference a piped command. Any output from that command will get written to *fileid*.

To continue the example, you can read all the data associated with a piped command using the following procedure:

```
proc read_pipe { command } {

    # Initialize.
    set data ""

    # Start piped command.
    set fileid [open $command r]

    if { $fileid != "" } {

        # Read data.
        set data [read $fileid]

        close $fileid
    }

    return $data
}
```

On UNIX, you can test the read_pipe procedure with the following command:

```
read_pipe "|ls"
```

You should see a listing of all the files in the current directory. For example:

```
arsearch.tcl
canvas.tk
hello.tk
jah_lion.ppm
mryuk.gif
multlist.tk
newtext.tk
peace16.xbm
picdir.tk
pr_argv.tcl
```

On Windows, try this command:

```
read_pipe "|DIR"
```

You'll see slightly different output, such as:

```
Directory of C:\TCL\BIN

.            <DIR>           10-14-95    1:52p
..           <DIR>           10-14-95    1:52p
CW3215   DLL       176,128 08-29-95    4:52a
TCL75    DLL       143,360 10-05-95    1:05p
TK41     DLL       462,848 10-06-95   10:08a
WISH41   EXE        16,384 10-06-95   10:08a
TCL1675  DLL         1,382 10-05-95    1:05p
DIRVIEW  TK          3,749 10-09-95   11:26a
MULTLIST TK          1,659 10-09-95   10:58a
TMP2     BAT            18 10-20-95    6:43p
        10 file(s)      805,528 bytes
                     39,026,688 bytes free
```

You can also open pipes for writing or for reading and writing. This is useful if you want to create an application that presents a graphical user interface on an older command-line program. See the online documentation on exec and open for more on pipes.

Executing Tcl Scripts from within Tcl

In addition to exec and open, you can use the source command to execute files of Tcl scripts. The source command loads in a Tcl file and executes all the commands in it, using the following syntax:

```
source filename
```

With the open, gets, close, and exec commands, you could easily build your own version of the source command. See Chapter 6 for more on these file commands.

Many friendly applications provide a means for users to customize the applications and store these customizations so that every time the programs run, the user's customizations take effect. In Tcl, I've found the source command most useful for this purpose. Since Tcl works quite well at executing Tcl commands, it makes sense to leave any customization file in Tcl format as well. This means you won't have to write a parser for a customization file. Instead, you just source it in.

It's very common to combine the catch command, described in Chapter 8, with source. The reason is so that errors in the file "sourced in" don't stop your Tcl script.

Executing Scripts After a Time-Out

You can use the after command to execute Tcl scripts, including the exec command, after a time-out. You'll find this handy for commands that should execute on a given time cycle, such as a clock display (run the command once a minute) or animation (draw each frame after a very short but even time period) and so on.

The after command requires the following syntax:

```
after milliseconds tcl_script
```

The after command returns immediately. Sometime later, at least after the given number of *milliseconds*, the *tcl_script* gets executed. Don't assume the time delays will be exact. Factors such as system load or simply poor resolution system clocks can alter the actual amount of time delayed.

The *tcl_script* gets executed once, after the given time delay. This means that if you want to set up a periodic task, you need to call after again in your *tcl_script*.

For example, if you have a time-consuming task, you may want to display a message, such as *Working...*, to let the user know your program hasn't locked up. To continue showing that the program hasn't locked up, you may want to flash this message or in some way alter its appearance every so often. This will tell the user that the program is indeed continuing. One way to do this, using the after command, is shown here:

```
proc disp_working { widget show_text } {

    if { $show_text > 0 } {
        $widget configure -fg lightgray

        set show_text 0
    } else {
        $widget configure -fg black

        set show_text 1
    }

    # Set up command to run again.
    after 400 "disp_working $widget $show_text"
}

label .label -bg lightgray \
    -text "Working..."
pack .label

disp_working .label 0
```

This code makes the foreground and background colors the same on every other iteration. By doing this, the *Working...* message will appear to flash on and off.

You can look up more options for the `after` command in the online documentation.

Summary

The exec command allows you to execute programs on your system. These programs are likely to be very different between Windows and UNIX, which makes writing portable Tcl scripts with exec difficult.

You can combine the `eval` command with exec to break up a variable into its component parts and create a better command line for `exec`.

You can create a pipe to an application if you pass a pseudo filename of *|command* to the open command.

The `source` command allows you to execute Tcl script files from within Tcl.

The `after` command allows you to run a Tcl script after a given time-out. This time-out only occurs once. So, to set up a periodic command, you must call `after` in your Tcl script each time it gets invoked.

Tcl/Tk Commands Introduced in this Chapter

```
after
exec
source
```

## CHAPTER 11

Embedding Tcl in Your Applications

This chapter covers:

- Calling Tcl from C
- Creating your own Tcl interpreter
- Compiling and linking
- Adding Tk into your interpreter

Calling Tcl from C

Tcl was originally created to allow you to embed the interpreter within your C programs. You can use Tcl as an application language, much as you would a macro language for a spreadsheet program. To make such an application language work, you'll need to add in your application-specific commands to the base set provided by Tcl. That's the topic of Chapter 12. But first, you must embed the Tcl interpreter within your application, the topic of this chapter.

Tcl is really a library of C functions. Tk is another library. You normally don't notice this because the **wish** and **tclsh** programs obscure this fact. These programs are merely very simple routines linked with the Tcl and Tk libraries.

This chapter covers a lot of C and C++ programming issues necessary to add new commands in C to the set provided by Tcl. If you're not familiar with C programming, or don't need to add new commands, you can skip ahead to Chapter 13, which covers advanced application issues.

When to Code in Tcl and When to Code in C

In your applications, every part you can write in Tcl will be easier to modify, but Tcl code does have its limitations, such as the fact that Tcl is an interpreted language, leading to inherent performance problems. The right mix of Tcl and C code is up to you—do what makes sense for your applications.

There's a lot of power in the Tcl interpreter, power you can harness in your applications.

The Simplest Tcl Interpreter

From a Tcl-centric point of view, an interpreter contains three parts:

- Interpreter initialization
- Feeding input to the interpreter, usually in some form of command loop
- Cleaning up before termination

Of course, if you embed Tcl within your application, a number of parts are missing—your entire application, for one! You'll need to mesh the Tcl calls with your application calls.

For simple Tcl interpreters, all the initialization you need to do is to call Tcl_CreateInterp:

```
Tcl_Interp* Tcl_CreateInterp()
```

Tcl_CreateInterp allocates memory for a Tcl_Interp structure, which holds all the information about the current state of the Tcl interpreter.

After calling Tcl_CreateInterp, you'll need to register any new commands you create. See Chapter 12 for more on this. For now, though, all you need to do is call Tcl_CreateInterp.

Tcl_CreateInterp returns a newly allocated Tcl_Interp structure, which has only a few fields, as shown here:

```
typedef struct Tcl_Interp{
    char *result;
    void (*freeProc) (char *blockPtr);
    int errorLine;
} Tcl_Interp;
```

Tcl_CreateInterp actually creates a much larger structure that shadows the Tcl_Interp structure used in your code. This structure is private to the Tcl library. The important point about the Tcl_Interp structure is that just about every Tcl function requires a pointer to the structure returned by Tcl_CreateInterp.

Once you've initialized the Tcl interpreter, you can start feeding commands. The Tcl_EvalFile function reads in a file and executes the Tcl commands in the file. Tcl_EvalFile takes the following parameters:

```
int Tcl_EvalFile(Tcl_Interp* interp,
    char* filename)
```

Tcl_EvalFile returns an integer code, one of the error codes listed in Table 11.1.

Table 11.1 Tcl Error Codes

Code	Meaning
TCL_ERROR	An error occurred
TCL_OK	Everything is hunky-dory
TCL_RETURN	A request that the current procedure return
TCL_BREAK	A request to exit the innermost loop
TCL_CONTINUE	A request to jump to the top of the innermost loop

Tcl_EvalFile should return only TCL_ERROR or TCL_OK. The other values appear when you're executed one command at a time with Tcl_Eval, as covered later in this chapter.

These codes are the same as the ones in Table 8.1 in Chapter 8, except that the values are C language defines rather than Tcl strings.

N O T E

If you get an error from Tcl_EvalFile, the result field in the Tcl_Interp structure will contain an error message in string format.

Don't free the result string. If you want to keep it around, make a copy. The Tcl interpreter owns the memory for this string and may overwrite the contents at any time.

N O T E

If Tcl_EvalFile returns TCL_OK, then the result field will hold the returned data from the script (usually passed by the Tcl return command).

To evaluate a single Tcl command instead of a whole file, use the Tcl_Eval function, which takes the following parameters:

```
int Tcl_Eval(Tcl_Interp* interp,
    char* command)
```

You must pass a writable variable for the *command*. A literal string won't work. Tcl writes into this command, although it usually restores any changes when complete. Avoid the following code:

WARNING

```
status = Tcl_Eval(interp, "puts ouch"); /* Wrong */
```

Instead, use something like the following:

```
char  command[100];

strcpy(command, "puts ouch");
status = Tcl_Eval(interp, command);
```

In addition to `Tcl_Eval`, you can use `Tcl_VarEval` to build up a command from a variable number of arguments, which uses the following syntax:

```
int Tcl_VarEval(Tcl_Interp* interp,
    char* string,
    ...
    NULL)
```

Since `Tcl_VarEval` takes a variable number of arguments, you must provide a sentinel value to tell the function where the end of the list lies. This sentinel value is `NULL`, as shown here:

```
status = Tcl_VarEval(interp,
    "puts",
    "ouch",
    NULL);
```

You can use literal strings with `Tcl_VarEval`, because it creates a new command string from the full set of arguments. But don't forget the `NULL` sentinel value.

When you're done with your Tcl interpreter, free it with the `Tcl_DeleteInterp` function:

```
void Tcl_DeleteInterp(Tcl_Interp* interp)
```

You'll usually call `Tcl_DeleteInterp` at the end of your program.

UNIX systems should free all memory allocated by your program on exit, making `Tcl_DeleteInterp` redundant. Windows 3.1, on the other hand, does not free all memory on exit. Therefore, it's important to call `Tcl_DeleteInterp` before exiting your application.

All Tcl definitions are found in the include file **tcl.h**, which should be installed with your copy of the Tcl libraries.

Pulling this all together, one of the simplest Tcl interpreters in a C program follows:

```
/*
 tclint.c, a simple Tcl interpreter.
*/

#include <stdio.h>
#include <stdlib.h>
#include <tcl.h>

int main(int argc, char** argv)

{    /* main */
    Tcl_Interp* interp;
    int         status = TCL_OK;


    interp = Tcl_CreateInterp();

    if (argc > 1) {
        status = Tcl_EvalFile(interp, argv[1]);

        /* Print result string. */
        if (interp->result != NULL) {

            printf("TCL: [%s]\n", interp->result);
        }

    }

    /* Free memory for interpreter. */
    Tcl_DeleteInterp(interp);

    /* Report errors. */
    if (status != TCL_OK) {

        printf("TCL Error: %d\n", status);
        exit(1);
```

```
    }

    exit(0);

}    /* main */
```

```
/* end of file tclint.c */
```

Compiling and Linking Your New Interpreter

How you compile and link depends on which system you use.

On UNIX, you need to link in the Tcl and **m** (math) libraries. The actual library name for the Tcl library may vary on your system (e.g., **libtcl7.5.a**).

You may also need options for the C compiler to tell it where the Tcl include files and libraries are located. If your Tcl include files are located in **/usr/local/tcl/include**, for example, you'll need the following command:

```
cc -o tclint -I/usr/local/tcl/include \
    tclint.c -ltcl7.5 -lm
```

If your Tcl libraries are also located in a nonstandard directory, such as **/usr/local/tcl/lib**, then you'll need the following command to compile and link the example interpreter program:

```
cc -o tclint -I/usr/local/tcl/include \
    tclint.c -L/usr/local/tcl/lib -ltcl7.5 -lm
```

On Windows, your setup will vary depending on the compiler and integrated environment you use. Regardless of the compiler, you need to build a Win32 application and need to link in the Tcl library, which is usually named something like **TCL75.LIB**.

If you use the integrated environment that comes with Microsoft's Visual C++, you need to specify the proper options, include files, and libraries. The Tcl include files will, by default, appear in **C:\TCL\INCLUDE**.

Running the Example Interpreter

Our simple Tcl interpreter needs a script file to execute. You can use the following short script or create your own:

```
# Test of our simple Tcl interpreter.
puts "Inside Tcl interprter."

set var 55
set var2 [expr $var + 83]
puts "var2 holds $var2"

# Data to pass back to program
return "Hello out there"

# end of file simple.tcl
```

When you run this new interpreter with the preceding Tcl script file, you should see output such as the following:

```
Inside Tcl interprter.
var2 holds 138
TCL: [Hello out there]
```

The third line lists the data from the result field of the Tcl_Interp structure.

You cannot run the **tclint.c** interpreter on Windows 3.1, as the DOS shell cannot execute Win32s applications (you must execute these programs fully within the Windows environment). But on Windows NT, with its enhanced DOS Command Prompt, you can run the **tclint.c** interpreter.

WINDOWS

Creating More Complex Applications

The **wish** and **tclsh** interpreters do a lot more than our simple Tcl interpreter in **tclint.c**. Because of this, you may want to take advantage of the main functions inside the Tcl and Tk libraries, called Tcl_Main and Tk_Main, respectively. These main functions set up all sorts of Tcl commands, such as the unknown procedure, from a Tcl library directory. In addition, the values of argc and argv get placed in Tcl global variables, along with all the initialization needed—it is quite extensive for Tk especially.

To take advantage of all this, you don't call Tcl_CreateInterp from your main function. Instead, you call Tcl_Main for Tcl-only applications and Tk_Main for Tk applications (see the section on Tk later in this chapter). With both of these functions, you pass in an application initialization function to call, usually a function called Tcl_AppInit.

The Tcl_Main and Tk_Main functions call Tcl_AppInit (or whatever function you pass in) just before entering the command loop. Inside your Tcl_AppInit function, you can initialize any commands you create (see Chapter 12 for more on this topic) and set up any data necessary for your program.

The basic format for Tcl_AppInit follows:

```
int Tcl_AppInit(Tcl_Interp* interp)
{

    /* Insert your code here... */

    return TCL_OK;
}
```

Usually, you'll want to invoke a function called Tcl_Init from within your Tcl_AppInit function, as shown here:

```
#include <tcl.h>

int Tcl_AppInit(Tcl_Interp* interp)
{
    int    status;

    status = Tcl_Init(interp);

    if (status != TCL_OK) {
        return TCL_ERROR;
    }

    /* Insert your code here... */
```

```
    return TCL_OK;
}

        /* From tclAppInit.c */
int
main(int argc, char** argv)
{
    Tcl_Main(argc, argv, Tcl_AppInit);
    return 0;
}

/* end of file tclapp.c */
```

The Tcl_Init function sets up the unknown procedure and something called **auto-loading**. See the online manual information on Tcl_Init for more on this subject.

For Tcl_Main, pass in the command line, in the form of argc and argv. You also need to pass a function to execute, normally Tcl_AppInit.

Adding in Tk into Your Programs

The Tk add-on to Tcl weighs in much larger, code-wise, than Tcl itself, because graphical interfaces require a lot more code than the very simple Tcl language. If you use the Tcl_AppInit method described earlier, all you need to do is call Tk_Main instead of Tcl_Main (as called in the code in **tclint.c**), and link with both the Tk and Tcl libraries. You may need other libraries on your system.

To start up Tk functions, your Tcl_AppInit function should call Tk_Init as well as Tcl_Init. You can use the example file, **tkapp.c**, for the minimalist C program with Tk functionality. The code follows:

```
/*
 tkapp.c, Test of Tcl_AppInit().
*/
```

```c
#include <stdio.h>
#include <stdlib.h>
#include <tcl.h>
#include <tk.h>
```

```c
int Tcl_AppInit(Tcl_Interp* interp)
{
    int     status;

    status = Tcl_Init(interp);

    if (status != TCL_OK) {
        return TCL_ERROR;
    }

    /* Initialize Tk values. */
    status = Tk_Init(interp);

    if (status != TCL_OK) {
        return TCL_ERROR;
    }

    /* Insert your code here... */

    return TCL_OK;
}

        /* From tclAppInit.c */
int
main(int argc, char** argv)
{
    Tk_Main(argc, argv, Tcl_AppInit);
    return 0;
}

/* end of file tkapp.c */
```

With the preceding code, you effectively get the **wish** interpreter built into your program. Of course, you'll probably want to customize your program.

Linking with Tk

You can link the **tkapp.c** program in much the same way as the **tclint.c** program, only you now need the Tk library as well.

UNIX

On UNIX, you'll need the Tcl, Tk, X11 (X Window System) and math (**m**) libraries. You can use a command like the following to compile and link the **tkapp.c** program:

```
cc -o tkapp tkapp.c -ltk4.1 -ltcl7.5 -lX11 -lm
```

You may need special options to tell the compiler and linker where your include and library files reside, as with the preceding Tcl example (**tclint.c**). On a system such as Linux, for example, you may require options for the libraries and include files. In addition, you may need to link in specific versions of libraries, such as tcl7.5 and tk4.1, as shown here:

```
cc -o tkapp -I/usr/local/tcl/include \
  tkapp.c -L/usr/local/tcl/lib -ltk4.1 \
  -ltcl7.5 -L/usr/X11R6/lib -lX11 -lm
```

WINDOWS

Win32 applications typically define a WinMain function instead of a main function (although this is not required) as the program's entry point, as shown here:

```
int APIENTRY
WinMain(hInstance, hPrevInstance, lpszCmdLine, nCmdShow)
    HINSTANCE hInstance;
    HINSTANCE hPrevInstance;
    LPSTR lpszCmdLine;
    int nCmdShow;
{
    /* Insert your code here. */

}
```

On Windows, you'll need to link with the Tcl and Tk libraries, usually **TCL75.LIB** and **TK41.LIB**, and you'll need to have the corresponding Tcl and Tk Dynamic Link Libraries (DLLs) in your path, or your new program will fail.

PORTABILITY

The difference between main and WinMain creates a problem if you're trying to write cross-platform applications. Luckily, the difference in the code is not that great.

The preceding example isn't exactly like **wish** on Windows. On Windows, **wish** creates an extra window called *Console* for your input. This makes **wish** act more like UNIX, where terminal windows are still the norm. If you embed Tcl and Tk in your applications, it's not likely you'll need such a Console window, as this goes against the Windows interface style guidelines. Look in the Windows source code on the CD-ROM for more Windows differences.

Running the tkapp Program with Tk

Try running the new Tcl interpreter with the **hello.tk** script file from Chapter 1, or with any script file you want. The scripts should execute much like they do for **wish**.

Summary

This chapter introduced the C language functions you need to embed Tcl within your application.

You can create a Tcl interpreter with Tcl_CreateInterp. The returned data value, a pointer to a Tcl_Interp structure, will be used in just about every Tcl function call.

The Tcl_EvalFile function executes a script file of Tcl commands. Tcl_Eval evaluates a single command, as does Tcl_VarEval, which builds up the command from a list of text strings.

In most of your applications, the main work to initialize your commands should be done within a Tcl_AppInit function. You can redefine this function to set up any Tcl commands you need and perform any other initialization you feel appropriate.

In Chapter 12, you'll extend your Tcl interpreter with new commands. You'll find this essential for virtually all applications.

334

Tcl and Tk Library Functions Introduced in this Chapter

```
Tcl_AppInit
Tcl_Main
Tcl_Init
Tcl_CreateInterp
Tcl_DeleteInterp
Tcl_Eval
Tcl_EvalFile
Tcl_VarEval
Tk_Main
```

Extending Tcl

This chapter covers:

- Making new Tcl commands in C
- Returning data and error messages
- Evaluating arguments and handling string data
- Registering your new commands

Making New Commands

You can write new procedures entirely in Tcl, using the `proc` command. But if you need to add something beyond the capabilities of Tcl and Tk, you're out of luck, unless you start writing commands in C. This chapter covers how to create new commands in the form of C language functions that extend the base Tcl language into new areas—whatever areas you desire.

You'll find extending Tcl essential if you try to embed Tcl within an application. In most cases, the application already provides some significant functions. You can then use Tcl commands to provide user access to those functions.

The best plan is to extend Tcl by adding primitive operations. Each primitive operation should become a new Tcl command. Combine these primitive operations with Tcl procedures, not C code. By taking this approach, you'll find that your resulting code becomes reusable in ways you never imagined, and you won't be locked into a single method of execution.

Your C functions also need to add in the application glue code to combine your application with Tcl. For example, if you create a spreadsheet program, you'll need to add Tcl commands to access cells in a spreadsheet. You'll likely add a set of new math functions. If you have a factory control application, you might want to add Tcl commands to turn on and off factory devices.

This chapter covers how to create new Tcl commands in C and goes over a number of Tcl utility functions to aid in making your commands.

Creating Your New Tcl Commands

All commands in Tcl are implemented as C functions. All these functions take the following parameters, as defined in the Tcl_CmdProc data type:

```
typedef int Tcl_CmdProc(
    ClientData clientData,
    Tcl_Interp *interp,
    int argc,
    char *argv[]);
```

Much like the traditional main function, *argv* holds all the arguments to the command and *argc* contains a count of the number of values in *argv*.

The *argv* value includes the command name. This allows you to have multiple Tcl commands share the same C function if you wish.

N O T E

For example, you can use the following as a template for your own commands:

```
int MyCommand(
    ClientData client_data,
    Tcl_Interp* interp,
    int argc,
    char *argv[])
```

```
{

    /* Your code goes here... */

    return TCL_OK;

}
```

Your function can do whatever it wants. It must, however, return a code, as listed in Table 12.1.

Table 12.1 Tcl Error Codes for your Command Functions

Code	Meaning
TCL_ERROR	An error occurred
TCL_OK	Everything is hunky-dory
TCL_RETURN	A request that the current procedure return
TCL_BREAK	A request to exit the innermost loop
TCL_CONTINUE	A request to jump to the top of the innermost loop

In most cases, the value returned will be TCL_OK or TCL_ERROR. In addition to the returned code, each Tcl function must return data in the result field of the Tcl_Interp structure.

Returning a Result

Each Tcl command needs to return some value in the result field of the Tcl_Interp structure. On a successful execution, the value stored should be whatever data your command intends to return. On errors, the value should be an error message. When placing data in the result field, though, you must follow the memory management conventions the Tcl interpreter expects.

To store a result, you can use the Tcl_SetResult function, but you will be responsible for managing the memory yourself. A far easier method, and less prone to errors, is to call Tcl_ResetResult and then Tcl_AppendResult.

Tcl_ResetResult resets the result value and takes the following parameter:

```
Tcl_ResetResult(Tcl_Interp* interp)
```

Don't call this routine if you don't want to destroy any previous result data. In your Tcl commands, chances are you do want to reset the result string. Then you can append new strings onto the result by calling Tcl_AppendResult, which takes the following parameters:

```
Tcl_AppendResult(Tcl_Interp* interp,
    char* string,
    ...
    (char *) NULL)
```

Like Tcl_VarEval shown in Chapter 11, Tcl_AppendResult takes a variable number of parameters. You can append more than one string to the result. You must, however, end the input with NULL, the sentinel value that tells Tcl_AppendResult the input is complete.

For example, we can create a simple Tcl command to reverse two arguments passed to it. A trial run of this command is:

```
% reverse a b
b a
% reverse [expr 10+1] 12
12 11
% reverse a
ERROR: reverse requires two arguments.
```

To implement this new reverse command, the C code needs to check the number of arguments and generate an error. If enough arguments are provided, then the first and second arguments should be reversed and placed in the result. The initial code for this command follows:

```
/*
 revcmd.c
 Tcl sample command to
```

```
 reverse two arguments.
*/

#include <tcl.h>

int RevCommand(
  ClientData client_data,
  Tcl_Interp* interp,
  int argc,
  char *argv[])

{    /* RevCommand */

      /* Reset result data. */
      Tcl_ResetResult(interp);

      /* Check number of arguments. */
      if (argc < 3) {
            Tcl_AppendResult(interp,
                  "ERROR: reverse requires two arguments.",
                  (char*) NULL); /* Sentinel. */

            return TCL_ERROR;
      }

      /* Reverse arguments. */
      Tcl_AppendResult(interp,
            argv[2], " ", argv[1],
            (char*) NULL); /* Sentinel. */

      return TCL_OK;

}    /* RevCommand */

/* end of file revcmd.c */
```

While this command returns an error code if it detects problems, it does not
return any special error code information for use by the Tcl interpreter.

Returning an Error

When you function returns TCL_ERROR, you can also add in additional information with the Tcl_SetErrorCode function:

```
Tcl_SetErrorCode(Tcl_Interp* interp,
    char* info,
    ...
    (char *) NULL)
```

The values you pass are the ones listed in Table 8.2 in Chapter 8.

You can also call Tcl_AddErrorInfo with stack trace information if you want. See the online documentation for more on this.

Accessing Tcl Variables in Your Commands

One of the key tasks you'll need to do in your commands is access Tcl variables. To access the value of a variable, call Tcl_GetVar:

```
char* Tcl_GetVar(Tcl_Interp* interp,
    char* varname,
    int flags)
```

The flags can be any of the bitmasks listed in Table 12.2. You can "or" together one or more of these masks.

Table 12.2 Bitmasks for Tcl_GetVar and Tcl_SetVar

Mask	Meaning
TCL_GLOBAL_ONLY	Look up the value only as a global variable
TCL_LEAVE_ERR_MSG	If an error occurs, a message is placed in interp->result
TCL_APPEND_VALUE	For Tcl_SetVar, appends value to existing value.
TCL_LIST_ELEMENT	For Tcl_SetVar, converts data to list element before writing

To set a variable value, call `Tcl_SetVar`:

```
char* Tcl_SetVar(Tcl_Interp* interp,
    char* varname,
    char* data,
    int flags)
```

In addition to `Tcl_GetVar` and `Tcl_SetVar`, there are a few other routines you can use. Look up `Tcl_GetVar2` and `Tcl_SetVar2`, for array variables, in the online documentation.

Allocating Text Strings

Since everything in Tcl is text, you'll find you need to allocate text strings. Tcl's C library comes with a number of routines for creating, copying, and appending dynamically allocated text strings.

For this task, Tcl uses a data type called `Tcl_DString`, short for dynamically allocated string. Inside this structure, Tcl takes care of all the memory management. This is very handy because Tcl strings tend to get very long (and you'll use many such strings).

When first declaring a `Tcl_DString`, you need to call `Tcl_DStringInit` to initialize all the data in the structure:

```
Tcl_DStringInit(Tcl_DString* ds)
```

To append data to the string, call `Tcl_DStringAppend`:

```
char* Tcl_DStringAppend(Tcl_DString* ds,
    char* string,
    int length)
```

To extract out the value, call `Tcl_DStringValue`:

```
char* Tcl_DStringValue(Tcl_DString* ds)
```

Note that `Tcl_DStringValue` returns a pointer to the data. Don't write to this data directly, call `Tcl_DStringAppend` instead.

To get the length of a dynamic string, call `Tcl_DStringLength`:

```
int Tcl_DStringLength(Tcl_DString* ds)
```

When you're done with a dynamic string, call `Tcl_DStringFree` to free any allocated memory:

```
Tcl_DStringFree(Tcl_DString* ds)
```

Converting Strings

Tcl provides a number of handy routines for converting string data to and from numeric data. `Tcl_GetInt` converts a string to an integer:

```
int Tcl_GetInt(Tcl_Interp* interp,
    char* string,
    int* value)
```

If an error occurs, `Tcl_GetInt` returns `TCL_ERROR` and stores an error message on `interp->result`. Otherwise, `Tcl_GetInt` returns `TCL_OK`. The converted value is returned in *value*.

`Tcl_GetDouble` and `Tcl_GetBoolean` act similarly:

```
int Tcl_GetDouble(Tcl_Interp* interp,
    char* string,
    double* value)
```

```
int Tcl_GetBoolean(Tcl_Interp* interp,
    char* string,
    int* value)
```

Evaluating Arguments

In addition to working with text strings, you may need to evaluate the arguments passed to your command function. To convert an expression (of the form given to the expr Tcl command) to a double value, use `Tcl_ExprDouble`:

```
int Tcl_ExprDouble(Tcl_Interp* interp,
    char* expression,
    double* value)
```

Tcl_ExprDouble handles errors like Tcl_GetInt. If everything succeeds, Tcl_ExprDouble returns TCL_OK and the result of the expression in value.

Tcl_ExprBoolean, Tcl_ExprLong, and Tcl_ExprString work similarly:

```
int Tcl_ExprBoolean(Tcl_Interp* interp,
    char* expression,
    int* value)
int Tcl_ExprLong(Tcl_Interp* interp,
    char* expression,
    long* value)
int Tcl_ExprString(Tcl_Interp* interp,
    char* expression)
```

Tcl_ExprString acts slightly different in that it stores the results of the expression in interp->result.

Looking Up Objects

Tcl uses text names for all objects, rather than the more common pointers in C and C++. This means that any object or structure created in your C and C++ code must have a name. You also must be able to look up the name and return the object or structure pointer.

Tcl provides hash table routines that can help in this regard, if your application doesn't support object lookup by name. See the online documentation for Tcl_InitHashTable and Tcl_GetHashValue for more information.

Registering New Commands with the Interpreter

Once you've written your new Tcl command, you need to register the command with the Tcl interpreter, so that this command can be used in Tcl scripts.

To do this, call `Tcl_CreateCommand`:

```
Tcl_Command
Tcl_CreateCommand(Tcl_Interp* interp,
    char* commandname,
    Tcl_CmdProc* function,
    ClientData client_data,
    Tcl_CmdDeleteProc* deletefunction)
```

`Tcl_CreateCommand` associates a *commandname*, such as `reverse`, with a function pointer. The *function* is the C function you wrote for your command and takes the parameters shown earlier in the section on creating new Tcl commands.

WARNING

Function pointers are inherently dangerous. If you pass the wrong value, the Tcl interpreter won't know and will try to execute the code at whatever address you pass, leading to interesting and wrong results.

The *client_data* is any value (integer or pointer) that you want passed to the *function* and *deletefunction*.

N O T E

You can normally skip the *deletefunction*. It is intended as a clean-up function before your command gets deleted from the interpreter. See the online documentation on `Tcl_CreateCommand` for more on this.

To put this all together, you can register the new `RevCommand` function for handling the `reverse` Tcl command within the `Tcl_AppInit` function, as shown here:

```
#include <tcl.h>

extern int
RevCommand(
  ClientData client_data,
  Tcl_Interp* interp,
  int argc, char *argv[]);

int Tcl_AppInit(Tcl_Interp* interp)
```

```
{
    int    status;

    status = Tcl_Init(interp);

    if (status != TCL_OK) {
        return TCL_ERROR;
    }

    /* Insert your code here... */
    Tcl_CreateCommand(interp,
        "reverse",    /* Command name */
        RevCommand,   /* C function */
        NULL,         /* Client data, unused */
        NULL);        /* Delete function, unused */

    return TCL_OK;
}

int
main(int argc, char** argv)
{
    Tcl_Main(argc, argv, Tcl_AppInit);
    return 0;
}

/* end of file tclcmd.c */
```

When you compile and link this example, be sure to link in **revcmd.c**, too. See Chapter 13 for more on compiling and linking with the Tcl libraries.

N O T E

Summary

This chapter shows how to create your own Tcl commands using C functions. If you embed Tcl in your applications, chances are you'll need to create a number of Tcl commands.

Each command function must return an error code, usually `TCL_ERROR` or `TCL_OK`, and fill in the `result` field of the `Tcl_Interp` structure. You can use `Tcl_ResetResult` to clear the `result` and `Tcl_AppendResult` to store in new `result` data.

Inside your new command function, you can use `Tcl_GetVar` to access the value of a variable and `Tcl_SetVar` to store in new data to a variable.

You must register each new command with `Tcl_CreateCommand`. `Tcl_CreateCommand` associates a command name, such as `reverse`, with a C function pointer, such as `RevCommand`. Typically, you'll register new commands in your `Tcl_AppInit` function.

Chapter 13 finishes up by describing how to put the final touches on your applications.

Tcl and Tk Library Functions Introduced in this Chapter

```
Tcl_AppendResult
Tcl_CreateCommand
Tcl_DStringAppend
Tcl_DStringFree
Tcl_DStringInit
Tcl_DStringLength
Tcl_DStringValue
Tcl_ExprBoolean
Tcl_ExprDouble
Tcl_ExprLong
Tcl_ExprString
Tcl_GetBoolean
Tcl_GetDouble
Tcl_GetInt
Tcl_GetVar
Tcl_ResetResult
Tcl_SetErrorCode
Tcl_SetVar
```

Advanced Applications

This chapter covers:

- Finishing the application
- Setting up an icon
- Color schemes
- Updating widgets
- Sending commands to applications
- Cross-platform issues
- The option database

Finishing the Application

This chapter focuses on how to finish off professional-looking applications with Tcl, whether you embed Tcl in your applications or just use Tcl alone.

Setting up an Icon

In Windows, you usually associate the icon with the application from the **Program Manager** or when you install a program.

UNIX

In UNIX, the icon must be set up from within the application's code itself. You can set up an icon with the wm iconbitmap command:

```
wm iconbitmap widgetname bitmapname
```

You can use any valid bitmap or bitmap file. See Chapter 9 for more on bitmaps. To set up an icon for the main application window, use the following command:

```
wm iconbitmap . bitmapname
```

You can set up a name for the icon (the default name is the application's name) with the following command:

```
wm iconname . name
```

You'll want to keep this *name* short, because there usually isn't much space for an icon name.

To set the title bar of the application, use the following command:

```
wm title . titlestring
```

UNIX

Under UNIX, you'll also want to set the **WM_COMMAND** X Window property with the application's command line. You can do this in UNIX and Windows, it just doesn't do anything under Windows:

```
wm command . "$argv0 $argv"
```

The purpose of this command is to allow your application to be restarted again in another session.

Cursors

You can change the mouse cursor shape with the -cursor option supported by most widgets. You can request just a cursor shape, or you can ask for a shape with a particular foreground and background color, as shown in the following syntax:

```
widgetname configure -cursor cursorname
widgetname configure -cursor { cursorname foreground background }
```

The latter form, where you can specify the colors, works only on UNIX, not Windows, with the current version of Tk.

The available cursor names come from the X Window System's **cursor** font. Only a few are available on Windows, and they are listed in Table 13.1.

Table 13.1 Some Cursor Names for Tk

Name	Shape
arrow	Left-pointing arrow (Windows); points right on UNIX
center_ptr	Arrow pointing up
crosshair	Crosshairs
gumby	My favorite; the Gumby cartoon character; UNIX-only
fleur	Arrows pointing in four directions
icon	Square box
left_ptr	Arrow pointing to upper left
right_ptr	Arrow pointing to upper right
sb_h_double_arrow	Double-pointed arrow, left and right
sb_v_double_arrow	Double-pointed arrow, up and down
size_nw_se	Double-pointed arrow, NW and SE; Windows-only
size_ne_sw	Double-pointed arrow, NE and SW; Windows-only
watch	Busy-wait watch or hourglass
xterm	Text-entry "I-beam" cursor

On Macintosh systems, only the cursor names listed in Table 13.2 are available.

Table 13.2 Macintosh Cursor Names

Name	Shape
arrow	Left-pointing arrow
ibeam	Same as xterm
text	Same as xterm
xterm	Text entry "I-beam" cursor
cross	Crosshairs
crosshair	Crosshairs
cross-hair	Crosshairs
plus	Plus-shape
watch	Busy-wait watch or hourglass

Future versions of Tk will probably support more cursors.

Color Schemes

Older Tk applications displayed a tannish color scheme based on the X Window System color called **bisque**. You can use the tk_bisque routine to restore that color scheme, as shown below:

```
tk_bisque
```

The tk_bisque procedure sets up a color scheme for all Tk widgets. Of course, you could do this yourself by setting the colors for each widget, but it tends to get rather tedious.

You can set a different Tcl color palette for all widgets using tk_setPalette, as shown here:

```
tk_setPalette option color option2 color2 ...
```

You need to pass which options you want to set and the color for that option. The available options appear in Table 13.3.

Table 13.3 Color Options for `tk_setPalette`

Option

```
activeBackground
activeForeground
background
disabledForeground
foreground
highlightBackground
highlightColor
insertBackground
selectColor
selectBackground
troughColor
```

Updating Widgets

If you change some values and a widget does not appear to get updated, you can call the update command:

```
update
```

Tk widgets usually don't get updated until a script completes. This means that intermediate results that you want to display may not get seen by the user. If you face this situation, call update.

Sending Commands to Applications

The send command sends a Tcl command to another application. If that application accepts the command, your Tcl script gets that command's result. The basic syntax for send follows:

```
send options application command arguments
```

The send command accepts a few options, including -async to send the command asynchronously (rather than waiting for completion) and -displayof with an X Window display name. If the application name begins with -, you can use the -- option, which terminates the scanning for options.

Each Tcl application is named, by the tk appname command:

```
tk appname name
```

You can change your application's name with this command. The default name is something like *wish4.1*. To get the names of all registered Tcl applications, call the winfo interps command:

```
% winfo interps
wish4.1 app2 app1
```

For send to work, of course, you must have more than one Tcl application running.

To try out the send command, run two copies of **wish**. In each, set up a unique application name with the tk appname command. For example:

```
% tk appname app1
app1
```

In the second **wish** window, try the following name:

```
% tk appname app2
app2
```

Next, try to send a command from one interpreter to another, using the following command and assuming the second application is named *app2*:

```
send appz {button .b -text Remote ; pack .b }
```

This should create a button widget in the second **wish** window.

Security Issues with Send

The ability to send commands to other applications opens up a whole new world of Tcl capability, but it also opens up a gaping security hole. In UNIX,

you need to use the **xauth** security system for controlling access to your X
display, or send won't work between displays although you may still be able
to use send between applications running on the same display, depending on
your X display's security setup.

On Windows, the send command is disabled in the current release.
Hopefully, a later version of Tcl will allow this handy command.

Cross-Platform Issues

Just as the send command runs only on UNIX so far, there are a number of
cross-platform issues to deal with when writing Tcl scripts. Of course, if you
don't intend to run your scripts on more than one platform, it isn't an issue.

So far, Tcl is clearly written from a UNIX point of view. Tcl scripts and
programs run best on UNIX, but the Windows version gets better with each
release. If you do write cross-platform scripts, you'll need to perform a lot of
testing on Windows.

Windows and UNIX file names differ. You'll also need to be careful about
path names.

While the file names differ, the basic interface conventions only differ
slightly. See Chapter 4 for more on menu and interface conventions. Generally,
you'll find Tcl applications appear close enough to the Windows style guide.

Another set of commands that aren't support on Windows yet includes
the option database.

The Option Database

The **option database** is a fancy way of saying X resource files. Under the X
Window System, users can modify the text, colors, fonts, and so on in applications by editing X resource files. Applications then load these text files at
runtime. See Appendix A for more information on X resource files.

Tk also supports X resource files on UNIX. For example, the common
widget -activeforeground option corresponds to the *activeForeground*
resource. In addition, each widget also has a class name in resource files. To
see the resources available, you can look in the online documentation on
each widget.

The option add, option get, and option readfile commands allow you to modify the option database. None of these commands runs on Windows. See the online documentation on option for more information.

The Future of Tcl and Tk

The ultimate goal of Tcl and Tk are to provide a scripting language where scripts can execute—without change—on all major computing platforms, including Windows, UNIX, and Macintosh systems. This goal hasn't been reached yet, although Tcl gets closer with every release.

To help achieve this cross-platform nirvana, Tcl and Tk are going through a lot of changes. The support for Windows and Macintosh platforms raised a lot of questions about Tk's dependencies on the X Window System. Expect to see a lot of changes at the Tk level, including look and feel changes to better mimic the system your scripts run on as well as the syntax for file names. Check the Sun Labs Internet Web pages (see Appendix A) for more on this topic as things progress.

Other changes in the works include better internationalization, improved security and a graphical interface builder called **SpecTcl**. On the more mundane level, a table-based geometry manager should help augment the packer and allow you to lay out widgets in rows and columns that line up. The image command should one day also support JPEG images.

Summary

Use the wm iconbitmap command to set up an application's icon. The wm iconname sets the name displayed with this icon. You should use a short name or the user may not see the whole name.

You can use the tk_setPalette command to set up a palette of colors for use with all Tk widgets. This is helpful if you create a number of color schemes. One such color scheme is the set of bisque colors that older versions of Tk used. To restore the older bisque colors, use the tk_bisque command.

The send command allows you to execute a Tcl script inside another Tcl application.

You should now be more than ready to tackle the wide world of Tcl/Tk applications. See Appendix A for more sources of information and reference material.

Tcl/Tk Commands Introduced in this Chapter

```
send
tk
tk_bisque
tk_setPalette
```

APPENDIX A

For More Information

Tcl/Tk Books

This book concentrates on how to create graphical applications with Tcl and Tk, but there's a lot more to Tcl and its Tk toolkit. The main reference comes with Tcl in the form of online manual information, accessible on Windows or UNIX, as discussed in Chapter 1. In addition, there are a few more Tcl books you might find helpful:

- *Tcl and the Tk Toolkit*, John Ousterhout, Addison-Wesley, 1994. Written by the creator of Tcl, this book contains a lot more reference material, but for an older version of Tcl, Tcl 7.3 and Tk 3.6. Most of this material is still valid, but some is out of date.

- *Practical Programming in Tcl and Tk*, Brent Welch, Prentice Hall, 1995. This book covers the UNIX version of Tcl and Tk in great depth. It uses Tcl 7.4 and Tk 4.0 so it isn't fully up to date, but UNIX developers will find this book handy.

- *Exploring Expect*, by Don Libes, O'Reilly and Associates, 1995. **Expect** is a UNIX package written with Tcl and Tk that allows you to place a graphical interface on top of many UNIX commands. Instead of typing away at the unfriendly command line, **Expect** users interact with a graphical interface.

UNIX Books

Tcl was written with the UNIX and X Window System in mind. It was only later that Windows and Macintosh versions appeared. If you're unfamiliar with the basics of UNIX, you'll find *Teach Yourself UNIX* helpful.

- *Teach Yourself UNIX*, third edition, Kevin Reichard and Eric F. Johnson, MIS: Press, 1995. Aimed at the UNIX beginner, you'll find clear explanations for Unix file permissions (used with the Tcl open command) and more on where globbing came from.

- *Advanced Programming in the UNIX Environment*, W. Richard Stevens, Addison-Wesley, 1992. By far the best book on programming UNIX applications, Stevens' book is an essential part of my bookshelf. If you need to program advanced applications on UNIX, this book is essential.

- *Teach Yourself C++*, fourth edition, Al Stevens, MIS: Press, 1995. If you're new to C++ programming, you'll find this book of great help.

X Window System Books

The X Window System has become the de facto graphics engine on UNIX. While not written for UNIX alone, it is UNIX where X has been most successful. Tcl and Tk on UNIX use X for all graphics, and many of the concepts of Tk, such as selections and events, come straight from X.

One of the trickier concepts of X is the separation between the window manager and the windowing system. Neither Windows nor the Macintosh make this separation, a fact that tends to confuse many when they migrate to UNIX. In X, a window manager is a separate program. The user can run any window manager desired, but few ever change the default configuration. Even so, every system seems to come with its own different window manager. The tough part of all this is that X enforces a nasty rule: the window manager controls the screen layout. For more on these issues, you can try the following books:

- *Advanced X Window Applications Programming*, second edition, Eric F. Johnson and Kevin Reichard, M & T Books, 1994. This book covers programming with the X library, or Xlib. You'll find a lot of similarities with the internals of Tk, since Tk also uses the X library. Tk even goes so far as to port a number of Xlib C functions to Windows and Macintosh systems. The extensive window manager section in this book will go a long way toward providing a background for the Tk wm command. The sections on X events will help understand the Tk bind command and all its permutations. Furthermore, I'm biased—I'd love for you to buy this book.

- *UNIX System Administrator's Guide to the X Window System*, Eric F. Johnson and Kevin Reichard, M & T Books, 1994. If you use the Tk send command, you'll often need to delve into X Window System security, covered in this book. If you use the option command for X resource files, you'll also like the sections on the multitude of locations X resource files can be found.

Tcl Information and Code on the Internet

This book comes with a CD-ROM containing the latest versions of Tcl and Tk as of this writing. You can acquire even later versions from the following Internet sites:

The official Tcl FTP site is located at **ftp.smli.com/pub/tcl**. This is the machine provided by Sun Labs, where John Ousterhout, creator of Tcl, now works. Sun Labs provides a Web page at **http://www.sunlabs.com:80/research/tcl/**, but you'll often have difficulty connecting to this site.

The main contributed application FTP site is **ftp.aud.alcatel.com**, which also mirrors the Sun Labs site for Tcl updates.

A good starting point for general Tcl information is the set of pages from SCO, a PC UNIX vendor, at **http://www.sco.com/Technology/tcl/Tcl.html**.

You'll find an extensive set of online manuals for Tcl and Tk at **http://www.elf.org/tcltk-man-html/contents.html**.

Usenet News

The **comp.lang.tcl** Usenet newsgroup is a great source of information on Tcl and Tk. Every day, many users pose questions and receive answers from a number of Tcl experts. Chances are if you face a problem, someone else has already faced it and solved it.

In the **comp.lang.tcl** newsgroup, you'll also see compiled lists of common questions and answers. These postings go a long way for answering most common questions. Included among these frequently-asked questions lists, or FAQs in Internet speak, is the Tcl and Tk on Windows FAQ list (maintained by yours truly).

APPENDIX B

Installing Tcl and Tk

Installing Tcl and Tk on UNIX

The instructions for installing Tcl and Tk differ based on your platform. The UNIX instructions are a lot different from those on NT. In addition, different UNIX versions may require you to make minor modifications to Tcl files to get things to compile.

What You Need

For Tcl, you'll need a C compiler and the standard libraries and header files that come with C compilers.

For Tk, you'll also need X Window System libraries, as Tk provides a handy front end to making graphical X programs. In addition, you need to set up the directories properly for the Tcl runtime library to find certain files it needs.

Although the rules may change with later releases (always check the README files that come with Tcl), you should create a top-level directory for all of Tcl, such as **/usr/local/tcl**.

Then, in this directory (**/usr/local/tcl** in our example), create a directory for Tcl and call it **tcl7.5**. Create a directory for Tk and call it **tk4.1**.

Later versions of Tcl and Tk will, of course, require different directory names.

362

Copy the Tcl 7.5 release source code to your new **tcl7.5** directory. In this directory, you'll see subdirectories for the UNIX (**UNIX**), Macintosh (**mac**), and Windows (**win**) versions of Tcl. For Tcl, the source code only differs slightly between systems. For Tk, though, the source code is radically different.

On the accompanying CD-ROM, these sources are stored in the **tcl/tcl7.5a2** directory.

Copy the Tk 4.1 release source code to your new **tk4.1** directory. You'll also see **unix, mac,** and **win** subdirectories.

On the accompanying CD-ROM, these sources are stored in the **tcl/tk4.1a2** directory.

If you acquired the Tcl and Tk sources over the Internet, now is the time to check for patches. A **patch** is a file that corrects problems in source code. Patch, the program that updates the code, uses **context difference** files in the form of those generated by the UNIX utility **diff**. If there is a patch file, you'll want to apply the patch before compiling and installing Tcl and Tk. This will ensure you have the latest versions of the code and all the up-to-date fixes.

On the accompanying CD-ROM, any latest patches for both Tcl and Tk have already been installed.

Installing Tcl on UNIX

Now you're ready to install things. Change to the **tcl7.5** directory and look at the **README** file. This file goes over the basic installation instructions.

The next step is to run **configure**. This program searches through your system and builds a—hopefully—correct **Makefile** with all the necessary options to build Tcl on your system. To do this, use the following command:

```
./configure
```

After **configure** completes, you should edit the **Makefile** it generated. You may need to change some of the entries in the **Makefile**.

The key entries to look for are prefix, the general directory path prefix and exec_prefix, the directory path where the resulting executables should go.

The default values for these entries are the following.

```
prefix =        /usr
exec_prefix =   ${prefix}
```

You may want to change these values to something different, such as **/usr/local /tcl** as shown here:

```
prefix =        /usr/local/tcl
exec_prefix =   ${prefix}
```

For example, I built Tcl on a Linux system that had an older version of Tcl and Tk already installed. Because I didn't want to damage a working version of Tcl until I was sure the new version worked, I choose to install Tcl and Tk in alternate directories to allow for testing without overwriting any of the existing versions.

The next step is to run **make**, to build all the source code:

```
make
```

Once **make** is finished, if it works successfully, then you should have **libtcl.a** and **tclsh** built. The library, **libtcl.a**, is used when you want to embed the Tcl interpreter within your applications. (This library may be named differently, such as **libtcl7.5.a** on your system.)

Tclsh is the Tcl shell program (much like **ksh** or **csh**, two other shells), that allow you to execute Tcl programs and discussed in Chapter 2. (You'll probably make much more use of **wish**, the Tcl shell with Tk support, than merely **tclsh**, which does not support graphical applications with Tk.)

If **make** fails, then you need to edit the **Makefile** and correct whatever problem was discovered. Sometimes this is not an easy task.

To help with this, there is a file named **porting.notes** in both the Tcl and Tk directories that may contain useful information for your platform.

Once Tcl is properly made, you can run **make install** to install the proper files in the directories you listed in the **Makefile**, as shown here:

```
make install
```

Installing Tk on UNIX

The process for installing Tk is almost exactly like that for Tcl.

1. Run **./configure** in the **tk4.1/lowercase** directory.
2. Edit the **Makefile** generated by configure to change the prefix and exec_prefix entries, if necessary.
3. Run **make** to build the programs and library.
4. When **make** completes successfully, run **make install** to install Tk.

Since there is a lot more code for Tk, generally, this process will take longer than for Tcl.

Cleaning Up after the Installation

After you are sure Tcl and Tk both work (running some of the examples from this book may help test your interpreters), you can run **make clean** to clean up all the extra object modules and associated debris left over from compiling and installing Tcl.

Merely run the following command in both the **tcl7.5/lowercase** and **tk4.1/lowercase** directories:

```
make clean
```

WARNING

Do not run **make clean** until you have built both Tk and Tcl. Building Tk requires **libtcl.a** from the **../../tcl7.4** directory. If you run **make clean** too soon, you may need to rebuild parts of Tcl to get Tk to build.

Installing Tcl and Tk on Windows NT, Windows 95, or Windows 3.1

The main problem on UNIX is the difference between UNIX versions. The main problem on Windows is differences between compilers.

Tcl and Tk require the Win32s subsystem. You'll also need either the Borland or the Microsoft compiler to build Tcl from source code. Each of these compilers uses a different format for the important **Makefile**, which is why you need be concerned about these compiler differences.

Installing the Binary Version

If you can avoid it, don't compile the libraries. Instead, just install the binary version that comes on the CD-ROM as a self-extracting archive. Just execute the **WIN41.EXE** program and it will lead you through the installation. (The actual file name for the self-extracting archive may differ for different versions of Tcl, for example, **WIN41A2.EXE**.)

Compiling from Source Code

If you do need to compile Tcl from source code, look for the **README** files in the **win** subdirectories. These files contain the latest instructions for using both the Borland or Microsoft compilers.

With the Microsoft compilers, the typical command to build the libraries is as follows:

```
nmake -f makefile.vc
```

You'll need to run this command in both the **tcl7.5/win** and **tk4.1/win** directories to build the Tcl and Tk libraries, respectively. You may need to set up INCLUDE and LIB environment variables to tell Visual C++ where your C++ compiler support files are located.

The Tcl and Tk source code uses long file names, which will be a problem under Windows 3.1. Windows 95 and Windows NT both allow for longer file names.

WARNING

When you're all done with this, you can copy the executables (**.EXE** files) and Dynamic Link Libraries (**.DLL** files) to your installation binary directory, such as **C:\TCL\BIN**. You'll need to add this directory to your **PATH**. At the same level as the **BIN** directory, (e.g., **C:\TCL**), create a **LIB** directory with **TCL7.5** and **TK4.1** subdirectories under **LIB**. Copy the Tcl and Tk support files to these directories. See the **README** files for more on which files are necessary.

APPENDIX C

The CD-ROM

The accompanying CD-ROM uses Rock Ridge extensions to the standard ISO-9660 format. This allows for longer file names than the old-fashioned DOS eight-character names with three-character extensions. This was necessary because the Tcl source code uses long file names.

You'll find these main subdirectories on the CD-ROM:

- **book**, which holds examples from this book
- **contrib**, containing Tcl freeware from around the world
- **tcl**, the source code
- **win**, Windows binaries

INDEX

X